The Development of China's Information Resource Industry

The industrialization of information resources has been a growing trend across the world in recent years, especially in China, where the information resource industry has expanded exponentially for more than a decade.

While analyzing the development conditions of China's information resource industry, this book clearly defines the implications and strategic value of the industry, summarizes basic information resource industry theories, and clarifies the history of its development and special regional characteristics within the Chinese context. Drawing on the statistics and measurement of various economic indicators of the information resource industry, the authors propose four stages of development: a germination period, an initial development period, a subsequent rapid development period, and lastly, a steady development period.

At the same time, the book draws upon various theoretical models such as the "Dynamic Resource Triangle" model, the "Information Resource Industrial Symbiosis" model, the value chain model, and the explanation model of information consumption in order to shed light on the information resource industry's elements and the optimization of its management. In addition, the authors present the Information Resource Industry Development Index (IRIDI) to evaluate the industry's development in different provinces and cities across mainland China and monitor its dynamics from the point of view of industrial value and the external environment.

While the book lays a solid theoretical foundation for the growth of China's information resource industry, it will also give international readers a clear picture of China's emerging industries in the current era.

Feng Huiling is Professor of the School of Information Resource Management at Renmin University of China and specializes in information resource management, archival science, electronic document management, and digital memory.

Zhao Guojun is Professor of the School of Information Resource Management at Renmin University of China and specializes in e-government affairs and information resource industry policies.

Qian Minghui is Associate Professor of the School of Information Resource Management at Renmin University of China and specializes in information resource industry and management.

China Perspectives

The *China Perspectives* series focuses on translating and publishing works by leading Chinese scholars, writing about both global topics and China-related themes. It covers Humanities & Social Sciences, Education, Media and Psychology, as well as many interdisciplinary themes.

This is the first time any of these books have been published in English for international readers. The series aims to put forward a Chinese perspective, give insights into cutting-edge academic thinking in China, and inspire researchers globally.

Titles in information resource management include:

The Development of China's Information Resource Industry
Theory and Evaluation
Feng Huiling, Zhao Guojun, and Qian Minghui

The Development of China's Information Resource Industry
Policy and Instrument
Feng Huiling, Zhao Guojun, Qian Minghui

For more information, please visit www.routledge.com/series/CPH

The Development of China's Information Resource Industry
Theory and Evaluation

Feng Huiling, Zhao Guojun, and Qian Minghui

LONDON AND NEW YORK

First published 2020 by Routledge

2 Park Square, Milton Park, Abingdon, Oxon OX14 4RN
605 Third Avenue, New York, NY 10017

Routledge is an imprint of the Taylor & Francis Group, an informa business

First issued in paperback 2021

Copyright © 2020 Feng Huiling, Zhao Guojun, Qian Minghui

The right of Feng Huiling, Zhao Guojun, and Qian Minghui to be identified as
authors of this work has been asserted by them in accordance with sections 77
and 78 of the Copyright, Designs and Patents Act 1988.

All rights reserved. No part of this book may be reprinted or reproduced or
utilised in any form or by any electronic, mechanical, or other means, now
known or hereafter invented, including photocopying and recording, or in
any information storage or retrieval system, without permission in writing
from the publishers.

Notice:
Product or corporate names may be trademarks or registered trademarks,
and are used only for identification and explanation without intent to
infringe.

Publisher's Note

The publisher has gone to great lengths to ensure the quality of this reprint
but points out that some imperfections in the original copies may be apparent.

English Version by permission of China Renmin University Press.

British Library Cataloguing-in-Publication Data
A catalogue record for this book is available from the British Library

Library of Congress Cataloging-in-Publication Data
A catalog record for this book has been requested

ISBN: 978-1-138-33195-2 (hbk)
ISBN: 978-1-03-217281-1 (pbk)
DOI: 10.4324/9780429446986

Typeset in Times New Roman
by Apex CoVantage, LLC

This book is published with financial support from
B&R Book Program

Contents

List of figures	viii
List of tables	x
Foreword I	xii
Foreword II	xv
Preface	xviii

1	The information resource industry and its strategic value	1
2	Basic theories on the development of China's information resource industry	26
3	Development trajectory of China's information resource industry	75
4	The supply–demand relation of China's information resource industry	96
5	Structural features of China's information resource industry	115
6	Regional features of China's information resource industry	130
7	Evaluation of the development of China's information resource industry	149
	Afterword	171
	References	172
	Index	179

Figures

1.1	Relationships between the information resource industry and related industries	7
2.1	Progress of study on model of "resource triangle"	28
2.2	Displacement path of DRT barycenters in different social formations and DB curve diagram	33
2.3	Explanation model for features of information consumption	39
2.4	Structural features of information consumption	42
2.5	Symbiosis model of information resources in parallel and symbiosis model of other resources in series	49
2.6	Analysis of policies and management on "industrial symbiosis based on information resources"	54
2.7	Schematic diagram of industrial chain	59
2.8	Enterprise replacement in a traditional industrial chain	64
2.9	Increase in number of enterprises in information resource industry chain	65
3.1	Changes of subdivided industries of the information resource industry from 2004 to 2007	80
3.2	Proportions of subdivided industries of the information resource industry from 2004 to 2007	81
3.3	Regional distribution of the information resource industry from 2004 to 2007	82
3.4	Increase tendency of the information resource industry in all regions from 2004 to 2007	83
3.5	Development tendency of operating incomes of all regions from the information resource industry from 2008 to 2011	85
3.6	Development tendency of operating incomes from subdivided industries of the information resource industry from 2008 to 2011	86
3.7	Proportions of subdivided industries of the information resource industry from 2008 to 2011	88
3.8	Regional distribution of operating incomes from the information resource industry from 2008 to 2011	89
3.9	Development tendency of the information resource industry in all regions from 2012 to 2014	91

3.10	Development tendency of subdivided industries of the information resource industry from 2012 to 2014	92
3.11	Proportions of subdivided industries of the information resource industry from 2012 to 2014	93
3.12	Regional distribution of the information resource industry from 2012 to 2014	94
4.1	2009–2013 demographic change in Beijing Information Resource Industry	103
4.2	Bar chart of average provincial attention and output of the surveying and mapping industry in seven regions	109
5.1	Mix of the information resource industry's operating revenue and employees by category (2009–2013)	125
5.2	The information resource industry's operating revenue and employees by dependence (2009–2013)	126
5.3	The information resource industry's operating revenue and employees by region (2013)	127
6.1	Industrial value and industrial environment scores of provincial-level administrative regions of East China	134
6.2	Industrial value and industrial environment scores of Central China provinces	139
6.3	Industrial value and industrial environment scores of provincial-level administrative regions of West China	144
7.1	Level 2 indicators for the information resource industry's development in China (2013–2014)	163
7.2	Average information resource industry development index of provincial-level administrative regions (2013–2014)	165
7.3	Information resource industry development index scores and rankings of provincial-level administrative regions in 2014	166

Tables

1.1	Classifications of the information resource gathering industry, the subdivided industry of the information resource industry	7
1.2	Classifications of the information resource processing industry, the subdivided industry of the information resource industry	8
1.3	Classifications of the information resource providing industry, the subdivided industry of the information resource industry	8
2.1	Reflections of features of resource structure at different stages of social development	31
2.2	Types of information consumption markets	41
2.3	Evolution features of information consumption	44
2.4	Six basic types of "industrial symbiosis relationship based on information resources"	50
2.5	Government's intervention in the information resource industry: purposes, theories, and specific goals	71
3.1	Development periods and features of China's information resource industry	76
4.1	China's information resource industry development index rankings 2013	105
4.2	Subscriber size of the network information resources industry (partial)	106
4.3	Government attention to and development of the surveying and mapping industry in seven regions	108
4.4	Average provincial attention and output of the surveying and mapping industry in seven regions	108
5.1	Frequency of keywords to identify information resource industry segments (non-exhaustive list)	117
5.2	List of keywords to identify information resource industry segments	118
5.3	First categorization of the information resource industry	118
5.4	Second categorization of the information resource industry	119
5.5	Information resource dependence of the information resource industry	121
5.6	Estimation of missing data for the information resource industry development index	124

5.7	Operating revenues, legal entity, and employees of the information resource industry (2009–2013)	124
6.1	China's information resource industry development index rankings 2014 (provincial-level administrative regions)	131
6.2	Information resource industry development index scores and rankings of provincial-level administrative regions of east China	133
6.3	Industrial value scores and rankings of provincial-level administrative regions of East China	135
6.4	Industrial environment scores and rankings of provincial-level administrative regions of East China	137
6.5	Information resource industry indicator scores in East China (2013 & 2014)	138
6.6	Information resource industry development index scores and rankings of Central China provinces	139
6.7	Industrial value scores and rankings of Central China provinces	140
6.8	Industrial environment scores and rankings of Central China provinces	141
6.9	Information resource industry indicator scores in Central China (2013 & 2014)	142
6.10	Information resource industry development index scores and rankings of provincial-level administrative regions of West China	143
6.11	Industrial value scores and rankings of provincial-level administrative regions of West China	145
6.12	Industrial environment scores and rankings of provincial-level administrative regions of West China	147
6.13	Information resource industry indicator scores in West China (2013 & 2014)	148
7.1	Level 1, 2, and 3 indicators to evaluate information resource industry's development and their estimation	152
7.2	The weights of level 1, 2, and 3 indicators to evaluate information resource industry's development	154
7.3	Estimation of missing data for the information resource industry development index	156
7.4	China's information resource industry development index rankings 2014 (provincial-level administrative regions)	158
7.5	Industrial value ranking for China's information resource industry	159
7.6	Industrial environment ranking for China's information resource industry	161
7.7	Pearson correlation coefficient for per capita GDP and IRIDI	165
7.8	Information resource industry development index scores and rankings of provincial-level administrative regions in 2014	166

Foreword I

I have paid close attention to China's economy for many years, and especially to the development in management science, with a focus on the changes in China's emerging industries that are closely linked with the information age. I therefore was very interested to read the research results of the National Natural Science Foundation of China project and also pleasantly surprised and honored to be invited to write a foreword to this book.

The industrialization of information resources represents a general trend in the development of the world today. The rapid revolution in information technology has exerted a profound influence on modes of economic development. This revolution will promote a quantum leap in productivity and bring new opportunities for social and economic development. The information resource industry can create a number of new industries and, through the transformation and upgrading of traditional industries, expand their own development spaces. With the improvements in information technology and the wide application of electronic and information products, the information resource industry is bound to become an important force in promoting social transformation and economic restructuring. Recent progress in information technology has made the tendency toward economic globalization and information networking much clearer than before. Information technology and its application has become an important measurement index of a country's comprehensive strength and international competitiveness. Therefore, evaluating the problems and difficulties in the development of the information resource industry and identifying corresponding solutions has great value for practice and policy guidance.

From a strategic point of view, the information resource industry is a new impetus to promote economic growth and international economic competitiveness. It has become a new, commanding height in international economic competition. There are numerous challenges remaining. For example, in order to accomplish the transformation of economic development modes, industrial structural adjustment, improving people's livelihoods, optimization and upgrading of traditional industries, and the completion of fundamental social changes in order to solve a series of strategic problems and realize important strategic goals, the problems of resource allocation in economic and social development must be solved properly. A reasonable choice is to substantially reduce the consumption of raw materials and energy, which are limited and nonrenewable, and instead to explore inexhaustible

Foreword I xiii

information resources. Nowadays, many countries in the world have taken measures to promote information industry development. The United States, Britain, Ireland, many countries of the European Union, Japan, and many other countries have published documents about the development of their information industries that describe building industrial clusters in content and application areas with high added value, developing world-class information resource industries, and becoming world leaders in this area.

From the standpoint of enterprise organization, information resources play an important role in improving competitiveness, implementing strategic management, and speeding up technological innovation. Under fierce market competition, those who first possess and make full utilization of information resources will grasp the initiative and conquer their markets. The integration of information resources with enterprise development, therefore, constantly improves enterprise competitiveness. At present, more and more multinational companies are introducing new information resources into their production operations. This new competitiveness strategy – based on the Internet and information technology – has been successfully applied in companies such as Intel, IBM, and NEC, and has increasingly become a source of competitive advantage. Enterprises like Facebook, Google, Baidu, Tencent, and Alibaba know the importance of information resources. Google, as the leading company in the industry, expands their projects through resource sharing. This practice does not harm them in the game with competitors but instead improves their products by using the power of community and ultimately helps them go to the forefront of the industry. At this juncture of the information revolution, professionals from all fields need to seize the opportunity and hitch a ride on the high-speed train of the information revolution. Companies can survive and develop only by establishing their information superiority.

The book is based on the dynamic development of the global economy and focuses on the trend in China's economic transformation. This book analyzes key problems related to industrial development, such as the status and regional features of China's information resource industry. It lays a solid theoretical foundation for the development and growth of China's information resource industry. Moreover, this deeply thought-out book also will likely play a significant role in letting the world know about China's information resource industry. Many of the issues explored in this book have not been widely discussed in academia – for example, little has been said about the division of the scope of China's information resource industry. From a theoretical perspective, starting from philosophy, this book breaks the limitation of the static "Resource Triangle Model." It brings in the variable of time and establishes the "Dynamic Resource Triangle Model" in order to describe the features and evolution of social resource structure. Further, this book proposes the "Dynamic-resource-triangle Barycenter Curve" as well as its functional expression. This theory is an innovative improvement based on classical theories; it reveals the main features of the basic resource structure in different periods and its variation over time. This could provide theoretical guidance to policy-making departments regarding upgrading and optimization of industries. Moreover, to quantify the level of development of the information resource

xiv *Foreword I*

industry in different areas, this book attempts to develop an information resource industry evaluation index system to reflect the development status and features of the information resource industry from two dimensions: industrial environment and industrial value. Innovations like these can be seen everywhere in the book. As an outstanding piece of work – whether you are looking for a new economic growth point or intend to carry out industrial transformations through the information revolution – the book can be used as a handy reference for anyone who wants to make a difference in this information era. The insights and ideas may allow you to achieve more with less. The publication of this book can establish a theoretical basis for the information resource industry in China, assist the Chinese government in formulating appropriate development strategies, and guide and facilitate the development of China's information resource industry.

Nowadays, global economic development has entered into the information age, and information resources have become one of the essentials for economic and social development. While timely information can rescue a near-bankrupt enterprise, outdated information can lead to mistakes in strategy making. Readers are fortunate to read this book. From the book, we can enjoy the research team's commitment to excellence in scientific research, a rigorous scientific attitude, and an innovative spirit. It is no exaggeration to say that the publication of the book is opening up a new sphere for research on the information resource industry and its management policies in China.

Richard L. Priem
August, 2016

Richard L. Priem, professor at the School of Business of Texas Christian University and strategic management professor of Libera Università Internazionale degli Studi Sociali "Guido Carli" LUISS ROMA, acted as an editorial board member of such academic journals as *Academy of Management Journal* (AMJ), *Academy of Management Review* (AMR), *Journal of Management Studies* (JMS), *Organization Science, Oxford Research Reviews* (ORR), and *Strategic Management Journal* (SMJ), was a member of the Best Paper Selection Committee of the American Institute of Strategic Management for ten years and a member of executive committee and Doctoral Forum of business policy and strategic management group of American Management Society, and a review member of the National Science Foundation. Devoted to study on strategic management, organization theories, entrepreneurship, and senior management decisions for many years, Professor Priem came up with the strategic management idea of resource-based view (RBV) and published over 60 papers of significant academic influence in such leading international academic journals as *Academy of Management Journal, Academy of Management Review, Journal of Management Studies*, and *Organization Science*. His findings have not only received acceptance and respect – and are much quoted (many of his papers are quoted in Google Scholar over 2,000 times) – but exert a huge impact on the improvement of management ideas and concepts in actual enterprise operations. He has won many teaching and academic prizes, including the "Decade Achievement Award" of the Academy of Management for 2011.

Foreword II

Devoted to the emerging field of study with strategic prospect in recent years, the academic team led by Professor Feng Huiling has done the in-depth research on the basic theory and application of the information resource industry. The analysis and judgment of the strategic value of information resources for the Chinese economy and society and the digging into the structure of the information resource industry, policy orientation, and management mode are of high value and insightful. I feel very honored to be invited to write a foreword to this book.

In January 2014, President Xi said at the meeting of the Central Cyberspace Affairs Leading Group, "Information resources have become an increasingly important production element and social wealth, and how much a country grasps information signifies its soft power and competitiveness." As the overall size of China's information resource industry expands and the population of practitioners and the number of corporations persistently burgeon for over ten years from 2004 up until now, China's economic structure transformation and upgrading have sped up, and the information resource industry has become an important industrial type in the era of knowledge-driven economies. The hot spot of the new generation of information technology development is no longer the vertical upgrading of each branch of technology in the information field but the horizontal incorporation of information technologies into such industries as the manufacturing industry and the financial industry. The information technology research stays focused more on service technology than on product technology so as to form a new generation of information technology of "Internet+" with in-depth incorporation of informatization with industrialization as the main objective. China has begun to enter into the Information Age, which entails workers in all walks of life changing their ways of thinking so as to adapt to the tide of the times. The CPC Central Committee clearly pointed out that China entered into the "New Normal" of the economy, implying that China began to put the optimization of economic structure high on its agenda and that China stepped into a new stage where informatization drives new industrialization, urbanization, and agricultural modernization. Informatization as a driving force is a transition of socioeconomic management, but not a provisional initiative; instead, we will always keep on the track of the informatization.

Therefore, to develop the information resource industry in the future in the Information Age, China needs not only to make the related policies to provide

xvi *Foreword II*

guidance but also to strategically plan on the back of clear knowledge of real development. That is how China will strive to be the vanguard in the Information Age and shine in the global information industry competition. Set in the initial development stage of China's information resource industry, this book explores the development direction and strategic planning of China's information resource industry and exhibits a series of pretty creative theories and methods. With respect to basic theories, in this book, "Dynamic Resource Triangle Model" is creatively constructed through the introduction of a time variable on the basis of the "Resource Triangle Model" put forward by a professor at Harvard University. The "Dynamic Resource Triangle Model" can provide theoretical guidance for the governmental decision-making department that seeks the industrial upgrading direction and optimization path of industrial structure. Furthermore, with respect to the structure problems of China's information resource industry, in this book, industries of China's information resources are classified by use of the Delphi technique through a combination of subject term analysis methods with literature discovery theories, which defines the scope of and lays a foundation for subsequent work in industrial research, strategic planning, and other fields. This book is of academic and practical value for researchers in the information resource industry, decision-makers in the government, entrepreneurs, and various types of professionals. If the views in this book can be applied to industrial planning, industrial development, and other practices, detours may be avoided and a new road may be opened.

As a research result of the key project of the National Natural Science Foundation of China, this book provides guidance for the development of basic research of Chinese management science, stimulation of scientific discovery, and theoretical innovation and promotion of industrial revolution. In this age of "content first," I look forward to the author team's continued creativity in this promising field, and I hope that more people of insight will pay attention to and join in this field to explore a new path together that steadily drives the progress of China's informatization and helps to optimize and transform the economic structure.

Li Guojie

August 2016

Li Guojie, academician of Chinese Academy of Engineering and fellow of Third World Academy of Sciences, graduated from Peking University in 1968 and received a master's degree at the University of Science and Technology of China in 1981 and a PhD at Purdue University in 1985. He worked in the CSL Lab of the University of Illinois from 1985 to 1986, returned to China and worked in the Institute of Computing Technology, the Chinese Academy of Sciences (ICTCAS) in 1987, and was employed by the Institute as a researcher in 1989. He was appointed by the State Scientific and Technological Commission to be the director of the National Research Center for Intelligent Computing Systems in 1990 and once served as the director of ICTCAS. In May 2004, he also acted as the director of the Computer Science and Technology Department of the University of Science and Technology of China. Dr. Li published over 100 academic papers covering parallel processing, computer system architecture, artificial intelligence, combinatorial

Foreword II   xvii

optimization, and other subjects, and was the co-author of four English monographs. Over the past 20 years, Li Guojie has led ICTCAS and Sugon in making important contributions to the development of the Chinese high-performance computer industry and of the dragon-core high-performance universal CPU chip. He won the first prize and the second prize of national scientific and technological progress award, and received the scientific and technological progress award of the first Ho Leung Ho Lee Foundation and other awards. He was elected to be the academician of the Chinese Academy of Engineering in 1995 and fellow of Third World Academy of Sciences in 2001.

Preface

The information resource industry is a sector of the national economy in which information serves as an object of labor and as raw material for production; products and services in the form of information are outcomes and bring profits, and information is produced, processed, spread, and provided to consumers to generate economic and social value. China has impressed the world with its enviable economic development since the initiation of the reform and opening-up. That said, the issues concerning the transformation of the economic development mode, rebalance of the industrial structure, upgrading of the traditional industry, improvement in the livelihood of the general public, and employment increase are pressing. Considering that, the information resource industry is drawing attention from all walks of life as an emerging strategic industry and becoming more and more important for the rebalance of Chinese socioeconomic resource structure and scientific development.

Times of peace and prosperity usually appear in the post-war period and a new look takes on when changes begin . As the information resource industry booms such as Information resource collection industry, information resource processing industry and information resource supply industry, we must be sober with respect to some pressing problems, such as increasingly prominent monopoly phenomenon, regional development disparity, and lack of creativity, which have become the bottleneck of further development of China's information resource industry. To tell it like it is, compared with some developed countries, China's information resource industry is still at the initial stage and has a long way to go. Although the information resource industry can give strong impetus to the national economic development, governments at all levels do not try really hard to provide policy support and guarantees. To gain insight into the mechanism and function of policies on the information resource industry, we undertook the key project of the National Natural Science Foundation of China, titled "Policies for China's Information Resource Industry Development and Management Study," and this book is part of the research results. In this book, basic theories about the information resource industry are summarized, the general development history of China's information resource industry and regional development features are presented, and the corresponding evaluation of developments is made.

Preface xix

Specifically, this book covers seven chapters. In Chapter 1, the connotation and denotation of the information resource industry are discussed, and the role of economic, political, and social functions of the information resource industry in Chinese socioeconomic development are analyzed. The strategic value of the Chinese information resource industry development is analyzed from the perspectives of resource structure and social development trends. In Chapter 2, the conceptual model of the "Dynamic Resource Triangle," describing the features and evolution of social resource structure, is constructed on the basis of the "resource triangle" theory by the introduction of a time variable; based on that model, the "Dynamic-resource-triangle Barycenter Curve" is proposed to reflect the structural features and development trend of the social or industrial basic resources. The market features, structural features, evolution features, and policy demand features of information consumption are discussed in combination with the explanation model of information consumption features. The composition and features of "Industrial Symbiosis System Based on Information Resources," formations and types of the symbiotic relationship, influencing factors and measurement of symbiosis benefits, and demand of symbiosis for management and policies are elaborated through literature research, theoretical derivation, logical reasoning, case study, industrial development data calculation, etc. In Chapter 3, the development trajectory of China's information resource industry is explored, including the industrial germination period, the initial development period, the rapid development period, and the steady development period, Development trends of subdivided industries of the information resource industry in different periods are also discussed. In Chapter 4, supply and demand features of China's information resource industry are analyzed, including economic, political, people's livelihood improvement and cultural demands, and such key supply factors as labor input, capital input, urbanization level, and population density, so as to argue the relevance between demand and supply and its driving more rapid, steady, and sound development of China's information resource industry. In Chapter 5, the structural features of China's information resource industry are analyzed, and the specific industries encompassed by the information resource industry are defined. In Chapter 6, China's information resource industry is divided into eastern industry, middle industry, and western industry according to geographical position. The three categories are analyzed from such perspectives as industrial size, industrial contribution, industrial development, and industrial structure, and the development trend of each of the categories is predicted. In Chapter 7, three levels of indexes for industrial development evaluation are put forward. Those indexes are directed at comparing the development of the information resource industry in all provinces and cities in China as well as optimization of existing policies on the information resource industry. Positive analysis of the development situation of the information resource industry is made by use of related Chinese data from 2014, with a comparative study made based on 2013 data and 2014 data.

The 21st century is filled with opportunities. The rise of the mobile Internet, big data, cloud computing, the Internet of Things, smart home and other industries not only provides fertile ground for growth of the information resource industry but poses severe challenges. We believe that the information resource industry will definitely attain its priority in China's national economic and social development. I hope this book will be useful in promoting and guaranteeing the industry's sound development.

1 The information resource industry and its strategic value

China has impressed the world with its enviable economic development since the initiation of the reform and opening-up. That said, the issues concerning the transformation of the economic development mode, rebalance of the industrial structure, upgrading of the traditional industry, improvement in the livelihood of the general public, and increase in employment that arise from the recent socioeconomic development are pressing. Considering this, the information resource industry, which exerts strategic influences on the adjustment of the resource structure in the country's socioeconomic development, is drawing attention from all walks of life as an emerging strategic industry and one that is becoming more and more important for the scientific development of Chinese socioeconomic development. In this chapter, the connotation and denotation of the information resource industry are discussed, characteristics of the information resource industry are generally analyzed, and basic functions of the information resource industry and the strategic value for Chinese socioeconomic development are theoretically reviewed.

1.1 The connotation and denotation of the information resource industry

Though the expression "information resource industry" began to be used when the information resource concept entered China in the early 1980s and was formally applied by the CPC Central Committee and the State Council in the important documents on policies in the early 21st century,[1] its connotation and denotation have not been explained authoritatively yet.

1.1.1 Discussion of the connotation of the concept of the information resource industry

People do not agree on the meaning of "information resource industry," although they have conducted many beneficial explorations into the subject. In 1996, Zhu Youping and other Chinese scholars said, in effect, that the "information resource industry is an industry to exploit information resources."[2] In 1998, Pang Jing'an said that the information resource industry corresponded to "content" among 3C (communication, computer, and content).[3] According to the *Report for Development of*

2 The industry and its strategic value

Beijing Information Service Industry in 2004, the information resource industry is "an industry that develops, designs, distributes, packs and sells information products and services by use of information resources and other related resources on the back of digitization, media and network technologies, dominated by the digital content industry which comprise the industry along with the information consulting industry and the market survey industry."[4] As is described in the *Research Report of Information Resource Industry and Information Market Policies* by Chen Yu and others in 2005, more broadly measured, the information resource industry refers to all industries that provide products or services to society by producing and processing information resources. The products include printed materials, electronic publications, and audios and videos carried in various media. The industry is divided into traditional and modern industries (Beijing: Economic Science Laboratory of School of Information of Renmin University of China [2004–2005]; *Research Report of Oversight System for Information Resource Market* by Beijing Information Resource Center and National Information Center [ce.cn].

Some researchers of Chinese information resource management also came up with their own insights into the concept of the information resource industry, giving people a better grasp of the concept. According to Han Yun, "[The] information resource industry is an industrial group that focuses on making information content products and providing services concerning the information content products, which can be divided into information product manufacturing industry, information data transmission industry and information resource service industry."[5] Xuan Xiaohong said that the "information resource industry is a sector of the national economy that provides information resource content-based products or services to society by producing and processing information resources."[6] Nai Maosheng and others thought that the "information resource industry is also an information content industry, and it implies that (1) the sources of the industry are such information resources and information contents as remains to be exploited or have been exploited, (2) profits mainly derive from the operation of information content products or information services, (3) it represents the commercialization of exploitation of information resources, and (4) it takes the lead in the development of China's national economy in the Information Age."[7]

The academic community's perception of core characteristics of the information resource industry includes that the industry is targeted to produce information resources (or information contents) and that the outputs of the information resource industry are products or services in the form of information. Alongside that, the commercialized information products and services, digitization, the network-based and intelligence-based production process, and the dominance in the information economy are also crucial characteristics of the information resource industry.

The complexity in defining the concept of the information resource industry also lies in the overlap between it and other related industries. The information resource industry overlaps with such industries as the digital content industry, the cultural creative-related industry, the creative content industry, the cultural content industry, the copyright industry, and the cultural industry, either in concept or in substance.

The concept of the digital content industry is generally accepted globally. It was put forward at the "Information Conference for Seven Western Countries" early in 1995 and was popularly used. In the *Info 2000 (4-Year Work Program 1996–1999)* of 1996, the digital content industry is defined as "an industry that manufactures, develops, packs and sells information products and services."[8] As described in the special report of the Organization for Economic Cooperation and Development entitled *Content As a New Growth Industry* in 1998, the content industry is "a new industry where information and recreation industries producing contents provide services."[9] *Irish Development Strategies for Digital Content Industry* in 2002 points out that the "digital content industry, in a broad sense, refers to an industry that creates, designs, manages and releases digital products and services and provides technical support for the activities."[10] Afterwards, such organizations as the American Association of Software and Information Industries and the Japanese Association of Science, Technology and Economics, as well as such official documents as the *Japanese Content Promotion Law* (2004) and the *White Paper of Digital Content* (2007) have made similar explanations of the content industry. A lot of Chinese scholars also accept the concept of the digital content industry mainly because the concept is consistent with the internationally popular perception. A similar perception of core characteristics of the digital content industry is formed in the related fields in China and beyond. That is, information content is the subject matter and finally processed into products or services, with frequent use of modern information technologies (ITs) to conduct creative design and other intelligent activities. The concept emphasizes the application of modern ITs representing digital technologies to industrial activities and dependence of industrial activities on the ITs, excluding traditional information production activities generally. Virtually, the concept of the digital content industry has a large overlap with the concept of the information resource industry.

The concepts of such industries as the creative content industry, the cultural content industry, the cultural creative industry, and the copyright industry overlap much with the concept of information resource industry. According to the International Intellectual Property Alliance 1990, the American copyright industry was a part and parcel of the cultural creative industry, including literature publication, music, films and television, advertisements, software, painting, manufacturing, wholesale and retail of playback devices, clothing, jewelry, furniture, and interior design. In 1998, the British Special Working Team for Creative Industry defined the creative industry to be an activity that originates in personal creativity, skills, and talents and can create wealth and job opportunities by development and use of intellectual properties. A similar definition also appears in the *Basic Research Report for Creative Industry in Hong Kong* (2003) by the Cultural Policy Research Center of the University of Hong Kong from the perspective of intellectual property. KOCCA (The Korea Creative Content Agency) maintained in 2001 that the cultural content industry is related to all cultural products under the joint action of cultural traditions, lifestyles, ideas, values, and folk culture. All the definitions of the "cultural creative"-related industry are made mainly in terms of "intellectual

4 *The industry and its strategic value*

property." The core characteristics of the cultural creative-related industry lie in its intelligent work mode and contributions to cultural development.

1.1.2 Discussion of the denotation of the concept of the information resource industry

China and other countries not only disagree with the connotation of the concept of the information resource industry but differ in their perceptions of the concept of denotation itself. The difference in perception of the concept "denotation" leads to different standards adopted by people in subdividing industries, which renders the segmentation and management of industries uncertain or extremely difficult.

In the special 1998 report of the Organization for Economic Cooperation and Development entitled *Content As a New Growth Industry*, the content industry is classified into two categories; that is, "the one is traditional audiovisual and music content and the other is multimedia service integrating digital texts, materials and audiovisual contents and rendered through such new media as the Internet."[11] According to the report entitled *British Digital Content* that was released through the European website of content-village.org in 2003, the British digital content industry includes the publication industry, the software industry, the webpage design and creation industry, the graphic design industry, the game industry, and the radio and TV industry.[12] The European "i2010" strategy released in 2005 classifies the content industry into three categories, namely, film, video, and music, including production departments for printed materials, electronic publications (including databases and game software), and audiovisual transmission services expressed in various media.[13] Norway, France, Ireland, the United States, Canada, and Japan made a strong case for officially including industries relating to information resources into the national industrial statistics and classification system. In the cross-border industrial classification system, the content industry or cultural creative industry is not separately classified into one category but is scattered in other categories.

Industrial Classification for National Economic Activities (GB/T 4754-2002) does not specify that the information resource industry is a separate industry category, and the *Regulation on Classification of Three Sectors* issued by the National Bureau of Statistics in May 2003 also does not classify the information resource industry into one category. The Temporary Provisions on *Statistically Classifying Information-related Industries* developed by the National Bureau of Statistics in 2004 divide information resource-related industries into five categories, namely, the electronic information equipment manufacturing industry, the electronic information equipment sale and lease industry, the electronic information transmission service industry, the computer service and software industry, and other information-related service industries. The last two categories can be deemed to overlap with the information resource industry in concept.

It is easy to understand the reasons why the national standards or policy documents do not classify the information resource industry into one category. On one hand, those national standards or policy documents were developed early, when the information resource industry was not mature and the industrial boundary was not clear; on the other hand, the information resource industry has not made outstanding contributions to the national economy generally. However, documents of some provincial governments in China indeed cover the composition and classification of the information resource industry. In the *Report for Development of Beijing Information Service Industry* in 2004, the information resource industry falls into "digital content industry that can be subdivided into internet information industry, database industry, value-added telecommunications service industry and digital TV content, information consulting industry and market survey industry."[14] The Digital Content Industry Promotion Office of the Industrial Development Bureau, Ministry of Economic Affairs in Taiwan, China, subdivides the digital content industry into the digital game industry, the computer animation industry, the digital learning industry, the digital audio-visual application industry, the mobile content industry, the network service industry, the content software industry, and the digital publication and book reservation industry.

The academic community and the industry have different perceptions of the industries included in the information resource industry. It is generally agreed that the press and publication industry, the radio, television and film industry, the TV series and audiovisual production industry, the consulting industry, the database industry, the software industry, the social investigation industry, the advertising production industry, the Internet information resource service industry, the game industry, the animation industry, the mobile content industry, and the online learning industry among the related industries are included in the information resource industry. However, no consensus has been reached on whether various telecommunication transmission industries, including the public information resource service industry and the mapping industry, are encompassed by the information resource industry. CCID Consulting Co., Ltd. divides the digital content service industry into the core and peripheral industries in the *Annual Research Report for Investment Opportunities of Chinese Digital Content Industry from 2004 to 2005*. The core subdivided industries include the Internet service industry, the digital TV industry, the online game industry, the online education industry, the digital cartoon industry, and the wireless content, while the peripheral subdivided industry encompasses the game recreation industry, the TV and film industry, the education industry, the telecommunication industry, the music industry, the medical care industry, the radio industry, and the publication industry.[15]

1.1.3 Definition of the concept of the information resource industry

It is very normal and beneficial to discuss the connotation and denotation of the concept of the information resource industry, which, however, should be managed according to regulations of the State. Especially for setting public policies, a concept of the information resource industry that may not be absolutely thorough but can identify the basic features and boundary of the industry must be developed for solving practical problems.

6 *The industry and its strategic value*

We maintain that the information resource industry is a sector of the national economy in which information serves as an object of labor and as raw material for production; products and services in the form of information are outcomes and bring profits, and information is produced, processed, spread, and provided to consumers to generate economic and social value.

This expression reveals the connotation of the information resource industry in the method of per genus et differentiam. Firstly, it indicates that the information resource industry is a relatively independent sector of the national economy, like other industries. Next, it focuses on the main features that set the information resource industry apart from other industries; that is, information serves as the object of labor and as raw material for production, while products in the form of information and services that provide information are outcomes and bring profits. Economic and social value is created in such links as production, processing, spreading, and provision of information products and services. In terms of attributes, the information resource industry is a strategic emerging industry, a labor and knowledge-intensive industry, a high-input industry and high value-added industry; with respect to economic characteristics, the information resource industry is featured by high input, high intellectual and human capital, high risk, high "sunk cost," and industrial chain of special nature.

With respect to the relationship between the information resource industry and other industries, we hold that the intersection of the concepts has little effect on the government's industrial management practice, especially on the implementation of industrial policies. Nevertheless, it is imperative to define the boundary between the information resource industry and the cultural industry, which may help avoid management oversight and repetition. Specifically, the information resource industry and the information technology industry constitute the information industry together. The information resource industry intersects with but is distinguished from the cultural industry. The cultural industry contains part of the content in which information resource serves as the object of labor, but the material production should not be part of the information resource industry. Though the digital publication industry, the digital radio and TV industry, the digital film industry, the online game industry, the animation industry, the digital learning industry, and the network advertising industry are part of the information resource industry, they may be included in the cultural industry for management for the convenience of government's administration. Nevertheless, the value-added telecommunications service industry, the content software industry, the digital processing and digital library industry, the consulting and survey industry, and the agency industry (trade economy and agency) do not fall under the cultural industry management. The relationships between the information resource industry and the related industries are presented in Figure 1.1.

To understand the denotation of the information resource industry, we spent a long time in statistics, calculation, and analysis of data in the four-tier code industries specified in the *Chinese Industrial Classification and Code for National Economic Activities (GB/T 4754–2011)*. After that we define 93 industries that meet the characteristics of information resource industry. We view the 93 industries as subdivided industries of the Chinese information resource industry.

The industry and its strategic value 7

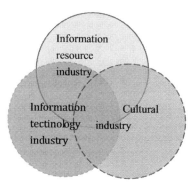

Figure 1.1 Relationships between the information resource industry and related industries

Table 1.1 Classifications of the information resource gathering industry, the subdivided industry of the information resource industry

General Classification	Category	Subcategory	
		Serial No.	Industry Name
Information Resource Gathering Industry (14)	Investigation and Monitoring Industry (8)	7410	Meteorological Service
		7420	Earthquake Service
		7430	Marine Service
		7640	Hydrologic Service
		7642	Ecological Testing
		7461	Environmental Protection Monitoring
		7450	Quality Inspection Technology Service
		7232	Market Survey
	Surveying and Mapping Industry (6)	7471	Energy, Mineral and Geological Survey
		7472	Geological Solid Mineral Survey
		7473	Geological Mineral Survey of Water and Carbon Dioxide
		7474	Basic Geological Survey
		7475	Technical Service for Geological Survey
		7440	Mapping Service

Next, we classify the information resource industry into the gathering industry, the processing industry, and the providing industry based on the nature of the main activities of the information resource industry. The information resource gathering industry encompasses 14 industries, the information resource processing industry 14 industries, and the information resource providing industry 65 industries. The compositions of the three industries are shown in Tables 1.1, 1.2, and 1.3.

Table 1.2 Classifications of the information resource processing industry, the subdivided industry of the information resource industry

General Classification	Category	Subcategory	
		Serial No.	Industry Name
Information Resource Processing Industry (14)	Data Content Production and Treatment Industry (9)	7240	Advertising Industry
		8510	Press Industry
		8610	Radio
		8620	TV
		8630	Film and Video Program Production
		8660	Record Production
		8710	Literary and Artistic Creation and Performance
		6540	Data Processing and Storage Service
		6591	Digital Content Service
	Design and Development Industry (5)	6510	Software Development
		6520	Information System Integration Service
		6550	Integrated Circuit Design
		7482	Engineering Investigation and Design
		7491	Professionalized Design Service

Table 1.3 Classifications of the information resource providing industry, the subdivided industry of the information resource industry

General Classification	Category	Subcategory	
		Serial No.	Industry Name
Information Resource Providing Industry (56)	Archive and Museum Industry (3)	8731	Books Service
		8732	Archive Service
		8750	Museum Service
	Consulting and Management Service Industry (14)	6530	Information Technology Consulting Service
		6790	Other Capital Market Services
		6891	Risk and Loss Assessment
		6940	Financial Information Service
		7221	Lawyer and Related Law Services
		7222	Notarization Service
		7231	Accounting, Audit and Tax Service
		7233	Social Economic Consulting
		7239	Other Professional Consulting
		7250	Intellectual Property Service
		7295	Credit Service
		6910	Financial Trusteeship and Management Service
		7481	Engineering Management Service
		7483	Planning Management

General Classification	Category	Subcategory	
		Serial No.	Industry Name
	Agency and Brokerage Industry	5181	Trade Agency
		5189	Other Trade Brokerage and Agency
		5821	Goods Delivery Agency
		5822	Passenger Ticket Agency
		5829	Other Transportation Agency Industries
		6850	Insurance Brokerage and Agency Industry
		8941	Entertainment Agent
		8942	Sports Agent
		8949	Other Cultural and Artistic Brokerage and Agency
		7030	Real Estate Agency Service
		7261	Public Employment Service
		7262	Employment Agency Service
		7263	Labor Dispatching Service
		7269	Other HR Services
		7292	Conference and Exhibition Service
		7520	Technology Agency Service
	Publication, Release and Lease Industry (15)	8521	Book Publication
		8522	Paper Publication
		8523	Journal Publication
		8524	Audiovisual Product Publication
		8525	Electronic Publication
		8529	Other Publication Industries
		8640	Film and Video Program Release
		8650	Motion Picture Projection
		5143	Book Wholesale
		5144	Paper Wholesale
		5145	Audiovisual Product and Electronic Publication Wholesale
		5243	Book and Paper retail
		5244	Audiovisual Product and Electronic Publication Retail
		7122	Book Lease
		7123	Audiovisual Product Lease
	Technology Promotion Service Industry (6)	7511	Agricultural Technology Promotion Service
		7512	Biological Technological Promotion Service
		7513	New Material Technology Promotion Service
		7514	Energy-saving Technology Promotion Service
		7519	Other Technology Promotion Services
		7590	Other Technology Promotion and Application Service Industries

(*Continued*)

10 *The industry and its strategic value*

Table 1.3 (Continued)

General Classification	Category	Subcategory	
		Serial No.	Industry Name
	Education and Training Industry (6)	8210	Preschool Education
		8291	Vocational Skill Training
		8292	Sports School and Sports Training
		8293	Cultural and Artistic Training
		8294	Ancillary Education Service
		8299	Other Education Not Covered
	Telecommunications Technology Service Industry (5)	6319	Other Telecommunications Services
		6420	Internet Information Service
		6592	Call Center
		6599	Other Information Technology Service Industries Not Covered
		6010	Basic Postal Service

1.2 Analysis of features of the information resource industry

As is described earlier, to fully understand the information resource industry, particularly to accurately define the connotation and denotation of the information resource industry, and to figure out what the industry is and what the industry is comprised of, it is of great significance to understand the basic features of the industry; that is, we must grasp the special attributes that set the industry apart from other industries. Here, we regard such attributes as features of the information resource industry.

1.2.1 Object of labor

Information serves as the main object of labor and the raw material for production in the information resource industry, which distinguishes the information resource industry from the traditional industries with material resources as the main object of labor and raw material for production. Although production activities of the information resource industry also involve the specific physical form of object and also consumes material resources (energy, various process and technological raw materials, carrier materials, etc.), the main object of labor in the information resource industry is information and its main raw material for production is information.

1.2.2 Profit output

Products and services in the form of information are outcomes and the main sources of profits in the information resource industry, which obviously distinguishes the information resource industry from traditional primary and secondary industries and other service industries. Firstly, the outcomes derived are not in physical form but in the form of information. Either a product or a service is a finished information product or an information service that aims to reduce people's certainty. Secondly, like any other industry, the information resource industry also needs to make profits; however, its sources of profits or main sources of profits are not material products and services – they are information products and services.

1.2.3   Source of value

The ultimate goal of an industry is, of course, to create economic and social value. Undoubtedly, the information resource industry is no exception. The "usefulness" of the information resource industry in socioeconomic development – its economic and social value – is mainly created in such links as production, processing, spreading, and provision of information products and services.

1.2.4   Functional positioning

For over 30 years, China witnessed its economic development at an ultra high speed and with impressive achievements. Nowadays, China has gradually ushered in a new stage that features a slowdown in economic growth and overall medium-and-high-end quality, benefit, ecology, and sustainability of economy. Information resources are of extremely special strategic value in such a historical period with issues concerning the fundamental transformation of economic development mode, adjustment of industrial structure and upgrading of traditional industries. To solve those strategic problems in China's socioeconomic development, essentially we need to fundamentally change the resource structure for economic development, need to reduce the consumption of material resources, and need to fully play the decisive role of information resources in creating and accumulating social wealth. As a brand-new industry in human history, the information resource industry is both a main provider of and the largest demonstrative consumer of information resources. It holds the key to solving strategic problems arising from China's socioeconomic development and dominates the scientific development of China's overall industrial system.

1.2.5   Features of elements

In the traditional social production field, the dependence of different industries on such elements as human labor, human technology, and human intelligence varies during the course of production. Industries highly dependent on human labor are known as labor-intensive industries, while those highly dependent on technology and intelligence and other knowledge elements are known as knowledge-intensive industries. China's realities and the law behind the economic development show that both types of industries are important.

China has the largest population of any country in the world, which means that a large number of people need to be fully employed, particularly many well-educated

12   *The industry and its strategic value*

people. Every year, seven or eight million students graduate from institutions of higher learning in China. Full employment, especially for the well-educated in China, is a critical social issue that is vital to individual development and social stability in China. In addressing the need for full employment, the information resource industry boasts an innate superiority because the output of the industry calls for well-educated and highly competent people. The nature of double intensity of the industry is crucial to full employment of Chinese well-educated population.

1.2.6   Economic features

With respect to economic features, the information resource industry features:

(1) High input. That is, there is a high threshold to enter into the industry. High technology content, high knowledge content, and an inclination toward monopoly require enormous amounts of economic input to enter the industry. Without a certain economic strength, it is impossible to step into the industry, let alone enter the development area.

(2) Huge growth. That is, there is a huge space for growth of the industry, and usually rapid growth of profits is fulfilled in the short term. Such well-known Chinese enterprises as BAT (Baidu, Alibaba, and Tencent) are typical information resource enterprises. All of them started from scratch and grew from small to large in a very short time, realized rapid growth of output value and profits, and quickly became famous high-value-added enterprises nationwide and globally.

(3) Large proportion of intellectual and human capital. That is, the information resource industry is highly dependent on highly competent people. Hence, human capital, particularly intellectual capital, accounts for a large proportion in the capital composition of the industry.

(4) High risk. That is, the industry is characterized by high uncertainty and unpredictability that may cause deviation from intended results after production, operation, investment, or credit granting. These characteristics mean there are increased chances of losses, increased chances of failure, and even increased chances of total failure that are far greater than those in other industries.

(5) High "sunk cost." That is, the cost that has been incurred due to past decisions that cannot be changed by any of the present or future decisions accounts for a large proportion in the cost composition of the industry. High sunk cost implies that time, money, and energy cannot be recovered once put into the industry in most cases. For example, the cost for information resource construction and the cost for setting up intellectual and human capital in high-quality talent teams can only be used for these specific purposes. Once no intended revenues are generated after input, the said cost and capital will be basically lose out, unlike the capital input for factories and general equipment that can be recovered (or may even bring in profits

because of appreciation in real estate). The high sunk cost often throws business decision-makers in the industry into a decision dilemma: on one hand, they dare not make investments because they are afraid of incurring "sunk costs" that do not bring in profit; on the other hand, they may be excessively obsessed with and regret the "sunk cost" and as a result, they go on with their original mistakes, causing more losses.

1.2.7 Industrial chain

An industrial chain is actually a vivid description of the close-link relation of technical and economic connections reflected in interindustries made by people. It is of great significance to construct a complete and valid industrial chain. That is, a complete and valid industrial chain helps reduce enterprise cost, makes for emergence of new enterprises, promotes the shaping of an atmosphere that encourages enterprise innovation, and fuels the scientific development of the whole industry. The information resource industry chain differs from that of other industries in many aspects, exhibiting obvious particularities, mainly including:

(1) Little substantial significance of the space chain that constitutes the information resource industry chain together with the value chain, enterprise chain, and supply and demand chain. The reason for that is the logistics concerning the information resource industry is basically ignored, economic benefits from the cluster of enterprises are not obvious, and it is not obvious to see the multiplied industrial value brought by optimized allocation of spatial position.

(2) Low relevance between the nature of and profits from economic activity and the overall regional economic development degree. The added value of economic activity, technological and capital content, labor intensity, and rough or finished machining regarding the information resource industry are not necessarily connected with the economic development degree in the region where an enterprise operates. Benefiting from this characteristic, underdeveloped areas are able to realize "overtaking at the turn" and give full play to their "late-starter advantages" by developing the information resource industry.

(3) Net structure. Vertically, the information resource industry chain is comprised of system equipment providers, basic network business providers, information resource developers, information content storers, information content integrators, information content service providers, regulatory agencies, and final users. Horizontally, there are numbers of more professional and elaborately divided enterprises of varied sizes in the same link.

(4) Three aspects highlighted for the conditions for composition of the information resource industry chain, namely, formation of the benefit sharing mechanism, maturity of information consumption awareness and behavior, and abundance and quality of information service content that can satisfy customers' needs.

14 *The industry and its strategic value*

(5) Prominent government factor. The strategic value of information resources determines the necessity for the State to control information resources. Meanwhile, information resources have strong cultural and ideological attributes. Therefore, the government plays a special role in such aspects as the enterprise ownership, property right, and market regulation with respect to information resources. The government intervenes more with the information resource industry than with other industries.

(6) Special mode of profitability. Indirect profits account for a large proportion. In a rare case, the existing information resource industries can gain profits directly through information products and services; instead, they often make profits indirectly. That is, information products and services are often provided to consumers free of charge or at a price lower than the cost, and profits made by information resource enterprises must be paid by third parties.

1.3 Basic functions of the information resource industry

Function often refers to the positive effect of a thing. The basic functions of the information resource industry discussed here are actually the positive effects the information resource industry exerts on China's socioeconomic development.

1.3.1 Economic function of the information resource industry

The economic function refers to the positive effect the information resource industry exerts on a country's economic development. The economic function is the primary function among the functions of the information resource industry as a sector of the national economy. The economic function is manifested mainly by the following two aspects: one is that the information resource industry can provide basic resources for economic development; the other is that the information resource industry can provide the entire society with consumption information products and services directly, becoming a new economic growth point in the Information Age.

The essential feature of economic activity is transforming resources into social wealth. Therefore, without resources, economic activity will lose its basic condition and even stop. As the world moves through the Information Age, information is applied to human economic activity on a large scale and constitutes a resource system like the three legs of a tripod together with raw materials and energy sources. In that new resource system that subverts tradition, information not only is put on a par with the other two physical forms of resources but obviously amplifies the effect of raw materials and resources; therefore, information is also called the "resource of resources." It is safe to say that information resources are the main source of the present and future social physical and mental wealth. The information resource industry fulfills its own mission to accumulate and create information resources and provide extensive social utilization. Both its main production object and main output are information. Therefore, the existence and

The industry and its strategic value 15

development of the information resource industry are basic conditions for present and future social and human economic activity. That implies human economic activity will lose the basic premise without the supply of basic resources that can be realized by the industry.

In a sense, consumption is the ultimate goal of economic activity. Human economic activity is desired to satisfy human consumption demand. An industry will be nothing if it cannot supply the society with the means of subsistence that sustains human survival. Another important function of the information resource industry is that it can supply the society with consumption information products and services directly and create a new economic growth point in the Information Age. With the development of the society, people will have more spiritual consumption demands, while their various material needs are satisfied; the more advanced the social formation is, the stronger the demands are. The information resource industry emerges to cater to these demands. Its emergence and development satisfy people's specific consumption needs and requirements, improve people's quality of life, and enrich the content of human economic activity. What cannot be ignored is that as the information resource industry advances, the applicable information products and services will promote people to further renew their ideas. In that way, more consumption needs are generated, persistently sustaining economic development and further fueling and driving faster economic development and a more rapid increase in social wealth.

1.3.2 Political function of the information resource industry

The political function of the information resource industry refers to various effects on the stability and development of national political life. The political function is reflected in several aspects, as follows.

Firstly, the information resource industry edifies people. Numerous products and services created by the information resource industry provide strong value guidance. When people receive and use information products and services, they are always educated and guided by the values recognized in the corresponding code of conduct and ideological and moral norms, which will exert explicit or implicit fundamental influences on the general mood of society and social conduct.

Secondly, the information resource industry safeguards national safety. This is especially true when provision of information products and services can effectively propagate correct ideologies in the fundamental interests of the State and nation and can constrain political behaviors of various social organizations and citizens by the law. That is how the information resource industry can safeguard the consolidation and stability of the State political power.

Finally, the information resource industry maintains social stability. On one hand, the information resource industry can scientifically and effectively allocate information resources, the core resource in the Information Age, by applying both market forces and government's macro-control featured by the socialist market economy system so that different types of social organizations and people in different regions receive resources required for development and share social wealth

16 *The industry and its strategic value*

created from such resources fairly and equally, maintaining social justice and steady social development in a more effective manner. On the other hand, some information products and services created by the information resource industry can culturally entertain and spiritually satisfy the citizenry. Thus, the citizenry can better enjoy their spare time, get physically and mentally relaxed and spiritually enriched, become happier and more satisfied, and have their lifestyle and quality improved. That undoubtedly promotes and guarantees social stability.

1.3.3 Social function of the information resource industry

The social function of the information resource industry refers to its effects on social development and progress. It is mainly shown in the following aspects.

Firstly, the information resource industry promotes and supports social governance modernization. In a sense, social governance modernization is essentially a national administration formation relying on information resources. Unlike the traditional government's administration of which the goal is realized by relying on energy sources and raw material resources, modernized social governance has viewed information resources as a core and main resource for national administration. Inevitably, the formation and development of the information resource industry will profoundly promote the exploitation of government's information resources objectively, because the majority of social information resources, particularly the best part, are under the direct control of the government, both in China and beyond. The huge demand of the information resource industry for raw materials for production will inevitably promote and guarantee the access to and profound utilization of the government's information resources beyond measure. Thus, on one hand, it will give surging impetus to the new formation of national administration (namely, social governance modernization), boosting the access to and profound utilization of the government's information resources; on the other hand, it will provide stronger resource condition support for national administration relying on information resources and ensure ongoing improvement of the degree of openness, fairness, and impartiality of the administration activities.

Secondly, the information resource industry improves the environment, increases employment, improves people's livelihood, creates more social justice and social welfare, and raises the quality of life. Low energy and material consumption along with low levels of pollution featured by the information resource industry can reduce environmental pollution and slow down the worsening of a series of human survival conditions that arise from economic development. The labor and knowledge intensity featured by the information resource industry will generate more opportunities for extensive social employment, especially for employment of the well-educated and highly competent population in modern society, and make contentment from social development and more social welfare and social fairness available to more members of society. Some information products and services produced by the information resource industry can also satisfy people's needs to physically and mentally relax, exercise, exchange feelings, refine the mind, spiritually fulfill themselves, and enrich their knowledge, improving society's life quality in all aspects. Entertainment function is an important and the most fundamental function of the information resource industry.

1.4 The strategic value of development of China's information resource industry

As is described earlier, the information resource industry is a strategic emerging leading industry. The development of the industry has strategic value to China's socioeconomic development. The strategic value is manifested in the following two aspects. On one hand, information resources are indispensable for development of almost all sectors and fields of China's national economy, and are of overall importance and fundamental. Nearly all industries, including the primary industry, secondary industry, and even tertiary industry, must regard information resources as a production element. On the other hand, the information resource industry, in which information resources serve as raw materials and information products and services are outputs, grows fast and fundamentally shapes the direction, mode, and state of socioeconomic development by supplying important resources for the whole socioeconomic development.

China has attracted the world's attention with its enviable achievements for over 30 years, since the initiation of reform and opening-up. Nowadays, the gross national economic aggregate of the whole country is dozens of times of that of 1978 every year, and more than a dozen times of that in 1978 every year, even if the rise in prices is considered. In 2013, China's economic aggregate ranked second in the world. If it is not specially stated, data in this book is exclusive of the Hong Kong Special Administrative Region, the Macao Special Administrative Region, and Taiwan. However, to accomplish the strategic objective of "double one hundred"[16] planned by the CPC Central Committee, great efforts must be made to transform the economic development mode, rebalance the industrial structure, update traditional industries, improve people's livelihood, and make fundamental social changes. To solve these strategic problems, it is imperative to finish strategic tasks and accomplish strategic objectives; that is, the resource structure issue arising from socioeconomic development in the new era must be properly addressed. That means to remarkably reduce consumption of nonrenewable raw material resources and energy sources in limited stock and devote more efforts to exploiting information resources that can be endlessly supplied. Developing the information resource industry in China is of indispensable and irreplaceable strategic value in such a historical period that is vital to China's socioeconomic development and fundamental interests.

1.4.1 The resource structure vital to China's economic development

The only fundamental solution to the strategic problems to be addressed in China's socioeconomic development in the new era, including transformation of the economic development mode, rebalance of the industrial structure and updating of

18 *The industry and its strategic value*

traditional industries, is to change the resource structure for economic development, reduce raw material and energy consumption, exert every effort to exploit information resources, and give full play to the strategic value of information resources.

The drawback of China's existing economic development mode is that China develops its economy basically by consuming quantities of raw materials and energy sources. In 2004, China's economic aggregate only accounted for 5.5% of the world's GDP, but China consumed 50% of the world's cement, 30% of the world's steel, and 15% of the world's energy sources. If China continues developing its economy in that way, the world won't allow it to do so because it is neither economical nor worthwhile. That kind of development causes deterioration of China's ecological environment. Essentially, that kind of development mode does not benefit our country and nation. The only solution is to become more dependent on information resources and to reduce material resource consumption.

The prominent problem of China's existing industrial structure is that the tertiary industry accounts for a small proportion of the total industrial output, while the tertiary industry of developed countries accounted for 70%–80% of total economic output around 2006 (Zheng Xinli. "Unswervingly Accelerating Transformation of Economic Development Mode." *Economic Daily*. 2010–06–28.). The tertiary industry of African countries generally accounted for about 50% of total economic output; China's tertiary industry accounted for less than 40% for a long time and the percentage dropped instead of increased in some years. For over 30 years, China has developed its economy by heavily relying on its industrial growth. According to statistical data, China's agriculture, industry, and services grew at annual average rates of 4.6%, 11.4%, and 10.7%, respectively, from 1979 to 2006, and at annual average rates of 4.1%, 11.1%, and 10.3%, respectively, from 2001 to 2006, with small changes. (Wang Tongsan. "Transformation of Economic Development Mode – Strategic Task Vital to Overall Socio-economic Development." *People's Daily*. 2008–01–04). The data indicate that there has been no structural improvement in China's economic growth mainly driven by industry. In particular, the symbolic proportion of industrial added value in GDP has not declined for a long time; instead, it rose to 48.9% in 2006 from 44.8% in 2002. In the same period, the proportion of China's tertiary industry in GDP did not go up but decreased from 41.5% to 39.4%.[17] Thanks to hard work, China's tertiary industry began to make up half of the national economic aggregate until 2015, accounting for 50.5%. Nevertheless, there is still a long way to go to reach the index value of 60%, the average proportion of the countries in the world. That kind of industrial structure reflects heavy dependence of China's economic development on resources in physical form.

Of course, for a socialist country with a population of more than ten million, to ensure safe and harmonious national development the position of agriculture as the foundation of the national economy must be strengthened no matter how the industrial structure is rebalanced so that Chinese agricultural production can grow strong from being weak. Meanwhile, we must continue improving the level of industrial production, growing the Chinese industry, especially the manufacturing industry, to be powerful instead of being large only. However, the top priority is to devote more efforts to accelerating the development of services so that services can develop more quickly and grow big and strong after being small and weak. That is how we can comprehensively achieve industrial collaboration and drive economic growth. To make this all come true, we must make efforts in the resource structure. That means we must continue reducing material consumption greatly by consuming more information resources.

It is a pressing task to upgrade Chinese traditional industries. Nevertheless, the solution for that is not simply rationalizing enterprises; instead, efforts must be made to "upgrade" primarily. In the final analysis, the efforts are about rebalance of the resource structure. For traditional industries featuring backward technologies and low knowledge content, upgrading mainly means improving the technological level of the industries and playing the role of knowledge and information in amplifying effects so as to reduce consumption of energy sources and raw materials and create more added value with information resources. The upgrading path of Chinese traditional industries is the integrative development of industrialization and informatization; essentially, it means adding more information resource elements to traditional industries, which the information resource industry is good at doing. Some analyses show that if the Internet drives the growth of industrial productivity by 1–1.5 percentage points every year, the average income level of enterprises will increase by 25%-40% in the next 20 years. General Electric predicts that the use of the Internet by industry will increase global GDP by USD 10–15 trillion in the next 20 years, almost equivalent to creating another American economy.[18] As is proved by practice in Japan, it can save about 2/3 of the time and 9/10 of the R&D cost to renovate traditional industries by bringing in foreign patents and using invalid patents. China shows great potential in that.

The rebalancing of the resource structure, which is the solution to the strategic problem of national socioeconomic development, means increasing the supply of information resources and replacing the material resources or amplifying effects of material resources with information resources. The necessity to use information resources determines the strategic value of developing China's information resource industry. The development level of the information resource industry as the main supplier of social information products, and services determines the overall supply level of social information products and services, the abundance of national quality information resources, the optimization of the resource structure for national socioeconomic development, and the satisfaction of needs and requirements for scientific socioeconomic development.

Comrade Jiang Zemin points out in *China's IT Industry Development in the New Era*,

> In modern society, the elements for economic development have expanded from capital, land and labor to technology, knowledge and information. As a production element that can be endlessly used, information can generate increasing returns, expand growth sources and spur sustained economic development. The exploitation of information renders such new production elements

20 *The industry and its strategic value*

as technology and knowledge vigorously fuel economic development, and such elements are contributing more and more to economic development.[19]

President Xi makes that view more direct and thorough. "Information leads technology flow, capital flow and talent flow, information resources have become an increasingly important production element and social wealth, and how much a country grasps information signifies its soft power and competitiveness," said President Xi at the first meeting of the Central Cyberspace Affairs Leading Group on February 27, 2014.

1.4.2 Basic tendency vital to China's social development

China has gained strong momentum economically and socially, and social and economic programs have made headway over the past 30 years since the initiation of reform and the opening-up. However, the problem of "one leg longer than the other" as Comrade Wen Jiabao said, has always existed during the course of economic development.[20]

1. Main strategic problems in China's social development

China has witnessed a large and fast economic development pace as a result of several factors over the past 30 years. Nevertheless, social programs highlighted by improvement in people's livelihoods have not progressed that much relatively. In other words, our economic development is not in much harmony with social development. That is reflected as follows.

Firstly, a modern scientific and technological system that ensures independent innovation has not been established yet. Independent innovation is not only an important sign that marks the maturity of the national modern scientific and technological system but also the core link in the transformation of the national economic development mode and rebalance of the economic structure. China has seen great headway in science and technology over the past 30 years since the initiation of reform and the opening-up. However, so far, China has not really established a modern scientific and technological system that ensures independent innovation yet, and it has not had strong original innovation and core technology innovation capabilities. If that situation is not changed, China will not gain the initiative in the new technological revolution and will not win the strategic initiative in the increasingly fierce global economic and technological competition.

Secondly, there is a huge gap between the real development of China's education and socioeconomic development needs and expectations of broad masses of the people. Although the Party and the State have made deployment, and the related parties have also made efforts over the past 30 years since the initiation of reform and the opening-up, the task of socialist education reform has not been finished throughout the country. There is still a long way to go to realize true educational fairness. The allocation of education resources remains to be optimized, and the schooling gap of different populations remains to be narrowed. Training people required by development of social programs is still onerous. China's education undertaking cannot really satisfy objective needs and requirements for socioeconomic development from such aspects as size, structure, and quality, and does not live up to the expectations of broad masses of the people well.

Thirdly, China's socialist culture has not really prospered. Undoubtedly, China has seen great improvement in people's material standard of living and some progress in socialist cultural undertakings as a result of reform and the opening-up. However, from the current development status quo, there is still a long way to go to meet the requirements of broad masses of the people to improve their own cultural quality and enrich their inner and cultural life. The gaps and bottlenecks in Chinese cultural undertaking development are prominent, and many aspects of the public cultural undertakings are yet to be developed.

Fourthly, China's basic employment system, income distribution system, social security system, and medical and health care system have not covered broad masses of the people. The socialist systems are essentially political and economic systems that benefit all of the people. However, over the past 30 years since the initiation of reform and the opening-up, it has not been the case that all of the people share the fruits of the reform and opening-up, and such employment and social security issues, income distribution issues and basic medical and health care issues as are highly relevant to the vital interests of broad masses of the people have not been addressed fundamentally. Firstly, the employment picture is not rosier. China has a large population, which means many people need jobs. In the future, over 20 million urban workers need jobs every year; however, China only generates job opportunities of 50% of that figure every year under normal growth conditions. Furthermore, the overall quality of national workers is low. A great amount of workers are only able to do simple physical work and are not competent to occupy positions with high technological requirements. Also, China does not have sufficient jobs to offer to intellectual laborers, so that it is difficult for some college graduates to find jobs. Secondly, the big income gap among people in different regions, industries, occupations, and levels, and unequal income distribution have begun to form social harms and bring about some severe social issues, which constrain the development of socialist systems. Thirdly, there is a big gap between the overall level of social security of China and that of other countries in the world. China's social security is characterized by unbalanced development of urban and rural social security, narrow coverage of the basic security system, and a low level of security. Social security for disadvantaged groups among people is very prominent. Finally, the reform of the medical and health care system is not successful, and the medical and health level of the whole society is not high. Since the initiation of reform and the opening-up, China has witnessed progress in the medical and health field; however, medical service is not sufficiently supplied as a whole, high-quality resources are mostly possessed by cities, and there are few big hospitals. Both urban and rural medical security systems are also not sound. The medical and health care system must be again reformed thoroughly and completely.

22 *The industry and its strategic value*

2. *The strategic problem facing China's social development is essentially about the development resource structure as well*

China's social development will keep pace with economic development so as to gradually realize balanced development. Social development not only needs physical resources for support but also cries for information resources for support. To realize the social development objective of benefiting people, physical resources are allocated to produce more and better material wealth so that the increased economic benefits are shared as widely as possible; meanwhile, nonphysical resources are also allocated to create more and better mental wealth so as to satisfy growing spiritual and cultural needs of a wider range of people. The resources for the human social development include three types, namely, raw materials, energy sources, and nonphysical resources. The former two types are physical resources, and nonphysical resources include only information resources. Therefore, directly or indirectly accomplishing the social development objective of benefiting people will need not only physical resources but also information resources. Virtually, most development results of such social undertakings as technology, education, and culture are carried in the form of information, and the resources necessary for their development are also information resources primarily. Without information resources, such social undertakings will not exist, let alone their development. Nowadays, increasing employment, strengthening social security, and improving the medical and health level for all need not only physical resources but also information resources. It is a defining trend that China will generate its job opportunities mainly by developing the tertiary industry through exploiting information resources. Even for strengthening social security and improving the medical and health level, the role of information resources must also be played to a great extent. The fact that both China and the wider community resort to informatization as a way to develop their social security and medical and health services can support our judgment. Applying information to the two fields is desired to reduce cost and input of physical resources and amplify effects by imputing information resources. The effect of information flow in guiding personnel flow and material flow is always amplified obviously.

It is an arduous task to achieve coordinated development between the city and the countryside, between industries, regions, and populations in China and to build a harmonious society. Therefore, we need to pay more attention to safeguarding the equal rights of different people to access and use information resources, which will contribute to coordinated and harmonious social development.

In the new era, China sees serious development imbalance between the city and the countryside, and between regions, industries, and populations, as a consequence of complex natural and social factors that will impede scientific and harmonious social development. In fact, much of inequality and unfairness in the Information Age, particularly unreasonable distribution of social wealth, is caused by inequality of access to information resources by different regions, industries, and populations, and that inequality is closely linked with the actual exploitability of information resources. Hence, it makes for eliminating various kinds of inequality to devote more efforts to exploiting information resources so that more information resources are available to people. It can be foreseen that when people can access and use information resources more equally and fairly, it will be highly conductive for relatively poor and backward areas, industries, and populations to play the later-starter advantage in economic development and social progress, boosting balanced, coordinated, and harmonious social development.

3. *We must devote more efforts to developing the information resource industry and pursue the coordinated social development of China*

As is described previously, to pursue coordinated social development of China, the resource structure that is vital to social development must be well addressed. That means we must highlight the role of information resources among the three kinds of resources, raw materials, energy sources, and information. That is how we can ensure the establishment of a modern, independent, innovative scientific and technological system, make educational development match socioeconomic development needs and expectations of broad masses of the people, achieve a booming and prosperous socialist culture, and get the Chinese basic employment system, income distribution system, social security system, and medical and health care system to really and completely benefit broad masses of the people. In view of this, it is vital and crucial to develop the information resource industry. If there are not so abundant information resources brought by the development of the information resource industry in China, the needs of social development for information resources will not be satisfied. As a result, coordinated social development will be theoretic only due to loss of strong resource support, just like water without sources and a tree without roots.

On one hand, development of the information resource industry can provide basic resources for development of China's social undertakings as well as full power and strong industrial support for coordinated social development, and can improve the quality of the nation, enrich the public's inner and material life, improve people's quality of life and offer benefits from the reform and opening-up, particularly from economic development, to more people by directly supplying quality information products and services. On the other hand, development of the information resource industry can generate exciting development opportunities for more people, especially those with knowledge-based talents, and can comprehensively improve Chinese people's livelihood. It can also make for income equality, sound social security, and availability of medical and health care to all people, and improve the scientific level of China's social development in an all-round way.

The top priority of improvement in the people's livelihood is to enhance employment so that a broad range of people, especially those with knowledge-based talents, are offered opportunities to develop themselves. It is highly commendable for the information resource industry to make great contributions to increase employment in a wide range of areas. On one hand, developing the information resource industry will enhance the size and development level of Chinese tertiary industry

24 *The industry and its strategic value*

a great deal so that more people will have opportunities to be employed. This is especially true at present when the Chinese secondary industry is characterized by severe overcapacity. On the other hand, the attribute of "knowledge intensity and labor intensity" of the information resource industry determines that the production process involves not only lots of technologies and such knowledge innovation activities as R&D but also frequent general work, such as data processing and product rendering. Therefore, the information resource industry has a strong capability of creating jobs. It not only can generate job opportunities for numbers of "blue collar" workers but can play an irreplaceable role in absorbing knowledge-based "white-collar" workers. The Chemical Abstract Service is a typical information resource enterprise. Its operation creates jobs for 500–700 doctors. The R&D and marketing of American SAS software provide jobs for several thousand people. Tokyo in Japan renders commercialized transport services by use of traffic information resources gathered by the government, which also generates job opportunities for several thousand people. In China, 26.15 million people worked in the information resource industry in 2012, and 28.87 million people were engaged in the industry in 2013. It is hard for traditional "labor-intensive" industries to attract college graduates who are knowledge-based talents; however, the information resource industry featuring "double intensity" can hold the key to providing jobs for knowledge-based talents.

The development of the information resource industry also plays a major role in enhancing national culture soft power, making education equality available to the social public and satisfying people's spiritual needs. It can meet needs of the population that had no access to quality education resources in the past to a great extent so that a wide range of people can enrich the contents of their knowledge and improve their knowledge structures by accessing more and more comprehensive information and knowledge. In that way, they can improve their own quality. Additionally, the products or services delivered by the information resource industry are obviously of entertainment nature. That is, when people are consuming such products or services, they are improving their life quality, particularly inner life quality. For instance, animation, film, and online game industries are of high value to enrich the public's inner life and improve the public cultural connotation, improving the public's life quality. In international cultural exchange, the development of the information resource industry improves national culture soft strength and nationally controls information resources. In the internationalization context, culture soft power is of great significance to strengthen national cohesion and form and uphold common values and cultural ethos of the Chinese nation.

Notes

1 "Several Opinions of the General Office of the CPC Central Committee and the General Office of the State Council on Strengthening Exploitation of Information Resources (Z.B.F. [2004] No.34)" issued on December 12, 2014.

2 Youping Zhu, "Ten Issues Concerning Development of Chinese Information Resource Industry," *China Soft Science*, no. 6 (1996): 102–107.

The industry and its strategic value 25

3 Jing'an Pang, "Development of Chinese Information Resource Industry in the Network Environment," *China Information Review*, no. 3 (1998): 810.

4 Beijing Information Technology Services Office, *Report for Development of Beijing Information Service Industry in 2004* (Beijing: China Development Press, 2005).

5 Yun Han, "Information Resource Industry and Strategies for Its Development in China," *Journal of Library Science in China*, no. 6 (2006): 41–44.

6 Xiaohong Xuan, *A Study on Fostering Information Resource Market* (Beijing: China Wenlian Press, 2008), 60.

7 Maosheng Lai, Hui Yan and Jian Long, "A Discussion over Information Resource Industry and Its Scope," *QING BAO KE Xue*, no. 4 (2008): 481–490.

8 European Commission, *Info 2000 (4-Year Work Program 1996–1999)* (European Commission, 1996).

9 OECD, *Content As a New Growth Industry* (DSTI/ICCP/IE(96)6/FINAL.OECD, 1998).

10 National Policy Advisory Commission of Ireland, "Irish Development Strategies for Digital Content Industry," ed. and trans. Jinjing Zhang, *Informationization Reference*, no. 5 (2004).

11 OECD, *Content as a New Growth Industry* (DSTI/ICCP/IE(96)6/FINAL.OECD, 1998).

12 "Historical Appearance of Modern Content Industry," [2010-12-31]. www.ssfcn.com/wenzhangdetail.asp?id=83366&wordPage=4.

13 European Commission, "I2000," [2010-12-31]. http://ec.europa.eu/information-society/eeurope/i2010/index-en.htm.

14 Information Technology Services Office, *Report for Development of Beijing Information Service Industry in 2004* (Beijing: China Development Press, 2005).

15 CCID Consulting, "Evolution Trend of 'The Strong Getting Stronger, and Extensive Development' of Chinese Geographic Information Resource Industry," [2014-01-04] (20150815), www.ccidconsulting.com/ei/gdcy/gdzb/sdpl/webinfo/2012/09/1346633865786936.htm.

16 The CPC Central Committee set two objectives of the struggle at the 18th National Congress of CPC, namely, building a moderately prosperous society in an all-round way at the 100th anniversary of CPC, and building a prosperous, democratic, civilized and harmonious socialist modern country at the 100th anniversary of the founding of new China.

17 Tongsan Wang, "Transformation of Economic Development Mode: Strategic Task Vital to Overall Socio-Economic Development," *People's Daily*, January 4, 2008.

18 "Industrial Internet Will Create another American Economy: Remarkable Economic Benefit," *Xinhuanet.com* [2015-06-21]. http://news.xinhuanet.com/fortune/201412/18/c_127314441.htm.

19 Zemin Jiang, "China's IT Industry Development in the New Era," *Journal of Shanghai Jiaotong University*, no. 10 (2008).

20 Jiabao Wen, "Several Issues Concerning Development of Social Programs and Improvement in People's Livelihood," *QIUSHI*, no. 7 (2010).

2 Basic theories on the development of China's information resource industry

Industrial development theories are about the law of development, the cycle of development and elements of an industry, industrial organization, industrial cluster, and research and development policies, etc. The research on industrial development theories enables the governmental decision-making department to take varied industrial policies subject to laws of industrial development at different stages and allows enterprises to adopt corresponding development strategies according to those laws so that they can gain some advantage in competition. In this chapter, such theories as dynamic resource triangle theory, information consumption theory, industrial symbiosis theory, information resource industry chain theory, and limited governmental intervention theory that guide the development of the information resource industry and the polices are illustrated in terms of philosophical vision, external impetus, endogenous structure, value driving, and policy reliance; the authors focus on introducing the backgrounds for formation of and basic connotations of these theories, and try to make a meaningful exploration of basic principles and basic laws of the development of the information resource industry and the policies.

2.1 Philosophical vision of the information resource industry: dynamic resource triangle theory

It is widely acknowledged in the domestic and foreign academic communities that the world is comprised of materials, energy, and information (Xu Cai et al., 1992; Sun Gennian, 1999; Wu Kun, 2002; Sun Dongchuan, 2004; Zhou Guangzhao, 2009), and that material resources, energy resources, and information resources constitute the three basic resources for human social development (Oettinger et al., 1990). A group of scholars represented by Professor Anthony G. Oettinger of Harvard University put forward the "resource triangle" model to describe the basic social resource structure. As information technology advances with each passing day and is comprehensively and profoundly popularized, information resources have gradually exhibited their strategic value in human social development and have gradually become an important strategic resource that helps a country and a territory realize economic and wealth growth and form international and regional influences. The application of a new generation of Internet technologies marked by

The basic theory of industry development 27

such new things as cloud computing, big data, and the Internet of Things empowers information resources to save and amplify effects of traditional material resources and energy resources more effectively. In this section, the research on basic theories, the concept model of "Dynamic Resource Triangle," describing the evolution features of social resource structure is constructed on the basis of the "resource triangle" theory by introduction of a time variable, and then "Dynamic-resource-triangle Barycenter Curve," and its function expressions are proposed, with the form features and the theoretical value of the curve explained. In subsequent studies, actually measured data is applied to draw the "Dynamic-resource-triangle Barycenter Curve" of a specific region or industry in a period with the foregoing curve as a tool so as to reflect structural features and the development trend of the society or basic resources of the industry that provides support for scientific decisions made by management.

2.1.1   Retrospective analysis of "resource triangle" theory

The Information Resource Policy Research Center led by Professor Anthony G. Oettinger first built a "equilateral triangle" model in its 1976 annual report that described the relations among materials, energy, and information, as shown in Figure 2.1(a). According to the research team, "[T]he resources of societies are materials, energy and information; without materials there is nothing; without energy all stands still; without information all is chaos." From 1978 to 1980, researchers tried discussing changes brought by application of information resources to the postal system, media system, international organization system, and computer communication system from the management's perspective. They believed that the exploitation of information resources would expand the industrial boundary and bring new benefit points to organizations. Particularly when using the "resource triangle" model to explain the related issues concerning "organization management," researchers adjusted the variable structure of the model, as shown in Figure 2.1(b). Thereafter, the researchers pointed out from the stakeholder's perspective that the model could reveal three attributes of information, namely, substance, format, and process, as shown in Figure 2.1(c) (Oettinger, et al., 1990; Oettinger, et al., 1998). Oettinger (2001) again extended the scope of application of the resource triangle as shown in Figure 2.1(d). In his view, information resources are playing an increasingly important role in driving the progress of modern civilization, and for all of us, information resources are one of the basic resources that sustain our lives, different from but as important as materials and energy.

From the existing findings, many scholars have made in-depth studies of features of three kinds of basic social resources as well as the relations among them (Ren Juan, 2006; Zhang Yuxiang, 2011; He Shaohua, et al., 2010). However, the research group identifies that there are still deficiencies as follows: one is that the "resource triangle" model cannot reflect the dynamic change of the social resource structure given that it is a dynamic model. That is, social development relies on the three basic resources variably, leading to the change of the basic social resource structure; the other is that the existing discussions of the academic

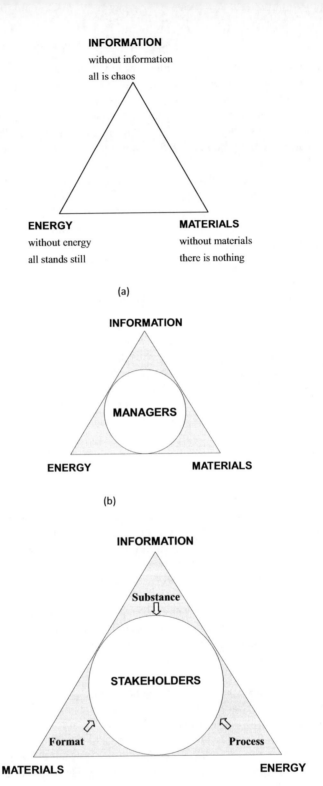

Figure 2.1 Progress of study on model of "resource triangle"

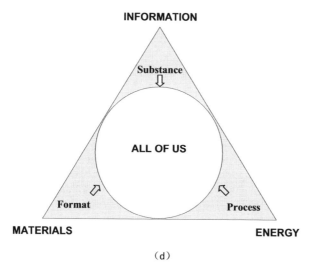

Figure 2.1 (Continued)

community over attributes of the three basic social resources are on the basis of descriptions of abstract concepts, and there is a lack of specific quantifiable indexes used for comparison of basic resource structures in different social formations.

2.1.2 Construction and characteristic analysis of dynamic resource triangle model

A group of scholars represented by Daniel Bell, an American sociologist, made a qualitative judgment of features of the resource structure in different social formations: In the traditional society (also called pre-industrial society), materials are input most, followed by energy and information; in the industrial society, energy input is obviously increased; however, in the information society (also called postindustrial society), information is input most (Bell, 1976; Bell, 1973; Sakaiya Taichi, 1987; Manuel and Aoyama, 1994; Servan-Schreiber, 1981; Naisbitt, 1982; Toffler, 1990). Hence, at different stages of social development, there should be different shapes of the "resource triangle" instead of the equilateral triangle only. Therefore, the research group added a time variable to the "resource triangle" model to build the "dynamic resource triangle" (DRT) model that reflects features of the resource structure at different stages of social development.

To better explain changes of the shape of the DRT at different stages of social development, the research group first introduced a three-axis coordinate system on the basis of the "resource triangle" model. To establish the three-axis coordinate system, three coordinate dimensions are led out from the center of the "resource triangle" as the origin, representing the percentages of consumption of material

30 *The basic theory of industry development*

resources, energy resources, and information resources in creating unit social wealth in a specific social formation, respectively, expressed by capital letters M (materials), E (energy), and I (information) respectively, in the coordinate system. Because the dimensions represent the percentages of the three kinds of basic resources, 1 is taken as the maximums of the M axis, E axis, and I axis (namely, the overall lengths of the axes). The three vertexes of the "resource triangle" are expressed by M_0, E_0 and I_0, respectively. Then, m_0, e_0 and i_0 are taken as their values in the corresponding coordinate axes, representing the percentages of material resources, energy resources, and information resources in social development in a general social formation, respectively. Hence, $m_0 + e_0 + i_0 = 1$. Because the "resource triangle" is an equilateral triangle, the included angle between any two axes in the three-dimension coordinate system is $120°$, and $m_0 = e_0 = i_0 = 1/3$. Based on the qualitative judgment of the academic community for main development resources and strategic resources in different social formations, the research group indicated the features of the resource structure at different stages of social development in the three-axis coordinate system, as presented in Table 2.1.

The previously-mentioned train of thought of provides theoretical thinking for a discussion of industrial structure upgrading. As basic resources (Oettinger, etc. 1990), materials, energy and information play a fundamental part in human social development, and any change of the resource structure exerts profound impacts on the evolution of human social formation. As such, the three kinds of basic resources are essential to develop various industries. Industrial structure upgrading means not only technological upgrading of traditional industries featuring high consumption of materials and energy so as to improve the development quality of such industries but also accelerating the development of strategic emerging industries in order to increase the percentage of such industries in the overall industrial structure (Zhao Yulin, etc., 2008). Hence, though the dynamic resource triangle model is built on the basis of analysis and reasoning of social formation evolution, it can, as an analysis tool, also be used to reveal the contributions of recyclable information resources to economic development during the course of the specific socioeconomic growth, and to analyze and explore changes of features of resource structures in various specific industries. In that way, industrial decision-making departments can keep track of the tendency of input of information resources during the course of industrial development and are provided with theoretical thinking to seek the goal of industrial upgrading and the path of industrial structure optimizing.

2.1.3 *Analysis of dynamic-resource-triangle barycenter curve*

The DRT model clearly presents features of the resource structure at different stages of human society. However, it seems not direct and convenient enough to apply the DRT model directly when a comparative analysis of the basic social resource structures in different periods, regions, or industries needs making. Therefore, the research group attempted to draw the dynamic-resource-triangle

Table 2.1 Reflections of features of resource structure at different stages of social development

Social Stage	Shape of Triangle	Mathematical Feature	Name of Triangle
Traditional society: material resources are utilized most, followed by energy resources and information resources		$m_1 \geq e_1 \geq i_1$	Left-leaning acute-angled triangle
Industrial society: more energy resources are used with the utilization ratio exceeding that of the material resources, while information resources are less utilized.		$e_2 \geq m_2 \geq i_2$	Right-leaning acute-angled triangle
Information society: as the utilization ratio grows fastest, information resources possibly become a resource type that accounts for the largest proportion in the whole resource structure; the consumption of energy resources and material resources decreases greatly, with material resources consumed least.		$i_3 \geq e_3 \geq m_3$	Middle-peak acute-angled triangle

32   *The basic theory of industry development*

barycenter curve (DB curve) as an analysis tool for revealing the law behind socio-economic development. By introducing a time variable, the DRT and DB curve theories will break through limitations of static studies of the "resource triangle." It means such theories will uncover main features of the basic resource structure at different social time points as well as the change tendency of the basic resource structure with the social change. Hence, the DB curve can reflect the main features of the economic development mode of a region in a period, which underpins the analysis of the quality of its economic development. The decision-making department in a region not only can view the DB curve as one of the tools for monitoring the regional economic development situation and grasping the change tendency of the economic formation but can also use it as a theoretical index for comparison of interregional economic development, thus providing reference for decisions for regional economic development.

1.   *Mathematical features of the dynamic-resource-triangle barycenter*

Any triangle has only one barycenter mathematically. In a rectangular coordinate system, if coordinates of the three vertexes of a triangle are known, it is easy to work out the coordinate of the barycenter. However, for a triangle of which vertexes can be arbitrarily changed, when the position of any of the vertexes changes so that the shape of the triangle changes, the position of the barycenter may remain unchanged. Nevertheless, the foregoing discriminant may become invalidated under some constraint conditions. Hence, we can infer that when the position of any of the vertexes of a triangle changes so that the shape of the triangle changes under some constraint conditions, the barycenter may be displaced.

So when the scenario of the researched problem meets the so-called "constraint conditions," values of the barycenter map the set of shapes of the triangle one by one; therefore, barycenters can be used to represent different shapes of the DRT. The research group proves that the revealed mathematical properties of the DRT can be said "constraint conditions" by use of the computational formula of the DRT barycenter; that is, any DRT barycenter can be used to represent the corresponding DRT. So when the scenario of the researched problem meets the so-called "constraint conditions," values of the barycenter map the set of shapes of the triangle one by one; that is, any DRT barycenter can be used to represent the corresponding DRT.

2.   *DB curve and features*

As mentioned earlier, with human social formation evolution, the shape of DRT changes from left-leaning acute-angled triangle to right-leaning acute-angled triangle and then to middle-peak acute-angled triangle. Such change can be shown through analysis of the displacement path of barycenters of each DRT. Therefore, the research group tried to find out the barycenters of the DRTs in the traditional society, industrial society, and information society, respectively, as shown in Figure 2.2(a–c). To highlight the displacement of the said barycenters, the research

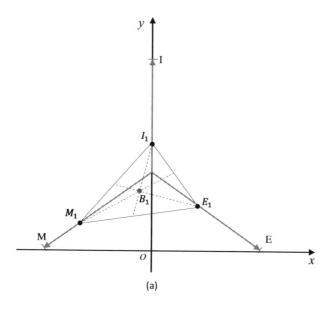

(a)

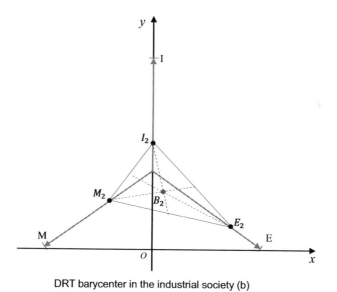

DRT barycenter in the industrial society (b)

Figure 2.2 Displacement path of DRT barycenters in different social formations and DB curve diagram

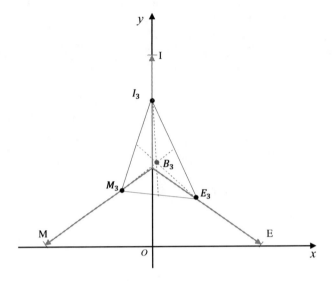

DRT barycenter in the information society (c)

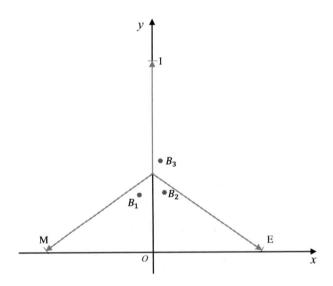

Displacement path of DRT barycenters in the three kinds of societies (d)

Figure 2.2 (Continued)

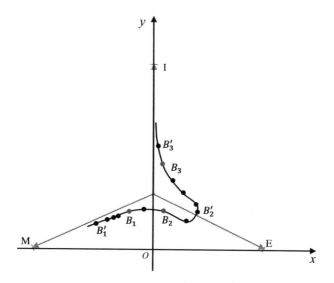

DB curve diagram (e)

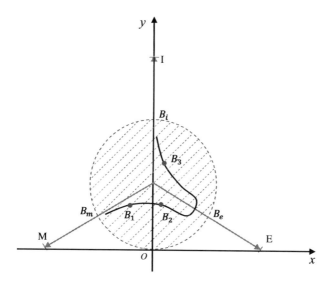

Movement range of "DRT" barycenter curve (f)

Figure 2.2 (Continued)

36 The basic theory of industry development

group placed the three barycenters in the same rectangular coordinate system and maintained the relative positions of the barycenters, as shown in Figure 2.2(d). Furthermore, to further present features and the tendency of displacement of the DRT barycenters during the course of social development, more DRT barycenters at different stages of social development can be drawn. When the points representing different DRT barycenters are sufficient, the displacement path will form a curve, as shown in Figure 2.2(e). [what should be noted is that the curve of inverted "ЛL" shown in Figure 2.2(e) is a possible typical form of the DB curve. The displacement from B'_1 to B'_2 indicates the growing proportion of energy resources in the basic social resource structure, reflecting the "industrialization" progress in human social development; the displacement from B'_2 to B'_3 indicates the growing proportion of information resources in the basic social resource structure, reflecting the "informatization" progress in human social development. The DB curve drawn based on actual data for a period for a country or a region or a specific industry may take on several different forms and may not be a complete line of inverted "ЛL".] The research group defines this curve as the "DRT barycenter curve." The function expression is as follows:

$$y = f(x), (x, y) \in \left\{ \left(\frac{\sqrt{3}}{6} (1 - i_n - 2m_n), \frac{2 + 3i_n}{6} \right) \right\}$$

The DRT theory implies that materials, energy, and information are three kinds of basic resources for human social development, sustaining any social formation. However, for further discussion, the following three "extremities" are theoretically assumed. That is, when only one of the three kinds of basic resources exists in the society, then the DRT will become a line segment. It is easy to prove that the value range of the DRT barycenter curve will be within the circle which is centered on the origin of the three-axis coordinate system (namely, [0, 1/2] in the rectangular coordinate system) and whose sides pass through barycenters B_n, B_e, and B_i (with the radius of 1/3), as shown in Figure 2.2(f). It can thus be seen that the following is always satisfied for the DB curve.

$$\left(\frac{\sqrt{3}}{6} (1 - i_n - 2m_n), \frac{2 + 3i_n}{6} \right) \in \left\{ (x', y') \mid x'^2 + \left(y' - \frac{1}{2} \right)^2 = \left(\frac{1}{3} \right)^2 \right\}$$

Apart from further enriching and developing the DRT theory, the DB curve also serves as an analysis tool for revealing the law behind socioeconomic development. By introducing a time variable, the DRT and DB curve theories will break through limitations of static studies of the "resource triangle." That means such theories will uncover the main features of the basic resource structure at different social time points as well as the change tendency of the basic resource structure with social change. Hence, the DB curve can reflect the main features of the economic development mode of a region in a period, which underpins the analysis of the quality of its economic development. The decision-making department in

The basic theory of industry development 37

a region not only can view the DB curve as one of the tools for monitoring the regional economic development situation and grasping the change tendency of the economic formation but can also use it as an theoretical index for comparison of interregional economic development, thus providing reference for decisions for regional economic development. Furthermore, the DB curve also provides a basis for explanation of features of the social modernization drive. Social modernization refers to the process where an individual applies modern science and technologies to improve material and mental conditions for their own survival in an all-round way (Lu Xueyi, etc., 2012). Different shapes of the DB curve reflect different shape features of the DRT at different stages of social development. The slope of the DB curve mathematically represents the speed of increase in the proportion of information resources in the basic social resource structure, essentially revealing the degree of the role of information resources in the evolution of social modernization. In a theoretically "typical" DB curve, the flat curve segment (as shown in Figure 2.2(f) $B_1 - B_2$) and the steep curve segment (as shown in Figure 2.2(f) $B_2 - B_3$) coexist. A flat curve segment with a small slope indicates the limited role of information resources in social development, and the reason for the movement of the curve is the growing consumption of energy resources, which virtually reflects features of the social industrialization process. However, when the DB curve begins to move upward with the slope of the curve increasing, it implies the growing consumption of information resources; that is, information resources are playing an increasingly important role in social modernization. That DB curve segment exposes features of social informatization. Therefore, analysis of shapes of the curve and changes of the slope can provide a theoretical basis for an explanation of features and development tendencies of the social modernization drive in different countries and regions.

2.2 Exploration of impetus to develop information resource industry: information consumption theory

The information consumption growth objectives were put forward in the *Several Opinions on Promoting Information Consumption and Expanding Domestic Demand* (G.F. [2013] No.32) issued by the State Council in August 2013. That is, projections showed that by 2015, information consumption would have exceeded RMB 3.2 trillion with an annual average growth by more than 20%, driving the new output of related industries of more than RMB 1.2 trillion; the Internet-based new information consumption would have exceeded RMB 2.4 trillion with an annual average growth of more than 30%. Consumption based on such information platforms as e-commerce and cloud computing would grow fast, with the turnover of e-commerce exceeding RMB 1.8 trillion and the turnover of e-retailing reaching RMB 3 trillion.[1] Once released, the document drew much attention from the industry and the academic community, rendering information consumption a new hot topic.

Notably, "information consumption" is a market behavior different from but linked with another concept, "information resource exploitation," which refers

38   *The basic theory of industry development*

to the process of gathering, processing, storing, spreading, serving, exchanging, sharing, and applying information resources based on social demands.[2] The concept also has broader connotations and denotations than "information resources," including not only non-market exploitation of information resources (such as inner exploitation) but also market exploitation of information resources (such as information consumption). To define that, the Chinese Government once published several documents, such as the *Remarks of President Xi at the First Meeting of the Central Cyberspace Affairs Leading Group, China's Twelfth Five-year Plan for Development of Strategic Emerging Industries, China's Strategies for Informatization Development from 2006 to 2020, Informatization Development Plan* issued by the Ministry of Industry and Information Technology, and *Several Opinions of the General Office of the CPC Central Committee and the General Office of the State Council on Strengthening Information Resource Exploitation* (Z.B.F. [2004] No.34).

Foreign literature covers few systematical findings of information consumption, and these limited findings are mainly about: (1) a discussion of such general issues as features and the mechanism[3] of information consumption, and construction of a model[4] on information consumption behavior, (2) analysis of consumption features of specific consumption groups, such as consumption features of students[5] or in rural areas,[6] (3) mention of information consumption in the discussion of other related issues such as personal information management aims at information production instead of information consumption.[7]

We hold that priority must be given to two important issues among the issues to be addressed in the study on the information consumption theory in terms of current socioeconomic development needs in China, namely, features of information consumption as an emerging market behavior, and special needs proposed by those features for the setting of related policies. We will briefly explain the preliminary research results in those two aspects. With the explanation model of features of information consumption as a basic clue, an exploration of market features, structural features, evolution features, and policy need features of information consumption will be made in the related contents, and investigation data of the Chinese network video industry serves as a basic argument support. The investigation data comes from the related research reports of the research group, as well as *Report for Research on Chinese Netizens' Application of Network Videos for 2013, Report for the 33th Statistics of China's Internet Development Status,*[8] *Annual Industrial Monitoring Report for Chinese Online Videos from 2013 to 2014* (iResearch Consulting Group), *Analysis Report for Network Video and Smart TV Industries for 2013* (iResearch Consulting Group), etc.

2.2.1   *Explanation model*

To make an in-depth explanation of basic features of information consumption, we, on the basis of field investigation, expert consultation, case analysis, literature study, and full inner discussion, have come up with an explanation model for

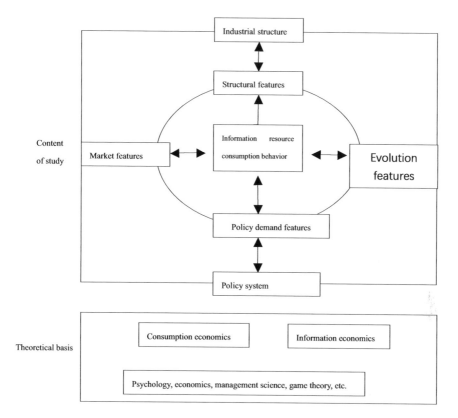

Figure 2.3 Explanation model for features of information consumption

features of information consumption after theoretical generalization (as shown in Figure 2.3). It can be seen from Figure 2.3 that for studying features of information consumption, we need to analyze and define the differences between information consumption and traditional consumption based on consumption economics and information economics theories, etc., giving priority to exploring the information consumption pattern, consumption structure, and the evolution law, policy demand, and inner links among them for the purpose of perfecting the information consumption theory and providing a basis for construction and development of the national related policy systems.

The following sections contain the research result produced on the basis of the explanation model for features of information consumption. The basic value of the result is to explore the mechanism for sound development of the information resource industry from the perspective of consumption and to define the policy demand and management demand of the information resource industry.

40 *The basic theory of industry development*

2.2.2 *Market features*

Compared with material consumption and energy consumption, information consumption features:

1. *Minimum marginal cost and maximum marginal benefit from the perspective of an operator*

In economics, marginal cost refers to extra or additional cost for an additional unit of output. Therefore, we can infer from the definition that marginal cost (MC) equals variation (ΔTC) of total cost (TC) divided by the corresponding variation of output (ΔQ), that is,

$$MC(Q) = \frac{\Delta TC(Q)}{\Delta Q}$$

Hence, when the cost is variable, the marginal cost and marginal benefit of a material product or a traditional service product often float as the output increases. Generally, as the output increases, the marginal cost of the material product or the traditional service product will decrease and then increase, while the marginal cost will increase and then decrease. However, information consumption is totally different from that. Because information products are featured with shareability and relatively fixed costs that are not obviously affected by output, they can be consumed repeatedly so that operators can gain profits from N units of products by paying costs for one unit of products. Therefore, information consumption can produce the minimum marginal cost and maximum marginal benefit.

The copyright royalty is one of the major reasons for the cost of Chinese network video consumption staying at a high level. Numerous video information platforms turn to producing videos by themselves from purchasing copyrights, aiming to reduce their costs. The shareability of network video information makes the marginal cost of consumption minimizable, leading to the difference from the general cost.

2. *Two-sided or multi-sided market as the main trading environment from the perspective of market environment*

Different from traditional material and service consumption, information consumption is often achieved through an intermediate platform for trading between the consumer and the provider, with profits made by the provider from the platform depending on the number of consumers joining the platform. Generally speaking, the more consumers there are, the more profits the information provider gains. In 2013, advertising revenues accounted for up to 72.1%[9] of Chinese online video market size. Thus it can be seen that the main income of the online video market comes from the advertising investment by third parties instead of payment by consumers for use. That exhibits the typical two-sided or multi-sided market feature.

The basic theory of industry development   41

Table 2.2 Types of information consumption markets

Types	Examples	Pricing Strategies
Market Maker	e-commerce platforms such as Taobao, JD.COM, and Amazon	Registration fees, service fees, or transaction fees
Audience Maker	Search engines such as Google and Baidu	Method for advertising pricing
Demand Coordinator	Intermediate platforms such as mobile value-added service platforms	More complex, including annuities, copyright royalties, and transaction fees.

The information consumption market covers three types of basic two-sided markets (market-maker, audience-maker, and demand coordinator),[10] leading to the diversity of pricing strategies and payment modes (as presented in Table 2.2). For example, such e-commerce platforms as Taobao, JD.COM, and Amazon fall under the market-maker for which prices are set based on registration fees, service fees, or transaction fees; such search engines as Google and Baidu belong to the audience-maker, where there are no direct transactions between users on both sides of the market, with prices set in the method for advertising pricing; such intermediate platforms as mobile value-added service platforms are categorized as the demand coordinator for which the pricing mode of information consumption is more complex, including annuities, copyright royalties, and transaction fees.

3.   Positive externality from the perspective of a consumer

In economics, externality means that non-reimbursable costs are imposed on and compensation-free profits are offered to other organizations during the production or consumption.[11] Externality falls into positive external economy and negative externality in terms of the effect. In light of shareability of information, a consumer of information can share information with other consumers free of charge during the consumption, resulting in the possible coexistence of paid consumption and free consumption in the information consumption chain. Sometimes, after one person pays for information, several persons use it free of charge, such as consumption of e-books. Externality of information consumption brings about some new issues, such as the necessity of copyright protection, identity authentication, and message discrimination. The statistical data in the *Report for Research on Chinese Netizens' Application of Network Videos for 2013* shows that the marginal cost of network video information is low; 54.1% of the users use the offline cache or downloading function of online video websites, while some users download videos via "sharing by friends or colleagues" (36.9%), "network disk or personal space" (27.4%), "video downloading forum or BBS" (20.1%), or any other source.[12] That tends to reflect positive externality.

42 *The basic theory of industry development*

2.2.3 Structural features

What sets information consumption apart from material and energy resource consumption is the consumption structure. Therefore, analyzing the consumption structure can contribute to consumption theory studies of the information resource industry. The particularity of information consumption renders the research variables and key analysis points of the consumption structure of the information resource industry different from traditional consumption economics and industrial economics. Hence, an in-depth analysis of information consumption structure entails methodology innovation.

For that, we classified information consumption into direct and indirect consumption based on the consumption modes of consumption objects. The former refers to direct consumption of information in its own right; the latter refers to the process of indirect consumption of information during the consumption of other resources, products, or services. Alongside that, information consumption can also fall into active consumption and passive consumption based on consumers' subjective wishes during the consumption. Therefore, there are four basic types of information consumption, namely, direct active type, direct passive type, indirect active type, and indirect passive type,[13] according to the proportions and combinational relationships of the consumption modes of consumption objects (direct consumption and indirect consumption) and consumers' subjective wishes during the consumption of information resources (active consumption and passive consumption), as shown in Figure 2.4. After an in-depth study on the information consumption structure, we found there are two prominent features of the structure.

	Direct consumption	Indirect consumption
Active consumption	Active behavior, often found in the consumers who are highly professional or have strong interest, such as scholars working on literature studies.	Active behavior, mainly involving evolution information, added-value services and derivative products based on information resources, such as sci-tech novelty retrieval
Passive consumption	Passive behavior, often seen in the information resource push service field, such as consumption of personalized push ads	Passive behavior, mainly involving evolution information, added-value services and derivative products based on information resources, such as indirect and passive consumption of information resources during the consumption of automobile products.

Figure 2.4 Structural features of information consumption

The basic theory of industry development   43

1.   Loose coupling between consumption behavior and motive

Unlike material and energy consumption, information consumption includes such different consumption types as active consumption and passive consumption, leading to the separation of "behavior" from "motive" in information consumption; that is, the motive and the behavior in the same information consumption activity may exist in different subjects. However, material and energy consumption is generally the active behavior of the consumption subject, and the consumption motive and behavior co-exist in the same subject, also consumer; that can be explained with the motive-behavior model. However, information consumption occurs in the two-sided market. The motive and the behavior often are separated from each other, and there may be inconsistency of the motive with the behavior subject. For example, during the passive consumption of advertising information, the consumption motive does not come from the consumption behavior subject but from the provider of information products or the third-party advertiser. In the structure of the Chinese network video information market, active consumption and passive consumption coexist. Video consumption mainly falls under active direct consumption, while advertising information consumption mostly belongs to passive direct consumption. The related statistical data show that, from 2013, users in the Chinese network video information industry began to actively search for videos they need by the site search function (45.7%) and by browsing by category (36%) and recently played videos (30.6%).[14] However, they have been very dissatisfied with various advertisements in network videos, particularly with the passive consumption process of pause advertisements (advertisements popping up when the videos are on).

2.   Tight coupling between information consumption and material (or energy) consumption

Unlike material and energy consumption, information consumption involves a ratio of direct consumption with indirect consumption, as well as integration of "information" with "material (or energy)." Information consumption is often accompanied by material or energy consumption and hard to separate from other types of resources. Hence, an indirect consumption mode existing in information consumption helps realize the integration of information consumption with material (or energy) consumption.

2.2.4   *Evolution features*

The evolution process of information consumption is divided into three basic stages from the type and change mode of the information consumption structure, namely, content consumption, integration consumption, and service consumption, corresponding to passive direct consumption, passive indirect consumption, and active indirect consumption in the information consumption structure, as presented in Table 2.3. Information consumption in the Chinese network video industry has stepped into the vertical integration consumption (integration consumption) stage from the consumption of pure video contents but has not entered into the service

44 *The basic theory of industry development*

Table 2.3 Evolution features of information consumption

	Content Consumption	*Integration Consumption*	*Service Consumption*
Evolution Stage	Initial stage	Key stage	Advanced stage
Consumption Granularity	Content	Content + supplies + materials	Content + supplies + materials + wisdom
Active or Passive Consumption	Active	Passive	Active
Direct or Indirect Consumption	Direct	Indirect	Indirect
Way of Consumption	Consumption by experiencing or subscription	Vertical integration consumption	Custom consumption
Example	Video content	Video content + video player (software) + video player hardware	Video industry data analysis, management consulting, or decision support

consumption stage. For instance, Youku.com and Tudou.com introduced three hardware products in 2014, namely, Youku Router, Youku Box, and Tudoupai, supporting vertical integration consumption and promoting the transition from content consumption to integration consumption.

1. From small-grained consumption to large-grained consumption

The granularity of the consumption object at the content consumption stage is the smallest, with information content most consumed. The consumption object at the integration consumption stage includes not only information but also materials and energy, with the consumption granularity larger than that of the content consumption stage. The consumption granularity at the service consumption stage is the largest beyond the realm of such specific resources as information, materials, and energy generally; given that plenty of human wisdom is incorporated in the consumption object, the granularity is often larger than those of the preceding two stages.

2. From passive consumption to active consumption

Passive consumption dominates the content consumption stage where the representations of information proactivity are complex. The integration consumption stage is often a passive consumption process from the perspective of information consumption; that is, information content is passively consumed during the consumption of material or energy resources. For example, during the consumption of a hardware product, information content bound to the product is passively consumed. However, the service consumption stage often involves highly active consumption; the service provider needs to tailor high-quality targeted services to consumers' individualized requirements.

3. From direct consumption to indirect consumption

Direct information consumption dominates the content consumption stage, while indirect consumption controls the integration consumption stage. At the service consumption stage, consumers do not consume the original content of information (primary information) directly but consume processed information.

4. From mass consumption to personalized consumption

Consumption by experiencing or subscription serves as the main consumption mode in the content consumption stage, while vertical integration consumption is applied to the integration consumption stage. Service consumption is a process of consumption guided by personalized customization.

From the evolution process of information consumption, content consumption and service consumption are the early stage and the advanced stage of information consumption, respectively, while integration consumption is the key stage of information consumption. Without integration consumption, it is hard for information consumption to evolve from the content consumption stage to the service consumption stage.

2.2.5 Policy demand features

The previous features of information consumption make special requirements on the setting of policies on the information resource industry. Content consumption is the basis for evolution of information consumption and determines the fundamental impetus to the whole information consumption market. However, characterized with a short life cycle, high cost, uncertainty, and many influencing factors, content consumption evolves into integration consumption with difficulty. Take consumption of book information as an example. Content consumption of a few books evolves into integration consumption. For instance, *Harry Potter* drives a huge industrial chain of integration consumption, including films, animation, games, toys, daily necessities, and tourism. Evolution from content consumption into integration consumption is a value-added process of information content, expanding the related industry scope and being the key link of realizing information service consumption. In terms of information consumption, the following three issues must be paid attention to for the setting of policies on the information resource industry.

1. Protecting rights and interests of the information content provider

It has become the most prominent challenge in the information consumption field to protect the rights and interests of the information content provider. Positive externality and indirect consumption form featured by information consumption

46 The basic theory of industry development

makes the producer of information content subject to damage, thus leading to a decline in the quantity and quality of content products and substantially impeding the development of the information resource industry. Therefore, it is imperative to protect the rights and interests of the information content provider in terms of policies and management. Take the Chinese network video industry for an example. The copyright of video information is the main bottleneck that hinders the development of integration consumption. To this end, the majority of the network video information service providers adopt the PGC (professional generated content) mode. That is, they change their operation mode of "purchase of copyrighted dramas" into "self-production of dramas" or into the combination of both, lowering their costs, becoming less dependent on copyright, averting legal risks, and improving their reputation.

2. Protecting personal privacy of information consumers

Personal privacy protection is possibly the biggest challenge in the information consumption field. Nevertheless, it is hard to directly apply traditional privacy protection technologies to information consumption, and it still takes time to develop a set of brand-new personal privacy protection technologies.[15] The multi-sided market nature and separability of motive from behavior featured by information consumption often result in the bidirectional flow of information or grey deals in information consumption, increasingly aggravating inadvertent collection, trading, or abuse of personal privacy of users. Take the Chinese network video industry for an example. The platforms have begun to improve the value of network video information through UGC (user generated content); however, the excessive capturing and abuse of data on users bring information consumers' concerns and even damage consumers' benefits. Therefore, China shall speed up setting policies on protection of consumers' privacy of information and of information security.

3. Standardizing the information consumption market order

Market order is a resource allocation status and benefit-based relationship formed during the market-driven allocation of resources, a relationship that embraces harmonious benefit, harmonious relationship, benefit sharing, moderate competition, orderly transactions, and steady structure.[16] Passive consumption of information and tight coupling between information consumption and material (or energy) consumption lead to conflict of interests, excessive competition, disorderly transactions, and other new problems in the information consumption market. Though the State and the industry published the *Administrative Requirements for Operation of Institutions with Internet TV License* (G.B.F.W. Zi No. [181]) and the policy of "one TV drama played on two satellite channels at most," we find from field investigation that the market order of the Chinese network video industry is still disorderly and that there is a lack of self-organized market order. Therefore, the State and the industry should put standardizing the information consumption

The basic theory of industry development 47

market order high on the agenda, formulate related rules and regulations, define market participants' responsibilities, and cultivate a self-organized market order.

2.3 Endogenous structure of the information resource industry: industrial symbiosis theory

The structure of the information resource industry prominently features the strong "convergence." That is, subdivided industries in the industry as well as the information resource industry and other industries are highly and frequently closely linked with each other, so it is hard to "define the boundaries" between industries in the industry and between the information resource industry and other industries. In other words, the subdivided industries in the information resource industry as well as the information resource industry and other industries are in a strong symbiotic relationship, so that they are inseparable from each other. This feature indicates that the information resource industry differs greatly from other industries in its endogenous structure. We can summarize the relationships among subdivided industries in the information resource industry and between the information resource industry and other industries as the "industrial symbiosis relationships based on information resources industry research group." Next, we will discuss the industrial symbiosis theory proposed by the research group in such methods as literature research, theoretical derivation, logical reasoning, case analysis, and industrial development data estimate, briefly explaining the composition and features of the "industrial symbiosis system based on information resources," formations and types of the symbiotic relationship, influencing factors and measurement of symbiosis benefits, demand of symbiosis for management and policies, etc.

2.3.1 Composition and features of the industrial symbiosis system based on information resources

The term "industrial symbiosis" made its first appearance in the economic geographic literature in 1947, describing the "organic relationship"[17] between or among different enterprises. The most widely accepted concept of industrial symbiosis is the definition[18] that means different enterprises cooperate with each other to improve their viability and profitability together and to save resources and protect environment, as set forth in *Industrial Symbiosis* published by the Danish Kahlenburg Company. The concept shows that industrial symbiosis will form a complete industrial ecosystem in which enterprises are in the symbiotic relationship because of sharing of the same kind of resources or complementation of different kinds of resources, improving the efficiency of resource allocation as well as benefits yielded by the system. In fact, industrial symbiosis carries both economic character and ecological character. It aims to pursue both economic value and environmental improvement, and it is highly susceptible to policies and regulations, technological changes, etc. Furthermore, the prime approach to gain symbiosis benefits is rational division of labor among symbiotic units. One of the essential features of symbiosis phenomenon is the cooperative–competitive relationship. Symbiosis

48   *The basic theory of industry development*

also features cyclic utilization of resources, relevance between the upstream and the downstream industries, and value addition of production results.[19]

The industrial symbiosis system is often comprised of symbiosis unit, symbiosis environment, and symbiotic relationship.[20] In an industrial symbiosis system, the enterprises have symbiosis relationship because of the same resource sharing or different resource complementation, so as to achieve the goal of improving resource allocation efficiency and industrial output efficiency. In this book, the elements comprising the industrial symbiosis system based on information resources are defined as follows: symbiosis units refer to subjects in the symbiotic relationship, including enterprises, governmental departments, and other various types of organizations; symbiosis environment includes internal environment of the organization and internal environment of the industry, as well as external political, economic, social, and technical environments across industries. In the symbiosis environment, symbiosis units form different symbiotic relationships through exchange of material, energy, and information resources out of the need to save costs, carve up the market, improve production efficiency, or maximize benefits.

The "industrial symbiosis system based on information resources" is more complex than other industrial symbiosis systems from the micro aspect. The most prominent feature of the system is that lots of information resources are frequently shared and exchanged among symbiosis units apart from material and energy resources, which sets the system apart from the traditional industrial symbiosis systems. The particularities of industrial symbiosis realized through sharing and exchange of information resources are mainly shown as follows: firstly, given that information resources are more external and shareable and can be used again and again, the symbiosis model "in parallel" dominates the sharing and exchange of information resources, being greatly different from the symbiosis model "in series" dominating the cyclic utilization of material and energy resources, as shown in Figure 2.5; secondly, in the symbiosis activity, information resources play a role that cannot be replaced by material or energy resources in improving efficiency of other industries, transforming the economic development mode, reducing consumption of materials and energy, and creating "green GDP."

We can say that because of the special role of information resources in industrial symbiosis, information resources, material resources, and energy resources are increasingly segregated from each other functionally, resources are shared and exchanged between and among industries more and more frequently, and the symbiotic relationship is getting closer and closer so that the industrial symbiosis formation is transiting from "physical symbiosis" to "chemical symbiosis."

2.3.2   *Formations and types of the industrial symbiosis relationship based on information resources*

Analyzing symbiosis by category is one of the important perspectives for researching development policies and management of the information resource industry. Virtually, there are several levels of industrial symbiosis. For example, the industrial symbiosis system can be divided into four levels by openness: internal

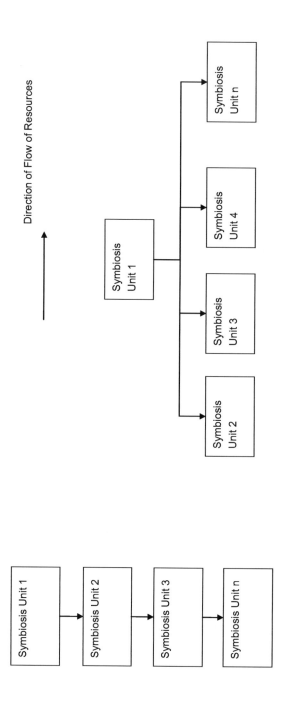

Figure 2.5 Symbiosis model of information resources in parallel and symbiosis model of other resources in series

50 *The basic theory of industry development*

symbiosis system I of the enterprise where corporate sectors are the symbiosis units, inter-enterprise symbiosis system II where corporate sectors are the symbiosis units, inter-enterprise symbiosis system III where independent enterprises are the symbiosis units, and interindustry symbiosis system IV where regional industrial clusters or leading industrial groups are the symbiosis units. The four levels of symbiosis systems generate symbiotic relationships through internal instructions of the enterprise, capital link, relational contract, and market exchange contract, respectively, as well as through several combinations of the foregoing means.[21] Based on that train of thought, the "industrial symbiosis relationship based on information resources" can be divided into six types by the level at which the symbiosis unit of the information resource industry is located and from internal and external aspects of the information resource industry, as presented in Table 2.4.

As presented in Table 2.4, the three levels and the internal and external aspects cross with each other, forming six types of industrial symbiosis relationships. Notably, governmental departments, public institutions, and commonweal

Table 2.4 Six basic types of "industrial symbiosis relationship based on information resources"

	Inside the Information Resource Industry/Interindustry	
Level at which the Symbiosis Unit is Located	Within the information resource industry: each of the symbiosis units is engaged in information resource businesses	Interindustry: some symbiosis units are engaged in information resource businesses, while others specialize in businesses of other industries
Between Different Departments of the Same Organization	Type 1 (such as resource flow between the map information gathering department and the processing department of an electronic mapmaker)	Type 2 (such as provision of data basis by the information department of a manufacturer for the raw material purchase department of the manufacturer)
Between Different Independent Organizations	Type 3 (for example, teachers' resource information of a commercialized education training institution may become an important resource of a vocational intermediary)	Type 4 (for example, market investigation data of a food producer are exploited by a market investigation company after such data become stale)
Between Different Industries	Type 5 (namely, between subdivided industries of the information resource industry. For example, the book or paper publishing industry provides goods for the book or paper retail industry)	Type 6 (namely, between the information resource industry and other industries. For example, information provided by the meteorological monitoring service industry may provide decision basis for agricultural production)

organizations may also be symbiosis units, but enterprises are the most important constituent units of the industry. In Table 2.4, organizations are used only to represent all organization types that possibly become symbiosis units.

Levels at which symbiosis units are at include between different departments of the same organization, between different independent organizations, and between different industries. When symbiosis units are at different levels, different governance means and management policies will apply. For example, symbiosis units in the same organization can be governed by instructions of the organization, symbiosis units of different independent organizations will be managed by contract, and symbiosis units of different industries are managed more by policies than the other two levels of symbiosis units.

Symbiosis activities are held inside and outside the information resource industry. In case of symbiosis inside the information resource industry, each of the symbiosis units is engaged in information resource businesses and shares and exchanges resources with each other inside the information resources industry. In the case of symbiosis between the information resource industry and other industries, resources are shared and exchanged across industries. Symbiosis inside the information resource industry highlights sharing and exchange as well as repeated use of information resources; for example, several database companies may use the same batch of governmental data for production and processing, making different information products. However, symbiosis between the information resource industry and other industries focuses on complementary sharing and exchange between information resources and material and energy resources as well as cyclic utilization. For instance, in the e-commerce and industrial Internet, information resources improve the efficiency of the logistics industry and the industry a great deal as well as the cyclic utilization rate of materials and energy; they also reduce unnecessary consumption of materials and energy of those industries, while the industry, agriculture and manufacturing industry provide necessary support in such hardware equipment as computer and such energy sources as water and electricity.

2.3.3 Influencing factors and measurement of industrial symbiosis benefits based on information resources

Which factors influence symbiosis benefits of the information resource industry? How can one judge whether symbiosis benefits of the information resource industry are positive and sufficient? Answering these questions is crucial to forming effective symbiosis policies for the information resource industry. And that involves measurement of industrial symbiosis benefits.

Measurement of general industrial symbiosis falls into three categories in the existing studies: (1) symbiosis model, describing the natural status of symbiosis relationship, such as form and manner of symbiosis, and stake between symbiosis units. For example, Xiao Zhongdong, Liu Yongqing, Sun Linyan,[22] and colleagues created $S = \frac{O-I}{I}$, where S represents the ratio of intake of residuum by the industry from the upstream industry, O means the quantity of output by the industry, and

52   The basic theory of industry development

I is the quantity of input by the industry and different from input by the industry; (2) symbiosis degree, such as tightness, diversity, and stability of symbiosis. For example, Hu Xiaopeng[23] sets the mass parameter derivation equation, describing the symbiosis degree of two symbiosis units. Specifically, A and B represent two symbiosis units, mass parameters Z_i and Z_j are set, and the symbiosis degree of A and B is defined as δ_{ij}, thus $\delta_{ij} = \frac{dZ_i/Z_i}{dZ_j/Z_j}$, $(d_{zj} \neq 0)$; (3) symbiosis benefit, including industrial efficiency and social welfare at least in terms of connotation. It can be expressed by several indexes. For example, symbiosis benefit can be known from the key variable, the cyclic utilization rate of resources that describes the symbiosis process, or from the output growth rate of the industry or cost saving rate that describes the production result. Cai Xiaojun, Li Shuangjie, and Liu Qihao[24] set the industrial chain symbiosis benefit function v(s) in the Shapley value method. A symbiosis industry chain is set for the function, including n entities whose set is denoted as $I = \{1, 2, \ldots, n\}$. S is a kind of cooperation among n individual sets in the set of n entities, and v(s) represents the benefit generated from cooperation S.

Among the three categories, the symbiosis benefit is the ultimate goal pursued for the industrial symbiosis. In fact, not all symbiosis systems will produce positive symbiosis benefits. Only when the symbiosis benefit is positive, will enhancement of the symbiosis degree further drive the maximization of the symbiosis benefit. However, for negative symbiosis, improvement of the symbiosis degree does not mean a better symbiosis result, and that needs the symbiosis environment to function. In the symbiosis environment, the government's policies are essential. The policy is used to guide and intervene with the symbiosis model and change the internal function mechanism of the symbiosis system. That is how the policy can ensure the realization of positive symbiosis benefit and avoidance of negative symbiosis benefit and maximize positive symbiosis benefit by adjusting the symbiosis degree.

Information resources are playing an increasingly important role in the information society as a production element, which is mainly reflected in the development of the information resource industry. However, after research, we find that the information resource industry does not develop independently but develops in a symbiotic relationship with other industries, which essentially reflects the permeability of the information resource industry as a production element into other industries. Hence, the measurement of benefits of the information resource industry is not only about the output value and added value of such industry but also about the increase in the output value and added value of other industries through symbiosis activities. Industrial economy is moving towards a cycle similar to that of the natural ecosystem through cyclic utilization of resources, contributing to the realization of industrial ecologicalization. It conforms to the advocacy of the construction of ecological civilization in the whole society. So the cyclic utilization rate of resources can better reveal the "symbiosis benefit" of the industrial symbiosis system.

Under the concept framework of "industrial symbiosis benefit based on information resources," the following equation can be tentatively set to express the

The basic theory of industry development 53

symbiosis benefit produced from the symbiotic relationship between the information resource industry and other industries in the train of thought for analysis of the enterprise's profit by the DuPont system:

$$Y = \beta \cdot \frac{\sum_{i=1}^{n} R_i \cdot K_i}{Q} \ (i = 1, 2, 3, \ldots, n) \text{ (Equation 1)}$$

Y represents the "industrial symbiosis benefit based on information resources" (equivalent to the return on equity in the DuPont system), namely, the net output brought by repeated or cyclic utilization of resources by each unit in the symbiosis system. The symbiosis benefit includes not only economic benefit but also social benefit and ecological benefit. Resources mentioned here include material and energy resources, etc. provided by other industries to the information resource industry as well as information resources the information resource industry supplies with other industries.

i represents the resource type, and one type or more is(are) information resources; n means the number of resource types.

R_i represents net output brought by one time of repeated or cyclic utilization of type i resources; K_i refers to times of repeated or cyclic utilization of type i resources. In fact, R and K represent the symbiosis degree together.

Q represents the total quantity of various types of resources in the "industrial symbiosis system based on information resources"

β represents the ratio of quantity of information resources with that of other resources for the repeated or cyclic utilization in the symbiosis system. The bigger β is, the larger proportion information resources account for in the industrial symbiosis. That means the resource structure is more optimized and there are greater symbiosis benefits and more improvement potential. The setting of variable β helps produce more social benefits in the symbiosis system, particularly ecological benefits.

2.3.4 New demands of new formation of industrial symbiosis for policies and management on the information resource industry

Policies and management are part and parcel of the symbiosis environment, are external conditions for symbiosis units, and are also the basis for formation and development of symbiotic relationships. As an important endogenous variable of a symbiosis system, industrial symbiosis policies will have implications for the symbiosis environment, symbiosis units, and symbiotic relationships in an all-around way. They not only hold the key to forming and improving the symbiosis system energy but also constrain functions and the efficiency of the symbiosis system. Therefore, it is necessary to fully leverage the role of industrial policies and management for the purpose of improving symbiosis benefits of the information resource industry. As shown in Figure 2.6, in fact, there are pressing demands

54 The basic theory of industry development

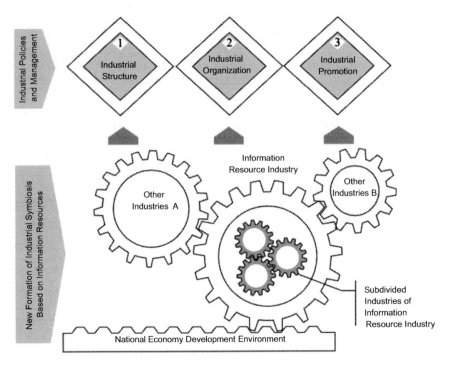

Figure 2.6 Analysis of policies and management on "industrial symbiosis based on information resources"

of the new formation of industrial symbiosis based on information resources for policies and management on the industrial structure, industrial organization, and industrial promotion of information resources.

1. Analysis of demand for policies and management on the industrial structure of information resources

China should, on the basis of various symbiotic relationships within the information resource industry, comprehensively manage the related industrial clusters but not purely manage the information resource industry. There are two levels of connotations of demand for policies and management. In terms of the macro structure of the information resource industry, full attention should be paid to the important strategic value of the information resource industry in the symbiotic relationship in upgrading other industries and transforming the economic growth modes of other industries; in terms of the micro structure of the industry, the symbiotic relationship between or among subdivided industries of the information resource industry proposes higher policy and management demand for sharing, complementation, and exchange of information resources.

The basic theory of industry development 55

2. Analysis of demand for policies and management on the industrial organization of information resources

The new formation of industrial symbiosis influences the horizontal and vertical organizations in the information resource industry and generates policy and management demands. Horizontally, in the same information resource market, symbiosis has implications for horizontal competitive–cooperative relationships between or among information resource enterprises, market concentration and industrial competitive features; vertically, different information resource enterprises need to frequently cooperate with each other in the links of the industrial chain on the basis of symbiosis. Because of the existence of the situation, a series of new knowledge of regularities should be developed with respect to such policy and management issues as symbiosis and monopoly control, symbiosis and vertical management of industrial chain, and symbiosis and coordinated innovation guidance.

3. Analysis of demand for policies and management on the industrial development of information resources

China should view promoting the improvement of industrial symbiosis benefits as one of the important objectives for industrial development, and make minor adjustments of specific goals of industrial development as well as the relationships between or among specific goals while staying focused on the macro objective. Meanwhile, it is imperative for China to take well-targeted measures to improve symbiosis benefits of the information resource industry by policy and management means, such as rebalancing the resource structure, increasing the proportion of information resources in the resource structure, and constructing symbiosis platforms to guide symbiotic relationships and drive symbiosis benefit improvement.

2.4 Value driver of information resource industry: information resource industry chain theory

2.4.1 Industrial chain theory

1. Theory evolution

As the social division of labor becomes more and more specialized, none of the products or services can be totally provided by one enterprise. Value provided by an enterprise to customers is restricted not only by its own capability but also by upstream and downstream enterprises, thus forming the industrial chain. Therefore, the foundation for competitive advantage modern enterprises boasts is beyond an individual enterprise's capability and scope of resources, and competition has spanned industrial chains from individual enterprises. As a new organization pattern coming into being in the new age to cope with fierce market competition, the industrial chain becomes the prime organization form in the 21st century to gain competitive advantage.[25]

56   The basic theory of industry development

The idea about industrial chain comes from the thesis of Adam Smith, the father of economists, on the division of labor. Taking needle making as an example, Adam Smith stated the significance of the division of labor and professionalism for economic development by describing the functions of the industrial chain inside the enterprise. The early concept of the industrial chain is limited to operation within the enterprise and highlights utilization of the enterprise's own resources. Marshall expanded the concept to inter-enterprise, which could be the origin of the industrial chain theory. The industrial chain is not only a product chain but also an information chain and function chain. Stevens regarded the industrial chain as a system that is comprised of suppliers, manufacturers, distributors, and consumers along with logistics and information flow run through (Stevens, 1989). That point of view indicates the same status information enjoys as products and emphasizes the feedback process existing in the industrial chain. In the early 1980s, Michael Porter, economics professor at Harvard Business School, came up with industrial chain in his value chain theory. Afterwards, he extended the nature of the industrial chain and further emphasized the role of the industrial chain in his study on competitive strategies (2000) and his study on national competitive advantage.[26]

2.   Connotation of industrial chain

An industrial chain is essentially a function network chain on the basis of knowledge division and collaboration where increasing returns are created by knowledge division and sharing, and value is created for customers. Manufacturing links of products and the resultant material flow are external manifestations of the industrial chain only.

Many scholars discussed and summarized the connotation of the industrial chain. The following are the representative views. Yang Gongpu and Xia Dawei (1999) defined the industrial chain as a value chain relationship comprised of all activities made up of relationships of continuous added value in the same industry.[27] In the view of Jiang Guojun and Jiang Mingxin (2004), industrial chain refers to the chain of strategic alliance relationships an enterprise with strong international competitiveness (international competition potential) in an industry within an industrial cluster establishes with enterprises in related industries.[28] Gong Qinlin (2004) held that an industrial chain is a chain-type association formation objectively formed among industrial sectors on the basis of certain technical and economic relevance as well as specific logical relations and time–space layout relations.[29] Yu Yihong and Guan Xizhan (2006) maintained that an industrial chain is an entire longitudinal chain comprised of all links encompassed by the production and processing process of a final product from mineral resources or raw materials at the beginning to arrival of the final product to consumers.[30] It can be seen that the foregoing scholars highlight different aspects in defining the industrial chain. Yang Gongpu and Xia Dawei defined the industrial chain from the perspective of chain value, Jiang Guojun and Jiang Mingxin defined the industrial chain in terms of strategic alliance, Gong Qinlin gave a definition from the perspective of industrial association, and Yu Yihong and Guan Xizhan focused on production technology process in defining the industrial chain. Additionally, other scholars researched the connotation of the industrial chain from the perspectives of ecology, knowledge sharing, etc., producing some results.

On the back of findings of other scholars, Liu Guifu (2007) gave a relatively comprehensive definition of the industrial chain after comprehensive analysis and summarization: the industrial chain is an up–down associated and dynamic chain-type intermediate organization formed on the basis of specific logical relations and time–space layout among enterprises in the same industry or in different industries which regard products as objects and input–output as the bond. The industrial chain is driven by value increment and aims to satisfy customers' needs.[31]

From the perspective of system economics, an economic system features a hierarchy that is always associated with a specific "resource-niche" phase. Furthermore, an economic system is characterized with structuredness, and economic system evolution is a process of structure shift. The structure of the industrial chain is the structure of work division within the industry. From the form of evolution, such structure shift undergoes from single structure (economies of scale) to specialized work division structure and then to modular structure. The force driving the structure shift is market competition which starts from value competition between or among enterprises and comes down to knowledge innovation and utilization efficiency. Different resource endowments serve as the basis for different work division structures and determine the comprehensiveness of the economic system.[32]

3. Structure of industrial chain

Liu Guifu (2008) explained the structure of the industrial chain comprehensively.[33] He pointed out that components of the structure of the industrial chain include enterprises, upstream suppliers, and downstream distributors and that there are different industrial chains according to the monopoly situation of each link. Wang Qiuju (2012) expanded the range of the structure of the industrial chain; that is, the industrial chain is comprised of chain, chain leader, and chain body. He emphasized the role of leading enterprises in the chain as well as the essence of the industrial chain as the economic "entity,"[34] apart from the "chain" we are used to understanding. Based on that, he also categorized the industrial chain by the relationship between enterprises in the industrial chain and spatial distribution of enterprises.

Among research results of the structure of the industrial chain, the "Bohr atom" model of the industrial chain put forward by Shao Chang and Li Jian (2007) is very novel.[35] In their opinion, node changes in the explicit and implicit transmissions between industrial chains features "fluctuation," while inter-enterprise integration at the nodes is characterized with "corpuscular property," and "wave corpuscle duality" of the industrial chain determines the particularity of the structure. The "Bohr atom" model of the industrial chain is comprised of atomic nucleus (terminal product enterprises), electron (supporting enterprises, key enterprises, and industrial chain bottlenecks), and track (industrial chain, nodes, industrial

58 *The basic theory of industry development*

supporting radius), in which quantum transition will occur (movement of intermediate products).

On the whole, there are not so many pure theoretical studies on the structure of the industrial chain in the academic community and more that are focused on the structure of the industrial chain of one specific industry, in which scholars study industrial chain upgrading and management. For example, Liu Ying, etc. (2014) researched the structure of the industrial chain of traditional Chinese medicine and made an in-depth analysis of causes for its complexity.[36] Yu Xiangping (2008) introduced each of the upstream, midstream, and downstream entities in the exhibition industrial chain and their activities, and analyzed the extension effects exerted within and without the industry.[37]

2.4.2 *The information resource industry chain*

1. Studies on the information resource industry chain

Although foreign scholars do not use the concepts of "information resource industry chain" and "industrial chain" directly in the studies on the information resource industry chain, there are still some related findings that can provide reference in terms of research content. With respect to the computer game industry, a typical information resource industry, Jockel, etc. (2008) highlighted the significance of users' participation for the computer game industry as well as the reconfiguration of the value chain in that industry.[38] Salehi-Sangari (2010) made a case study in Apple, finding that currently traditional suppliers in the media content industry have moved on to the digital field, and that there is a huge change of the industrial supply chain wherein those suppliers failing to step into the digital field will be phased out.[39] Hadida, etc. (2014) pointed out that technological advance would bring revolution to the digital music industry and that the value chain in that industry must be comprehensively and effectively managed in order to gain persistent competitive advantage.[40]

Currently, in China, few findings are relevant to the information resource industry chain. Among five research results from CJFD by insertion of key words "information resource industry + industrial chain," only two are highly relevant to the theme. Cui Hongming and Zhao Guojun (2013) pointed out that the information resource provider, the information resource owner, the information technology provider, and the information service provider in the information resource industry chain correspond to the content value, ownership value, technical value, and service value in the chain, respectively.[41] In another article, Cui Hongming (2014) took the digital publishing industry as an example, researching the structure of the information resource industry chain.[42]

However, scholars have made extensive studies on chains of the game industry, the animation industry, and other specific information resource industries, producing some results. Li Guifu (2007) researched the digital cable television industry chain, coming up with three mechanisms that maintained China's digital cable television industry in steady operation and sustained development.[43] Yang Chuanming

(2008) pointed out that the construction of modular industrial chains empowered online game enterprises to expand their cooperation networks.[44] Zhu Jiajun, etc. (2014) analyzed the structure of the animation industry chain and put forward strategies for integrated development of the entire animation industry chain around the structure and profitability mode of the animation industry.[45]

2. Definition of the information resource industry chain

At the early stage of human social development, commodity exchange behavior was simple, and commodities were often made and sold by small manual workshops. As industrialization advanced, people needed more and more articles that become more diversified, and it was hard for one enterprise to complete the whole production process independently. Thus, division of work in the same industry appeared, accompanied by the industrial chain.

In the market where work is divided, enterprises need to frequently trade with each other so as to obtain raw materials for production and to sell products. However, if enterprises need to seek suitable partners in the market before each transaction, they must pay high costs. Therefore, enterprises in supply–demand relationships often cooperate with each other in the long term, forming closer relationships than the pure market relationship. The form of organization generated among the enterprises is the industrial chain.

The authors think that the industrial chain refers to a vertical chain formed among enterprises in supply–demand relationships in the same industry that link with each other backward and forward in order to make a product. Enterprises in the industrial chain undertake raw material gathering, production and processing, and selling, respectively, based on the division of work, and finally delivering products.

Figure 2.7 is a brief description of the expressive form of the industrial chain in an industry. The following explanations need to be made with respect to the concept of the industrial chain we discussed earlier.

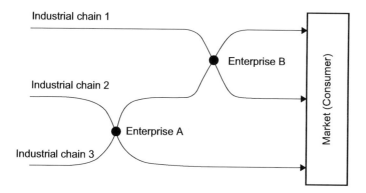

Figure 2.7 Schematic diagram of industrial chain

60   *The basic theory of industry development*

Firstly, the industrial chain is comprised of enterprises which are the entity nodes in the industrial chain and undertake different production links. One enterprise can exist in several industrial chains simultaneously. For example, an enterprise that supplies two manufacturers raw materials at the same time exists in the industrial chains where the two manufacturers are. Enterprises A and B in the Figure are at the cross-nodes of different industrial chains.

Secondly, enterprises in the same industrial chain are in demand–supply relationships. They are partners instead of rivals. Even though they have conflicts in other businesses, they can still cooperate with each other when considering the specific industrial chain where they coexist.

Thirdly, enterprises link with each other to form industrial chains for the purpose of delivering final products more effectively. There may be several industrial chains in the same industry, and products from different industrial chains are delivered to the same market. So such industrial chains are rivals. As presented in the figure, the three industrial chains lead to the sane market.

The information resource industry chain refers to a vertical chain formed among enterprises in supply–demand relationships in the information resource industry that link with each other backward and forward in order to make a product. To study the information resource industry chain, we need to analyze types of and relationships between nodes in the industrial chain, and we can further summarize features of the industrial chain so that we can provide guidance on improving and upgrading the industrial chain.

2.4.3   Effects of features of information products on the information resource industry chain

1.   Features of information products

Information products carry such information properties as both non-substantiality and independence and such economic properties as externality and network effect.[46] The authors focus on analyzing non-substantiality, independence, incomplete consumability, timeliness, and network effect in terms of the effects of information products on the structure of the information resource industry chain.

(1)   NON-SUBSTANTIALITY AND INDEPENDENCE

Non-substantiality of information products means that information products cannot live without specific physical carriers. Information cannot be seen and touched, and information products can be consumed or used by people only when they are attached to specific carriers. Professional writers cannot directly sell their "creativity" in their mind; instead, only after their "creativity" is printed into books can it be purchased and consumed by people. Meanwhile, the value of information products is not determined by the carriers; that is, information products are independent. For specific information products, changing their carriers will neither impair their use value fundamentally, damage consumers' interests, or provide consumers

The basic theory of industry development   61

with more information. For instance, a consumer may install an e-book purchased by him in his personal computer, copy it to his portable storage device, and again install it in his computer in his work location for use as long as the manufacturer does not specify that he cannot do that. The e-book in his personal computer and his computer in the work location is exactly the same in value. There is no difference in value, even though it is in different computers.

We not only can copy information products to the same type of carriers directly but can also change the carriers directly. We can enter a paper book into a computer, thus gaining the digital version, and we can also print an online book into a paper version. Though the paper version and the electronic version of the same book differ in the selling price, they are the same in value of content.

(2)   INCOMPLETE CONSUMABILITY

Incomplete consumability of information products, also called "no loss from consumption," means that information products will not disappear after consumers buy and use them. For physical products, loss and wear will inevitably arise from their consumption or use. From the perspective of the producer, once a consumer buys physical products, the producer will lose the ownership of and the right to use such products completely. From the perspective of the consumer, the consumer can only use food, daily necessities, etc. once after purchasing them, and such products will disappear as the use process ends. Although the consumer can use electric appliances, automobiles, and other durable consumer items again and again, such products will finally lose their use value and end up disappearing, given that there is certain service life for them. However, information products are different. When a consumer purchases an information product, he only obtains the right to use it and partial ownership of it. The producer is not deprived of the content value of the product owned by it and can still continue to further develop and sell the product. The product will not disappear or decrease in value because the consumer uses it after purchasing it. Take e-books for an example. After a reader purchases an e-book, the value of the book will not be impaired whether such a person reads it or not.

(3)   TIMELINESS

Though information products will not be lost and worn out because of consumption and use, they still possibly suffer intangible losses because of their timeliness. The timeliness of information products are manifested as follows:

Firstly, for some information products, their effectiveness is limited by time. That is, only when they are used in specific periods can benefits be maximized; over time their value will decrease greatly or they will even become useless. This property of information products is brought out best in the market. Many enterprises will entrust consulting companies with analysis before formulating development plans. Then the consulting companies will predicate the development trend of the market in the following years by gathering and analyzing information and guiding the entrusting enterprises in making further decisions. Information products delivered by the

62   *The basic theory of industry development*

consulting companies are of high value to the enterprises. However, if the consulting companies work inefficiently so that the market with development potential has been occupied by other enterprises when they provide the entrusting enterprises with consulting reports, the consulting reports will be useless.

Secondly, the value of information products will also decrease when more advanced substitutes appear. Compared with traditional industries, the information resource industry sees more frequent technical and product upgrading. According to Moore's Law, performance of computers at the same price will double every 18–24 months. In that case, the software industry and other industries relying on information technology witness ongoing generation of technologies and products. When the same type of software that is more sound and easier to operate makes its appearance in the market, the former product will be doomed to be knocked out. Therefore, with time passing by, information products will be phased out by the market finally even though their functions might still work, given that they no longer satisfy consumers' needs.

(4)   NETWORK EFFECT

The network effect of information products means that the value of information products changes with the size of the network. Information is a tool for people to communicate and needs passing on among different individuals. The play to the effectiveness of the majority of information products is affected by the size of the network, except the minority of the products provided in an one-way manner or separately used. The more people use them, the higher value the products boast.

The network effect should include direct network effect and indirect network effect.[47] Direct network effect should refer to that brought by Internet-based information products, which is common currently and easy to understand. For example, nowadays, there is much social networking software through which users can read contents written or shared by others and can also communicate with other users. If only one user uses the software, he cannot obtain any information from the software at all. As the number of users increases, others can also obtain more information, and thus the software becomes more valuable.

The indirect network effect is comes into play by development of complementary products. It seems not as direct as the direct network effect, but it is very important for market development. For instance, Amazon sells e-book reader Kindle at a lower price to promote sales of e-books; gradual popularization of the mobile 4G network spurs the development of the mobile software field. All those are manifestations of the indirect network effect.

2.   *Effects of features of information products on the information resource industry chain*

(1)   PHYSICAL EXCHANGE AMONG ENTERPRISES LESS HIGHLIGHTED

For traditional industries, physical exchange is the most important and the most fundamental contact activity among enterprises in the industrial chain, and orderly and effective physical exchange is a necessary condition that guarantees good operation of the industrial chain. Upstream enterprises in an industrial chain pass on raw materials to producing enterprises, semi-finished products are passed on among the enterprises in the production link, and finally finished products are passed on to distributing enterprises, thus realizing the flow of products to the market. There are many requirements for enterprise operating activities for the existence of physical exchange. Firstly, enterprises must consider the positions of the raw material market and the terminal product market in selecting sites so as to effectively control costs. Secondly, enterprises are also subjected to geographical limitations when cooperating with each other and must pay higher transportation costs for trans-regional cooperation. Thirdly, the existence of physical exchange also requires enterprises to effectively manage stock, because a large amount of stock occupies the enterprise space and causes difficulty in capital flow, while insufficient stock may reduce enterprise productivity or even damage their reputations.

Comparably, because of non-substantiality and independence of information products, the information resource industry is much less dependent on physical exchange. For some information products, because they can be transmitted and sold through the Internet directly, the whole process from production to flow into the market will not involve physical exchange; examples are software and databases. For information products that must be attached to specific carriers for selling, often it is unnecessary to introduce physical carriers at the initial stage of production, and instead the products are transferred to physical carriers in the final link of production for marketing. For example, some publications are proofread and revised through computer at the earlier stage and printed out only after they are finalized.

Therefore, physical exchange will not exist as an important activity anymore in the information resource industry chain. Even though manufacturing and selling of partial information products still involve transportation by physical carriers, the core value of the industry still lies in the information content of the products.

(2) NETWORK OPERATORS BECOMING IMPORTANT MEMBERS
OF THE INDUSTRIAL CHAIN

With physical exchange less highlighted in the information resource industry, it is inevitable that information exchange will increase. Information flowing among enterprises is made up of two parts. Part I is the same information as traditional industrial chains with respect to the process of product making, including discussions and plans among enterprises with respect to design, production, and sale of products; Part II is about information products in their own right, including content of each version during the design and improvement of the products.

Information exchange among enterprises entails support from network operators whose service abilities limit the degree of cooperation among enterprises in the industrial chain to a great extent. For example, early enterprises can only contact each other by telephone or fax; the monotonous form of conveying information makes it profoundly difficult for enterprises to cooperate with each other. As information technology advances, nowadays enterprises can communicate with each other through the Internet in various forms, including videoconferencing and remote control, making trans-regional in-depth cooperation among enterprises possible and even allowing workers in different regions and different enterprises to communicate and cooperate with each other as if they did that face to face. Furthermore, most information products must be pushed to mobile users through platforms provided by network operators during the distribution.

Meanwhile, network operators are becoming discontented with purely providing enterprises with network support; instead, they wish to have a hand in all industries more profoundly, in hope of improving their own status in the industrial chain while providing platforms for such industries as animation, music, and games by making full use of their own advantages, making their voice heard more and strengthening profitability.

(3) NEW ENTERPRISES TENDING TO ADD TO THE INDUSTRIAL CHAIN

The forms of traditional industrial chains are relatively fixed because of the relatively definite upstream–downstream relationship between enterprises. Even when there is any change of an enterprise in an industrial chain, it is often the case that the same type of rival replaces the said enterprise in the industrial chain by market forces. As shown in Figure 2.8, given that Enterprise A' is capable of undertaking the same activity as Enterprise A in the industrial chain, other enterprises in the industrial chain will select Enterprise A' to replace Enterprise A when Enterprise A' provides more favorable conditions for them. Because physical products will be completely used up during the consumption, there are no resources that can be used again within the industrial chains basically, and other types of enterprises beyond the industrial chains will find them hard to add to the industrial chains.

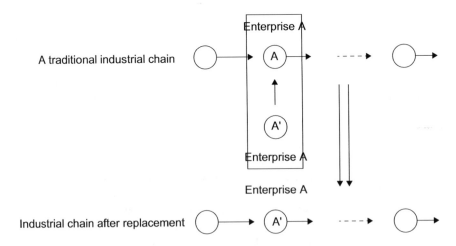

Figure 2.8 Enterprise replacement in a traditional industrial chain

The basic theory of industry development 65

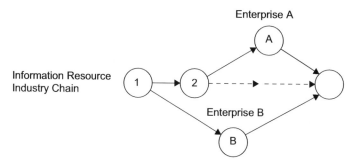

Figure 2.9 Increase in number of enterprises in information resource industry chain

However, the incomplete consumability of information products in the information resource industry renders repeated exploitation of information products by enterprises possible and generates exciting opportunities for enterprises beyond the industrial chain to add to the industrial chain. As shown in Figure 2.9, in the original industrial chain, Enterprise 1 supplies Enterprise 2 with information raw materials or information semi-finished products owned by it for further processing and selling. However, Enterprise 2 only obtains the right to use information resources provided by Enterprise 1. That means Enterprise 1 still reserves the ownership of such information resources, may further process them, or may change their forms. Therefore, Enterprise 1 can invite Enterprise B to join the existing industrial chain to process information resources owned by it. Similarly, other enterprises in the industrial chain can also invite enterprises in; for example, Enterprise 2 brings in Enterprise A as its downstream enterprise. In that case, Enterprises A and B joining in the industrial chain and the original enterprises are partners and complementors instead of rivals and substitutes, thus diversifying the product types in the industrial chain and expanding the target market.

(4) INDUSTRIAL CHAIN PRODUCTION TO BE MORE EFFICIENT

Although production efficiency is very important for all industries, production in the information resource industry must be more efficient in light of the timeliness of information products.

The increased complexity of modern industries makes it hard for a single enterprise to complete the whole production activity, so that enterprises in the industries have to divide work to improve their production efficiency; thus, the new form of organization, namely, industrial chains, has come into being. Indeed, enterprises can be more devoted to their own business activities after specialization of work and improve their own efficiency by technological reform and schedule management. However, flow of information and capital within the industrial chains is different from that within a single enterprise, and various objective factors will constrain the efficiency of the industrial chains to some extent. That kind of constraint may be acceptable for traditional industries, because products made by

66   *The basic theory of industry development*

traditional enterprises are relatively fixed; once production lines work normally, previous delays can be made up for and products can still be made continuously.

However, most products made in the information resource industry are original, especially such products as consulting reports, which are disposable consumables and which consumers will not need if enterprises fail to provide consumers with them within the time limit. Even software and other information products that can be duplicated in large numbers may be replaced by similar products at any time. If an enterprise fails to put its product into the market as soon as it's ready to sell and another enterprise launches a similar product in the market before the former enterprise, then the former enterprise will not be able to recover its sunk cost and may even become bankrupt. Therefore, production in the information resource industry chain must be far more efficient than that of traditional industrial chains. Only when enterprises maintain the efficiency of the industrial chain can they have a share in the market.

(5)   CONSUMER PARTICIPATION INCREASING

Consumers are playing an increasingly important part in the information resource industry chain, which is reflected by the following aspects:

Firstly, consumers provide other consumers with information on products. Consumers can directly observe superficial features of traditional physical products when they buy them, such as texture and color, and decide whether to buy them or not. Nevertheless, it is hard for consumers to obtain information on information products by directly observing them in light of their non-substantiality, so consumers often hesitate to buy them. In that case, consumers often rely on suggestions offered by other buyers. They will collect comments from users who have purchased an information product in the market as an important basis for them to buy such product or not.

Secondly, consumer participation improves the content of information products. For a traditional enterprise, once its product is put into the market and bought by a consumer, the whole process from production to selling basically ends, with the form and content of the product no longer changed and the value of the product purchased by the consumer remaining unchanged. The interaction between the enterprise and the consumer thereafter is mainly about the after-sale service; that is, the enterprise answers any question and repairs any problem arising from the consumer's use of the product. However, the value of some information products can still be increased after consumers buy them. Consumers can add information to such products in some cases after purchasing them. Different users of the same product interconnect with each other so that consumers can obtain more information and the information product can play a more important role.

2.5   Policy basis for the information resource industry: limited government intervention theory

The requirement of "improving social and economic benefits of the information resource industry" is clearly stated in the *Several Opinions of the General Office of the CPC Central Committee and the General Office of the State Council on*

The basic theory of industry development   67

Strengthening Information Resource Exploitation released in 2004. China is practicing the socialist market economy system, and all social resources, including information resources, are allocated by the market mechanism. Therefore, China must develop the information resource industry by market forces. However, China is a developing country and the information resource industry is an emerging industry, which inevitably results in more market failure phenomena during the course of development of the industry. Therefore, China needs to rely on the government's industrial policies, the "visible hand," to develop such a new industry on its land as soon as possible.

2.5.1 Market failure theory and its policy implications

Market failure is one of the basic reasons for the government's intervention in modern economics.[48] Remedying and correcting negative impacts that market failure exerts on economic development is often viewed as the basic function of industrial policies.

There are different causes for, manifestations of, and consequences from market failure in the information resource industry. Generally speaking, market failure in the information resource industry includes three types: Type I is mechanism failure. That is, the market mechanism lacks a necessary element, so that it cannot work efficiently, thus leading to failure in the optimal allocation of resources. For example, operation of the market mechanism entails sufficient information, but it is often the case in the market that information is insufficient or asymmetric, and thus the common market failure status forms. Another example is that operation of the market mechanism requires sufficient competition and corresponding systems and laws; however, in China, which has transformed from the planned economy to the market economy, there may be insufficient market competition or incomplete laws and systems. Type II is function failure. That is, the market mechanism in its own right runs normally but does not work in a specific field. For example, as content products, information resources are relevant to culture and civilizations, so they carry some nature of public products. To achieve effective supply, the government must, as the representative of public interests, make them by itself or promote effective supply by social and market players through public policies. Type III is effect failure. That is, although the market works well, it may exert adverse effects on society. For example, the market mechanism may lead to the formation of monopolistic industrial organizations, which not only hinders sound development of industries but may also stimulate the generation of information gap or reinforce its strength and lead to social inequality.

To address the types of market failure, different function objectives are set and different means are adopted in the policies on the information resource industry. Firstly, with respect to the mechanism failure, industrial policies aim to improve the market mechanism in its own right. For example, information disclosure systems for industrial organizations are established to make information in the market more sufficient and information grasped by different entities more symmetrical. The policy measure is strengthened to foster organizations in the information

68   *The basic theory of industry development*

resource industry and shape an environment that embraces benign competition between and among enterprises; the market monitoring system is improved to ensure sound and steady development of the information resource market. Secondly, with respect to the function failure, industrial policies aim to establish and improve special regimes and mechanisms to stretch out to the parts inaccessible by market forces. For example, the public welfare mechanism for exploitation and service of information resources is established and improved to enhance the abundance of social information resources. Thirdly, with respect to the effect failure, industrial policies aim to avoid adverse consequences or curb or eliminate adverse consequences through concurrent or post-event effective monitoring. For example, anti-monopoly acts are enacted and improved to prevent unfair competition, strengthen social control of the information resource industry, safeguard national fundamental interests, and protect legitimate rights and interests of social organizations and citizens.

2.5.2   *Economies of scale theory and its policy implications*

Economies of scale highlight gradual increase in scale and return; that is, the unit production cost keeps decreasing before the optimal scale with the lowest production cost is reached. So it is good for an industry or an enterprise to expand its scale (until it reaches the optimal scale).

The economies of scale theory often allows or even encourages monopoly to some extent. It is often applied to the following three cases. Number one, when the domestic or foreign market of an industry is monopolized by foreign enterprises, it is necessary for the government to adopt some policies to break down "joining barriers" so as to encourage domestic enterprises to reach some scale. Number two, if an economically backward country wants to achieve the catch-up effect, it must employ the policy means in a short time to improve the factory scale and even the strength of its industries. Number three, often the government makes direct investments in some natural monopoly enterprises so that they can reach the optimal scale of economy with the lowest production costs fast.

The economies of scale theory conflicts with the aforesaid market failure theory. Those advocates of new institutionalism economics may think that the economies of scale theory and its policies may relatively focus on the scale of enterprises instead of the scale of industries, which may reduce efficiency and competitiveness of enterprises. However, in relatively backward countries and industries, the economies of scale theory and its industrial policies turn out to be effective in some specific periods.

2.5.3   *Late-developing superiority theory and its policy implications*

The late-developing superiority theory originates from Li Jiatu's theory on the international division of labor and comparative production cost. According to the theory, each country's production costs vary from industry to industry, and

The basic theory of industry development   69

every country should give priority to developing industries with superiority in production cost (when several industries of the country preponderate in production cost, priority should be given to the one with the greatest advantage; when several industries do not preponderate, priority should be given to the one with the minimum disadvantage). Thus, every country can gain comparative profits through international trade.

Later, the comparative advantage theory was evolved by a Japanese scholar into the late-developing superiority theory generalizing that underdeveloped countries can absorb and apply capital, technologies, and management experience of developed countries by various means, and that as long as they reach the economies of scale under the support by national industrial policies, they may foster enterprises and industries superior to those in developed countries in light of their lower labor costs in the same period.

There are two key points about industrial policies on the basis of the late-developing superiority theory: one is carrying on the content of industrial policies for economies of scale, and embracing or even encouraging monopoly to some extent so as to expand the scale of enterprises; the other is keeping open to the outside, absorbing capital and technologies from the outside world and developing foreign trade.

2.5.4   Structural transformation theory and its policy implications

Economic growth is not only a process of quantity increment but also a process of economic structure change. The so-called "Petty-Clark Theorem" points out that with economic development, a country's labor will move from the primary industry to the secondary industry and then to the tertiary industry. Thereafter, Hoffmann and Kuznets put forward "Hoffmann Theorem" and "Kuznets Growth Theory," respectively, analyzing the law underlying the change of industrial structure in the economic growth.

The structural transformation theory is a development of theories mentioned earlier. The theories mainly involve the relationship between the economic growth process and industrial structure. However, views of the structural transformation theory are applied to industrial policy practice; according to the theory, the function of industrial policies is to promote change of a country's industrial structure and drive the evolution of whole country's industrial structure from low level to high level so as to achieve economic growth of the country and finally realize the economic catch-up strategy of the country.

Structural transformation is essentially a process of profit redistribution. Theoretically, it is driven by the market mechanism. However, in practice, to speed up structural transformation and spur fast economic growth, proper industrial policy instruments are needed to restrict, weaken, and phase out backward industries, sustain, strengthen, and develop competitive industries, and encourage, support, and develop emerging industries.

70   *The basic theory of industry development*

2.5.5   *Technological development theory, national interest theory, and their policy implications*

The technological development theory highlights the knowledge wealth nature of technologies. That kind of knowledge wealth is characterized with the nature of public goods, huge development risk at the earlier stage, and spillover of the development and utilization as well as social benefit being bigger than corporate benefit. Because of the previously-mentioned features, often private enterprises are unwilling or unable to conduct technological development. Therefore, it is the basic function of policies in the information resource industry to guide and encourage enterprises to undertake technological development for the purpose of laying technological foundations for and giving impetus to rapid development of the information resource industry.

The national interest theory focuses on protecting national safety and interests. According to the theory, underdeveloped countries' industries are often on a sticky wicket in the fierce competition from developed countries' industries. Then, the underdeveloped countries must set protection barriers and help expand domestic and foreign markets with their visible hands to protect their weak and small national industries, and gradually expand the access to such industries to the outside world until such industries grow strong and big.

2.5.6   *Summary: development of the information resource industry entails limited government intervention*

The foregoing theories reveal objectives and ways of government intervention in the development of the information resource industry from different perspectives. Those objectives and ways imply that the development of China's information resource industry entails government intervention and that the government is capable of intervening with the development of the information resource industry, provided that the intervention is limited. Usually, industrial policies are the main means to intervene with the accomplishment of specific goals. In reality, policies on the information resource industry are often comprehensive, covering several policy objectives, contents, and means, as presented in Table 2.5.

Table 2.5 exhibits the objectives and purposes of the government's intervention. They look varied but have something in common; that is, the government's intervention through industrial policies is limited, which is reflected as follows:

Firstly, the intervention is market-based. The government's intervention does not mean replacing the market but providing assistance and supplementing the market. Usually, the government does not provide products directly, except the public products that the market does not have access to delivering; instead, the government often functions indirectly by making industrial policies that focus on the market, interest orientation, and information guidance.

Secondly, the intervention is made with a view to the international market. The government makes industrial policies with a view to the international industrial division and the international market, whether the government does that for the

The basic theory of industry development 71

Table 2.5 Government's intervention in the information resource industry: purposes, theories, and specific goals

Basic Objectives	Theoretical Basis	Specific Goals
Addressing market failure	Market failure theory	• Fostering market players • Improving market systems • Optimizing the market environment • Providing information resource services • Anti-monopoly • Protecting consumer, social, and national interests • Maintaining social fairness and justice
Enhancing enterprise strengths	Economies of scale theory	• Improving scale strengths of large enterprises • Improving scale strengths of national industries
Improving competitiveness	Late-developing superiority theory	• Absorbing foreign technologies and management experience • Expanding the international market • Improving enterprise capabilities
Spurring economic growth	Structural transformation theory	• Fostering emerging industries • Phasing out backward industries • Developing competitive industries
Strengthening industrial technologies	Technological development theory	• Strengthening national technological R&D capabilities • Promoting enterprise technological R&D
Safeguarding national interests	National interest theory	• Protecting national industries

purpose of participating in the international division of work, international competition, or realizing economic growth. In this vein, industrial policies are essentially strategic economic decisions.

Thirdly, the intervention has an emphasis on guiding enterprise conduct. Industrial policies fall under microeconomic policies, and enterprises are the basic target group.[49] Although people argue whether industrial policies should be used to improve the scale of enterprises or competitiveness of enterprises based on the market failure theory and the economies of scale theory, on the whole, all the industrial policies must be finally realized through enterprises. Therefore, how to apply industrial policies to guiding enterprise conduct so that their allocation of resources moves towards the desired goal of the government is the key to success of industrial policies.

Fourthly, the intervention is ever-changing. That means the government's intervention keeps changing with socioeconomic development and industrial development needs. For example, when an underdeveloped country has a small scale of industry and at the lower level, it can often foster several important industrial sectors or large enterprise organizations by improving the market mechanism and implementing preferential policies. After its industries get developed with some

72 The basic theory of industry development

scale and strength, the country often begins to bring in foreign advanced technologies and management experience on the basis of late-developing superiority theory and the technological development theory in order to develop its basic studies, encourage its enterprises to take the initiative to undertake technological reform, and improve its international enterprise competitiveness. The government actively supplies public products and services, and strengthens and improves economic and social control of industries so as to build an enabling and fair competitive environment for enterprise development, allow survival of the fittest of enterprises, and improve the whole competitiveness of enterprises. Finally, when national industries and economic strength reach some level, the government must guide industrial structural upgrading and transformation through industrial policies, which can contribute to steady and sound national economic development.

Notes

1 General Office of the State Council, "Several Opinions of the State Council on Promoting Information Consumption and Expanding Domestic Demand (G.F. [2013] No.32)," (2013-08-14) [2015-1-6], www.gov.cn/zwgk/201308/14/content_2466856.htm.
2 Maosheng Lai, Xiudan Yang, Xiaofeng Hu and Bo Xu, "Study on Basic Theories about Information Resource Exploitation," *Information Studies: Theory & Application*, no. 3 (2004): 229–235.
3 M.A. Zhe-Ming, "Research on Mechanism of Information Consumption," *Information Science*, no. 12 (2012): 8.
4 P. Sepstrup, *Consumption of Mass Communication—Construction of a Model on Information Consumption Behaviour* (ERIC, 1977).
5 P. Sepstrup, *Consumption of Mass Communication—Construction of a Model on Information Consumption Behaviour* (ERIC, 1977).
6 Rozanski E.P. Yaccim, *Student Information Consumption Strategies: Implications of the Google Effect//Proceedings of the 2012 iConference* (New York: ACM, 2012), 248–253.
7 S. Whittaker, "Personal Information Management: From Information Consumption to Curation," *Annual Review of Information Science and Technology* 45, no. 1 (2011): 1–62.
8 China Internet Network Information Center, "Report for the 33th Statistics of China's Internet Development Status," (2014-03-05) [2015-1-26], www.cnnic.net.cn/hlwfzyj/hlwxzbg/hlwtjbg/201403/t20140305_46240.htm.
9 iResearch, "Chinese Online Video Market Size Was RMB 13.59 Billion in 2013, and Mobile App Commercialization Began," (2014-08-18) [2015-1-26], www.iresearch.com.cn/View/236618.html.
10 Hanlin Ji, "Study on Pricing Model for Two-Sided Market," *Industrial Economics Research*, no. 4 (2006): 11–20.
11 Manhong Shen and Lingqiao He, "Classification of Externality and Evolution of Externality Theory," *Journal of Zhejiang University (Humanities and Social Sciences)*, no. 1 (2002): 152–160.
12 China Internet Network Information Center, "Report for Research on Chinese Netizens' Application of Network Videos for 2013," (2014-06-09) [2015-01-26], www.cnnic.net.cn/hlwfzyj/hlwxzbg/spbg/201406/t20140609_47180.htm.
13 Feng Huiling and Lemen Chao, "Study on Law behind Evolution of Consumption Structure of Information Resource Industry and Optimization Strategies," *Information Studies: Theory & Application*, no. 5 (2014): 17–22.
14 China Internet Network Information Center, "Report for Research on Chinese Netizens' Application of Network Videos for 2013," (2014-06-09) [2015-1-26], www.cnnic.net.cn/hlwfzyj/hlwxzbg/spbg/201406/t20140609_47180.htm.

The basic theory of industry development 73

15 Yahui Liu, Tieying Zhang, Xiaolong Jin and Xueqi Cheng, "Personal Privacy Protection in the Big Data Age," *Journal of Computer Research and Development*, no. 1 (2015): 1–7.

16 Baocheng Ji, "A Discussion of Essence and Function of Market Order," *Journal of Renmin University of China*, no. 1 (2004): 26–32.

17 G.T. Renner, "Geography of industrial localization," *Economic Geography* 23, no. 3 (1947): 167–189.

18 "Industrial Symbiosis," [2015-12-15], http://wiki.mbalib.com/wiki/%E4%BA%A7%E 4%B8%9A%E5%85%B1%E7%94%9F.

19 Xiaopeng Hu, "Industrial Symbiosis: Theoretical Definition and Its Internal Mechanism," *China Industrial Economics*, no 9 (2008): 118–128.

20 C. Hood, *The Tools of Government* (London: Macmillan, 1983), 5.

21 Xiaopeng Hu, "Industrial Symbiosis: Theoretical Definition and Its Internal Mechanism," *China Industrial Economics*, no. 9 (2008): 118–128.

22 Zhongdong Xiao, Yongqing Liu and Linyan Sun, "Study on Food Chain in the Industry Symbiosis System," *Science&Technology Progress and Policy*, no. 3 (2008): 72–75.

23 Xiaopeng Hu, "Industrial Symbiosis: Theoretical Definition and Its Internal Mechanism," *China Industrial Economics*, no. 9 (2008): 118–128.

24 Xiaojun Cai, Shuangjie Li and Qihao Liu, "Study on Mechanism for Formation of Symbiosis Chain of Ecological Industrial Park and Stability," *China Soft Science*, no. 3 (2006): 12–14.

25 Mingjie Rui, Mingyu Liu and Jiangbo Ren, *Discussion of Industrial Chain Integration* (Shanghai: Fudan University Press, 2006).

26 M.E. Porter, "Location, Competition, and Economic Development: Local Clusters in a Global Economy," *Economic Development Quarterly* 14, no. 1 (2000): 15–34.

27 Gongpu Yang and Dawei Xia, *Modern Industrial Economics* (Shanghai: Shanghai University of Finance & Economics Press, 1999).

28 Guojun Jiang and Mingxin Jiang, "Study on Industrial Chain Theory and Stability Mechanism," *Journal of Chongqing University (Social Edition)*, no. 1 (2004).

29 Qinlin Gong, "Discussion of Construction of Industrial Chain and Holistic Urban-Rural Development," *The Economist*, no. 3 (2004): 121–123.

30 Yihong Yu and Xizhan Guan, *Vertical Control of Industrial Chain and Economic Regulation* (Shanghai: Fudan University Press, 2006).

31 Guifu Liu, "Study on Basic Connotation of Industrial Chain," *Journal of Industrial Technological Economics*, no. 8 (2007): 92–96.

32 Yang Wang, Xu Xiao and Shuyan Yu, *Study on Software Industry Development Mode* (Beijing: Science Press, 2009).

33 Guifu Liu, "Study on Structure Model of Chain Inside the Industrial Chain," *Taxation and Economy*, no. 2 (2008): 43–45.

34 Qiuju Wang, "Connotation of Industrial Chain and Structure Analysis," *Logistics Sci-Tech*, no. 5 (2012): 89–91.

35 Chang Shao and Jian Li, "Study on 'Wave Corpuscle Duality' of Industrial Chain: Discussion of Characteristics, Structure and Integration of Industrial Chain," *China Industrial Economics*, no. 9 (2007): 5–13.

36 Ying Liu, Qi Li and Xiaofan Wang, "Analysis of Complexity of Structure of Industrial Chain of Traditional Chinese Medicine," *China Journal of Chinese Materia Medica*, no. 16 (2014): 3187–3191.

37 Xiangping Yu, "Structure and Effect of Exhibition Industrial Chain," *Economic Forum*, no. 1 (2008): 67–69.

38 S. Jockel, A. Will and F. Schwarzer, "Participatory Media Culture and Digital Online Distribution: Reconfiguring the Value Chain in the Computer Game Industry," *The International Journal on Media Management* 10, no. 3 (2008): 102–111.

39 E. Salehi-Sangarie, A.K. Nath and P. Saha, "Transforming Supply Chains in Digital Content Delivery: A Case Study in Apple," *IFIP International Federation for Information Processing* 255, no.1 (2010).

74 *The basic theory of industry development*

40 A.L. Hadida and T. Paris, "Managerial Cognition and the Value Chain in the Digital Music Industry," *Technological Forecasting and Social Change*, no. 83 (2014): 84–97.

41 Hongming Cui and Zhao Guojun, "Study on Value Flow of Information Resource Industry Chain and on Value Beam of Information Resource Products," *Journal of Intelligence*, no. 8 (2013): 169–173, 168.

42 Hongming Cui, "Analysis of Structure of Information Resource Industry Chain: Taking Digital Publishing Industry as an Example," *Information and Documentation Services*, no. 1 (2014): 62–66.

43 Guifu Li, "Study on China's Cable Digital Television Industry Chain," *Journal of Industrial Technological Economics*, no. 1 (2014): 62–66.

44 Chuanming Yang, "Modular Study on Online Game Industry Chain," *Journal of Intelligence*, no. 7 (2008): 25–27, 36.

45 Jiajun Zhu, Hongzhen Tang and Jin Liu, "Comparative Study on Development Modes of Entire Animation Industry Chain," *Science and Technology Management Research*, no. 11 (2014): 92–95.

46 Feicheng Ma, Huai Wang and Xianjin Zha, *Information Economics* (Wuhan: Wuhan University Press, 1997), 115–127.

47 Feicheng Ma, *Information Resource Management* (Wuhan: Wuhan University Press, 2001), 206.

48 Charles Wolf, *Market or Government: The Truth of Market Government Failure*. Trans. Lu Jun and Xie Xu. (Chongqing: Chongqing press, 2009).

49 Xiuning Cao, Yinhua Tian and Haichao Jiang, "New Progress of Studies on Industrial Policies," *China Industrial Economics*, no. 12 (2007): 117–123.

3 Development trajectory of China's information resource industry

Many developed countries and regions worldwide have paid great attention to and given intensive policy support for the development of the information resource industry since the beginning of the Information Age, because information resources not only can create industrial value but also can reform the traditional process and help optimize the allocation of resources by combining with traditional industries and indirectly exerting the substitute effect on material resources and energy resources. Developing the information resource industry means lots of exciting development opportunities and the commanding height.[1] In this chapter, the development trajectory of China's information resource industry for the past ten more years will be exhibited through analysis of a series of data revealing the history of the information resources that grow to be a production element that is on the track of industrialization out of a factor that helps eliminate uncertainties.

It has been a very long time since information began to eliminate people's uncertainties, but it has been only decades since it started to serve as the production element and social wealth source in China. It has been more than ten years since information resources began to take off on the track of industrialization. We classify the development trajectory of the information resource industry in China into four periods: germination period, initial development period, rapid development period, and steady development period. The general development features are shown in Table 3.1.

3.1 Germination period

As China's socioeconomic informatization level keeps lifting, information resources gradually exhibit strategic value and attract an increasing amount of attention from all walks of life. Early in 1984, Comrade Deng Xiaoping clearly put forward the concept of "information resources" in his inscription "exploiting information resources and serving construction of four modernizations (industrial modernization, agricultural modernization, national defense modernization, and science and technology modernization)" for *Economic Information Daily*. However, according to the authors' survey, the wording of "information resource industry" had not been seen internationally. In the early 1990s, the core status of information resources in informatization was widely accepted, and the wording

Table 3.1 Development periods and features of China's information resource industry

Periods \ Features	Development Scale and Speed	Development of Subdivided Industries	Regional Distribution
Germination Period (from 1990 to 2003)	The concept of the information resource industry is not definite; such industries with features of the information resource industry as publishing industry, data industry, and Internet information service industry feature scattered distribution, small scale, and poor competitiveness.	The composition and structure of subdivided industries are not clear; traditional subdivided industries (such as publishing industry) and Internet-based and IT-based emerging industries (such as online game industry and online education industry) get developed to some extent.	The information resource-related industries get developed in developed provinces and cities (like Shanghai, Beijing, and Guangdong), while they are underdeveloped in other regions.
Initial Development Period (from 2004 to 2007)	Under the general concept, the information resource industry develops fast, but on a small scale.	Traditional subdivided industries (such as publishing industry) account for a large proportion, emerging or knowledge-intensive subdivided industries (such as consulting industry and brokerage industry) develop fast, and individual subdivided industries (such as archive and museum industry) do not start.	The information resource industry in all regions gets developed, particularly in developed provincial-level regions in North China, East China, and South China (such as Beijing, Zhejiang, and Guangdong).
Rapid Development Period (from 2008 to 2011)	The development scale expands obviously, and the information resource industry keeps developing fast.	Partial emerging industries (such as consulting industry and brokerage industry) account for an obviously increased proportion; traditional subdivided industries (such as publishing industry) account for a decreased proportion, and individual subdivided industries (such as archive and museum industry) start.	The information resource industry in more provincial-level regions gets developed, with a fast-expanding scale; provinces in East China take the lead in the development of the information resource industry.
Steady Development Period (from 2012 up until now)	The development scale keeps growing, and the information resource industry develops not that fast but still upward.	Subdivided industries get developed, and the structure of the subdivided industries tends to be steadier; emerging industries keep developing at a high speed, while traditional industries account for a steadily decreasing proportion to give way to emerging industries; the information resource industry and other industries combine with each other more profoundly, such as industrial Internet and e-commerce.	The regional layout of the information resource industry is basically steady. The information resource industry is mainly concentrated in the developed economic belts, shaping the distribution pattern of "strong East and weak West" with East China as the body and North China and South China as the wings.

Development trajectory of the industry 77

of "3C" (communication, computer, and content) began to be used. Content represents information resources in their own right. Considering the sudden expansion of the scale of information provision and consulting industries, the concept of "information content industry," also called "information resource industry," began to be used internationally to distinguish the new concept from the original "information service industry." In 1996, Zhu Youping, etc., pointed out that "the information resource industry is an industry that exploits information resources" for the first time.[2] In 1998, Pang Jing'an mentioned in his article that the "information resource industry" corresponded to "content" in 3C.[3] On December 27, 2001, Jiang Zeming pointed out in the preface of *Exploration and Practice of China's Informatization* that materials, energy sources, and information were three kinds of resources for modern social development and that information resource exploitation must be put high on the agenda to maintain sustained, fast, and sound Chinese economic development. According to the earlier descriptions, China's information resource industry indeed germinated, which could be seen from the development of the publishing industry, consulting industry, animation industry, radio, film, and television industry, market survey industry, online game industry, and Internet information service industry. Though those industries are not titled "information resource industry" in name, the content nature of the economic activity involved conforms to basic features of the information resource industry as mentioned earlier in this book.

3.1.1 Scale and competitiveness of related industries

Because the information resource industry is not clearly defined in the *Provisional Provisions on the Statistical Classification of Information-related Industries* promulgated by the National Bureau of Statistics in 2004 and before, data can be found only in subcategories related to information content, and we can only catch a glimpse of the development status of the germination period of the information resource industry by "splicing." For example, the output value of China's online game industry was only RMB 310 million in 2001 but increased to RMB 910 million in 2002 and reached RMB 2 billion in 2003, equivalent to that of the film industry. China's digital publishing-related industries boasted the direct output value of RMB 2.5 billion in 2003, and China's online education market size reached RMB 1.78 billion in the same year, a year-on-year increase of 55.3%.[4] China's online advertising revenues reached RMB 870 million in 2003, increasing by RMB 290 million compared with that in 2002, namely, an increase rate of 50%.[5] The content industry is the closest to the information resource industry in connotation and denotation. According to the findings, the total size of China's digital content industry was RMB 31 billion in 2003, mainly coming from network service, digital video animation, wireless content service, digital education, and digital publishing.[6]

However, the overall scale of the information resource industry was still small in this period. Except such industries as press and publishing industries with some features of traditional industries, it was often the case that enterprises in

78 *Development trajectory of the industry*

most industries, particularly emerging industries, were small scale and under-competitivene. Before 2003, among emerging enterprises with features of the information resource industry, Wanfang HC360.COM, and Tsinghua Tongfang could be counted as big enterprises, but they only had the business scale of RMB several hundred million. About 50% of the enterprises had registered capital of no more than RMB 10 million, from which we could infer that the overall scale of China's information resource industry (excluding traditional press and publishing industries) then was not likely to be more than RMB 3 billion and more than that it impossibly exceeded RMB 5 billion even though foreign enterprise sales in China were added. According to data of the State Information Center, information resource service enterprises suffered losses generally, and only few enterprises gained profits. In 2001, 55.6% of the enterprises suffered losses.[7] In this period, the information resource industry was characterized by lack of depth in information content and service product, unsteady customer base, and singleness of service forms. Furthermore, imperfect system building, weak policy intensity, overlapping management, and monopoly by public departments in terms of management and policies, as well as poor knowledge of the government administration of information resources as a production element, inadequate supervision of the information resource market, and rigid enterprise systems impeded the development of the information resource industry.

3.1.2 *Excessive concentration of industrial distribution*

In this period, the information resource industry was obviously concentrated in few developed regions. Take the information service industry for an example. Because there have been huge IT application demands in North China represented by Beijing, East China represented by Shanghai and Nanjing, and South China represented by Shenzhen and Guangzhou, the said regions gained a large share in the information service market, which would last for a long time.[8] Then take the online game industry for an example. Beijing, Shanghai, Guangdong, Fujian, and Sichuan were home to about 95% of the games and operators; in terms of regional distribution of profit shares, Shanghai enterprises represented by Shanda and Ninetowns undoubtedly had an overwhelming advantage, with 75% of the shares, higher than that of Beijing and Guangdong.[9] Finally, take the digital television industry for an example. Although the government approved extensive cities of undertaking the pilot project of digital television, digital television was mostly consumed in Beijing, Shanghai, and Guangdong, followed by Shandong and Zhejiang.[10]

3.2 Initial development period

The release of *Several Opinions of the General Office of the CPC Central Committee and the General Office of the State Council on Strengthening Information Resource Exploitation* (Z.B.F. [2004] No.34) in December 2004 could be counted as the start of large-scale development of China's information resource industry. In this programmatic document, "promoting sound and fast development of the information resource industry, and researching and developing policies and plans spurring the development of the information resource industry" were clearly put forward in the name of the highest Chinese party and government organs, affirming the significance of the information resource industry and making the explicit attitude of the Party and the State towards the development of the information resource industry clear. Thereafter, in *China's Strategies for Informatization Development from 2006 to 2020* issued by the General Office of the CPC Central Committee and the General Office of the State Council, it was further clearly highlighted that "information resources have become an increasingly important production element, intangible asset and social wealth," and it was pointed out that "information resource exploitation must be put high on the agenda," that "scientific outlook on information resources must be built, and information resources must be raised to the same important status as energy sources and materials so as to create conditions for developing knowledge-intensive industries," and that "more efforts must be devoted to the development of the modern information service industry featuring digitization and network orientation to promote information resource exploitation. The role of information resource exploitation in saving resources and energy sources and improving benefits must be fully played, and the effect of information flow in guiding personnel flow, material flow and capital flow must be exerted to promote the transformation of the economic growth mode and building of the resource-conserving society."

Driven by important strategic arrangements of the Party and the State that "craft overall plans, promote development and are well-thought with a long view," China's information resource industry grew big and strong from being small and weak from 2004 to 2007, with increasingly expanding scale and rising development level. Specifically, the development of the information resource industry in this period demonstrated the following features.

3.2.1 Development overview

From 2004 to 2007, China's information resource industry had the annual increase rates of operating incomes of 25.50%, 18.90%, and 18.40%, respectively, being on a steady rise on the whole. According to our conversion and calculation of the related statistical data, China's information resource industry gained the operating income of about RMB 563.6 billion in 2004 but boasted RMB 995.8 billion in 2007, meaning the initial development of the information resource industry.

As shown in Figure 3.1, the annual increase rates of operating incomes of the subdivided industries exceeded 15%, with most of the industries maintained at the level of high increase. The 30.2% annual average increase rate of the operating income of the technical promotion service industry was the highest among the subdivided industries, with the operating income increasing from RMB 21.8 billion in 2004 to RMB 47.7 billion in 2007, followed by the 27.7% annual average increase rate of the operating income of the exploration and mapping industry with the operating income increasing from RMB 3.8 billion in 2004 to RMB 7.5 billion in 2007. The agency and brokerage industry, the data content production

80 Development trajectory of the industry

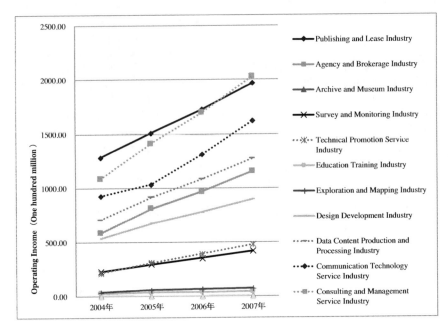

Figure 3.1 Changes of subdivided industries of the information resource industry from 2004 to 2007

and processing industry, the communication technology service industry, and the consulting and management service industry had a large scale and annual average increase rates of operating incomes of more than 20%, with operating incomes being RMB 115.5 billion, RMB 127.2 billion, RMB 162 billion, and RMB 203 billion, respectively, in 2007. The 15.3% increase rate of the publishing and lease industry was not high relatively among the subdivided industries, but with a large total scale being RMB 196.8 billion in 2007.

3.2.2 Industrial structure

The proportions of the subdivided industries of the information resource industry for the period from 2004 to 2008 were shown in Figure 3.2: the publishing and lease industry and the consulting and management service industry ranked as the top 2, accounting for about 20%, with the total operating incomes for that period being RMB 649 billion and RMB 622.1 billion, respectively; the communication technology service industry, the data content production and processing industry, and the agency and brokerage industry accounted for proportions ranging from 10% to 15%, with the total operating incomes for that period being RMB 489.1 billion, RMB 398.1 billion, and RMB 351.7 billion, respectively; furthermore, the design development industry, the technical promotion service industry,

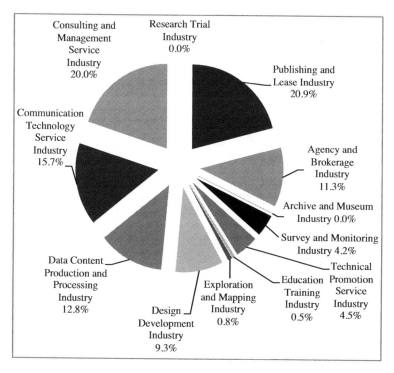

Figure 3.2 Proportions of subdivided industries of the information resource industry from 2004 to 2007

and the survey and monitoring industry also accounted for certain proportions, with the total operating incomes for that period being RMB 288.7 billion, RMB 139.8 billion, and RMB 129.8 billion, respectively; the exploration and mapping industry, the education training industry, the archive and museum industry, and the research trial industry accounted for small proportions, with the total operating incomes for that period not exceeding RMB 30 billion and therefore, such industries remain to be developed.

Furthermore, it can be seen from Figure 3.1 and Figure 3.2 that there are obvious differences between increase rates of part of the subdivided industries and the average increase rate of the industry. For example, the increase rate of the operating income of the consulting and management service industry was much higher than the average level of the information resource industry; although the consulting and management service industry ranked second among the subdivided industries by virtue of its operating income of RMB 108.5 billion in 2004, its operating income reached RMB 203 billion in 2007, exceeding RMB 196.8 billion operating income of the publishing and lease industry and rising to No. 1. Similarly, the technical promotion service industry achieved an operating income of RMB 21.8 billion in 2004, which was slightly lower than that of the survey and monitoring industry

82 Development trajectory of the industry

(RMB 22.9 billion); however, the technical promotion service industry gradually took the lead within two years after 2005, with an operating income of RMB 47.7 billion in 2007, exceeding RMB 41.8 billion of the survey and monitoring industry. That tendency in increase rate reflected the changing pattern in the information resource industry, which underpinned rapid development and structural rebalance for the next period.

3.2.3 Regional disparities

Operating incomes of China's information resource industry varied greatly from region to region for the period from 2004 to 2007. China can be divided into seven regions – North China, East China, Central China, South China, Northeast, outhwest, and Northwest – according to geographic features. Based on that division, it could be found from Figure 3.3 that operating incomes of the information resource industry both in North China and in East China accounted for 26.5% of all, with total incomes for that period being over RMB 820 billion, respectively, ranking first; then is South China, with an operating income accounting for 14.9% and the total income for that period being RMB 462.8 billion; next are Southwest, Central China, and Northeast, with operating incomes accounting for about 10%, respectively and total incomes for that period being about RMB 300 billion, respectively; finally is Northwest, with an operating income accounting for only 4.3%, and the total income for that period being RMB 134.4 billion.

The development of the information resource industry was unbalanced among provincial administrative regions. In North China, Beijing boasted total operating

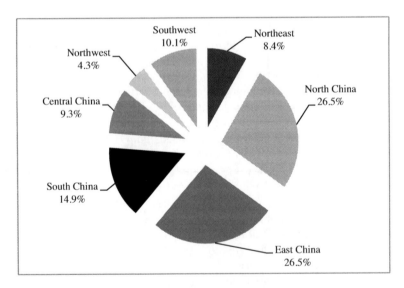

Figure 3.3 Regional distribution of the information resource industry from 2004 to 2007

income of RMB 528.6 billion from the information resource industry, ranking first among provincial regions in China and accounting for 65.5% of the total operating income of the whole of North China. In East China, the development of the information resource industry in all provincial regions was relatively balanced, with total operating incomes of Zhejiang, Shandong, and Shanghai, namely, RMB 217.2 billion, RMB 170.6 billion, and RMB 169.8 billion, respectively, accounting for more than 20% of the whole of East China. In South China, Guangdong Province contributed most to the total operating incomes of the whole region from the information resource industry; it boasted an operating income of RMB 361.8 billion, namely, 78.2% of the total of the whole of South China and ranked second among all provinces in China.

In this period, the regional pattern of the information resource industry changed greatly compared with that before 2004; most notable was the rapid development of South China. As shown in Figure 3.4, the information resource industry in South China was maintained at almost the same development level as that in Northeast, Southwest, and Central China before 2004, with a total operating income of over RMB 60 billion. However, it began to take off from 2006. When the other three

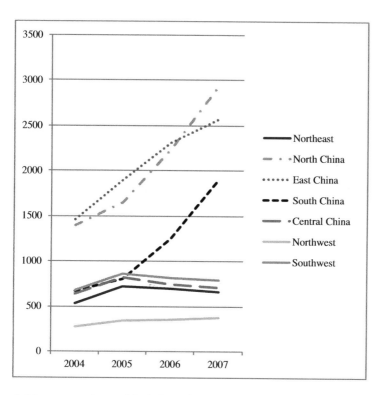

Figure 3.4 Increase tendency of the information resource industry in all regions from 2004 to 2007

84 Development trajectory of the industry

regions did not gain obviously increased operating incomes from the information resource industry (not exceeding RMB 85 billion), South China achieved an operating income of RMB 125.2 billion, far ahead of the other three regions considered in this chapter – East China, Central China, and West China – and ranking third among all regions all over China in terms of operating income.

On the whole, from 2004 to 2007, China's information resource industry was on the rise, got preliminarily developed, and reached a considerable scale under the guidance of national policies, which featured prominently in all industries of national economy (with an operating income accounting for about 5% of the GDP) and underpinned its future development. That said, China's information resource industry was in unbalanced development in terms of subdivided industries and regions, and some subdivided industries just started, a subject to which much attention should be paid.

3.3 Rapid development period

The operating income of China's information resource industry increased from RMB 995.8 billion in 2007 to RMB 1.3988 trillion in 2008, namely, a more than 40.47% increase in 2008 compared with that in 2007. The information resource industry provided 152.2 million jobs in 2008, with a steadily increasing number of people employed in the industry, which signified the entry of China's information resource industry into a rapid development period that lasted roughly until 2011. The development of the information resource industry in this period demonstrated the following features.

3.3.1 Development overview

From 2008 to 2011, China's information resource industry was maintained in faster development, with annual increase rates being 40.47%, 28.81%, 16.93%, and 19.51%, respectively, and it boasted total operating income of RMB 2.51795 trillion for 2011. For the four years, China's information resource industry achieved total operating income of RMB 7.8255 trillion, approximately 3.5 times of that for the initial development period, from which we could catch a glimpse of the development speed of the industry for this period.

The information resource industry in all regions grew at a good speed in this period. From Figure 3.5, East China, North China, South China, Central China, Southwest, and Northwest developed the information resource industry at levels from high to low, but all of them increased operating incomes. East China not only had the largest total of the industry but boasted the highest increase speed, with total operating income from the information resource industry being RMB 447.6 billion in 2008 and up to RMB 924.2 billion in 2011, a 206.5% increase, driving the entire rapid development of China's information resource industry for this period. North China and South China also achieved a remarkable increase in total operating incomes from the information resource industry. North China increased its total operating income at a lower speed but with a

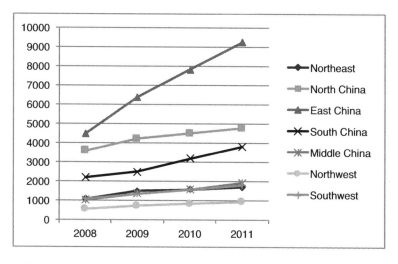

Figure 3.5 Development tendency of operating incomes of all regions from the information resource industry from 2008 to 2011

larger total operating income, reaching RMB 478.3 billion in 2011, a 133.6% increase; South China improved its total operating income at a higher speed but with a smaller total operating income, reaching RMB 381.3 billion, a 173.4% increase. Central China, Northeast, and Southwest had smaller total operating incomes which increased at a lower speed but achieved a total operating income of more than RMB 170 billion from the information resource industry in 2011. Northwest, with the smallest total operating income that increased at the lowest speed, also boasted total operating income of about RMB 100 billion in 2011, a 168.4% increase compared with that in 2008.

In this period, many subdivided industries of the information resource industry grew at a higher speed. From Figure 3.6, the operating income from the consulting and management service industry went up from RMB 296.1 billion in 2008 to RMB 542.9 billion in 2011, with the annual increase rates for this period being 31.4%, 18.2%, and 18.0%, respectively; the operating income from the agency and brokerage industry went up from RMB 190.2 billion in 2008 to RMB 381.8 billion in 2011, with the annual increase rates for this period being 39.3%, 19.5%, and 20.6%, respectively; the operating income from the data content production and processing industry went up from RMB 187 billion in 2008 to RMB 330.7 billion in 2011, with the annual increase rates for this period being 32.0%, 14.5%, and 17.0%, respectively. It can be said that most of the subdivided industries of the information resource industry achieved rapid development except such individual industries as the education training industry and the research trial industry.

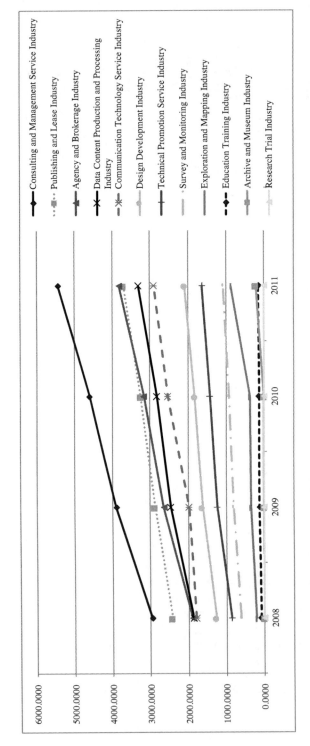

Figure 3.6 Development tendency of operating incomes from subdivided industries of the information resource industry from 2008 to 2011

Development trajectory of the industry 87

3.3.2 *Industrial structure*

From 2008 to 2011, subdivided industries of China's information resource industry continued to grow on the back of the previous period. As shown in Figure 3.6, the annual increase rates of the consulting and management service industry and the agency and brokerage industry (22.5% and 26.5%, respectively) went up further, while the developing speed of the publishing and lease industry continued dropping with an annual increase rate of only 15.2% for this period, which was the lowest among the subdivided industries. Additionally, the increased rate of the exploration and mapping industry for 2011 also exceeded that of the average speed of the industry. Those changes in development tendency brought the rebalance of the structure of the subdivided industries of the information resource industry.

The proportions of subdivided industries of the information resource industry for this period were shown in Figure 3.7. Most notably, the proportion of the publishing and lease industry dropped from 20.9% in the initial development period to the present 15.6%, and the total operating income of RMB 1.2241 trillion for this period rendered the publishing and lease industry rank second among all the subdivided industries; however, the proportion of the consulting and management service industry increased from 20.0% in the initial development period to 21.6%, and the total income of RMB 1.6882 trillion for this period made the consulting and management service industry rank first among all the subdivided industries. From Figure 3.6, the consulting and management service industry kept ahead of the publishing and lease industry in terms of operating income for the four years, leading the subdivided industries. The proportions of the communication technology service industry, the data content production and processing industry, and the agency and brokerage industry kept ranging from 10% to 15%; however, the proportion of the agency and brokerage industry obviously rose to 14.7%, with the total operating income for this period being RMB 1.1536 trillion, while the proportion of the communication technology service industry went down to 11.8%, with the total operating income for this period being RMB 921.5 billion.

Furthermore, the total proportions of the design development industry, the technical promotion service industry, and the survey and monitoring industry in the information resource industry went up to 19.7% from 18.0% in the initial development period, with total operating income increasing to RMB 1.5409 trillion in this period from RMB 558.1 billion in the previous period; the total proportions of the exploration and mapping industry, the education training industry, and the archive and museum industry in the information resource industry increased remarkably from the previous 1.3% to 3.2% in this period, with total operating income rising to RMB 250 billion in this period from RMB 39.5 billion in the previous period. That implied the subdivided industries accounting for small proportions in the information resource industry made great headway. On the whole, subdivided industries of the information resource industry were making headway in an all-round way.

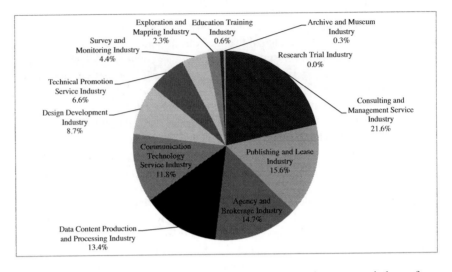

Figure 3.7 Proportions of subdivided industries of the information resource industry from 2008 to 2011

3.3.3 Regional disparities

In this period, regional development of the information resource industry was still unbalanced but differed from that in the initial development period in features. As shown in Figure 3.8, from 2008 to 2011, Shanghai, Zhejiang, Shandong, Jiangsu, Fujian, and Anhui in East China made outstanding achievements in the development of the information resource industry. Shanghai, Zhejiang, Shandong, and Jiangsu boasted operating incomes of more than RMB 500 billion from the information resource industry for this period, ranking third, fourth, fifth, and sixth in their own provinces; Fujian and Anhui had total operating incomes of about RMB 200 billion from the information resource industry, respectively, for this period, ranking ninth and twelfth in their own provinces, respectively. Only Jiangxi Province in East China performed relatively poorly, achieving total operating income of approximately RMB 100 billion from the information resource industry for this period, ranking 23rd in its provincial regional. It can be said that East China led the development of China's information resource industry for this period.

By contrast, only Beijing in North China developed its information resource industry at a skyrocket speed, with the total operating income of RMB 1.1278 trillion in this period almost doubling that in the previous period. Because other provinces in North China did not achieve an obvious increase in their operating incomes, the total strength of North China could not rival East China. The proportion of the information resource industry in South China was slightly lifted from 14.9% in the initial development period to the present 15.6%, and the total operating income of South China rose from RMB 4.628 billion in the previous period

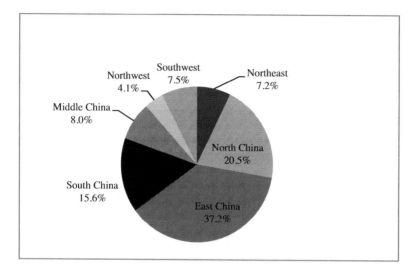

Figure 3.8 Regional distribution of operating incomes from the information resource industry from 2008 to 2011

to RMB 2.1101 trillion in this period; the total operating income of Guangdong Province reached RMB 9.627 billion, still ranking second among all provinces all over China. By contrast, Central China, Southwest, Northeast, and Northwest were still in the low ebb of the development of the information resource industry and had total operating incomes of RMB 1.11 trillion at the most for this period, accounting for no more than 8%, respectively.

3.4 Steady development period

After the germination period, the initial development period, and the rapid development period, China's information resource industry entered into the steady development period, from 2012. In 2013, China's economic situation was complex amid the persistently downward economic landscape worldwide. In the first half of the year, China's economic growth rate dropped for two quarters consecutively; however, in the second half of the year, strongly guided by the government's macro-policies, China's reforms further penetrated into all aspects of economic life, and the information resource industry showed unprecedented vigor and began to make a figure amid the complex economic landscape. In the same year, the State Council issued the *Several Opinions on Promoting Information Consumption and Expanding Domestic Demand*, stating that "the upgrading of information industries must be accelerated, content of information consumption must be enriched, the capability of protecting network security must be enhanced, and a long-term mechanism spurring persistent and steady growth of information consumption

90 Development trajectory of the industry

must be established so as to drive rapid and sound consumption growth of production, life and management information and play a greater part in steady and fast economic development and improvement in people's livelihood," that "barriers to entry into industries must be broken to promote sharing of information resources and fair competition among enterprises, market-oriented operation must be upheld in competitive fields, and the market mechanism must be introduced to the social management and public service fields so as to enhance the endogenetic impetus to information consumption development," that "new industry forms must be fostered, the effective supply levels of the product, service and content must be raised and consumption potential must be reached," that "production, life and management information products and services must be more diversified," that "emerging information service industry forms must be expanded," that "more efforts must be devoted to developing such emerging cultural industries as digital publishing industry, new interaction media industry and mobile multimedia industry so as to increase consumption of such cultural content animation game, digital music and online artworks," that "development of digital cultural content products and services must be strengthened, platforms for producing, converting, processing and pushing digital content must be established, and the supply of information consumption content products must be enriched," and that "the Internet-based new media construction must be strengthened and the network culture information content construction project must be performed to promote the spread of excellent cultural products through the Internet and encourage various online cultural enterprises to produce and provide healthy and positive information content." By virtue of strong support by policies, China's information resource industry advanced steadily upward.

3.4.1 Development overview

From 2012 to 2014, China's information resource industry developed at a slower speed but kept growing, with annual increase rates being 10.9% and 2.1%, respectively. Total operating income from the information resource industry as of 2014 reached RMB 3.1248 trillion, about five and a half times of that in 2004; the information resource industry provided 28.88 million jobs in 2013, almost doubling that in 2008. On the whole, China's information resource industry entered into the steady development period.

The information resource industry in all regions showed an obvious slowdown. From Figure 3.9, only East China and South China, which were highly developed, demonstrated a visible growth trend in the information resource industry, while other regions showed flat growth for the three years. East China not only had the largest total of the information resource industry growth but also grew the information resource industry fastest still, with the total operating income from the information resource industry increasing from RMB 1.063 trillion in 2012 to RMB 1.2136 trillion in 2014, a 14.2% increase. South China achieved total operating income of RMB 509.6 billion in 2014 from RMB 442.3 billion in 2012 from the information resource industry, a 15.2% increase. Central China, Southwest,

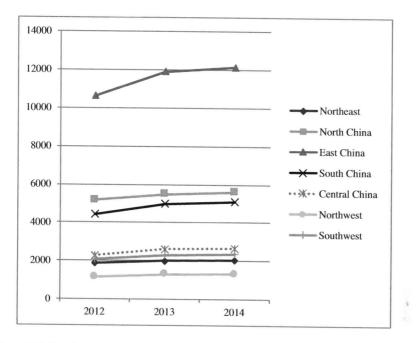

Figure 3.9 Development tendency of the information resource industry in all regions from 2012 to 2014

and Northwest had about 15% increase in operating incomes from the information resource industry but with relatively small totals, with the operating incomes from the information resource industry being RMB 266.8 billion, RMB 236.2 billion, and RMB 133.5 billion, respectively, in 2014. By contrast, North China and Northeast had a smaller increase, with the increase rate of the total operating income from the industry in 2014 being 10% less than that in 2012.

From the development tendency of subdivided industries of the information resource industry, the increase rates of most of the subdivided industries were relatively flat, and the annual increase rates of operating incomes from such subdivided industries ranged from 4.8% to 7.5%, as shown in Figure 3.10. Among all the subdivided industries, the agency and brokerage industry generated an operating income of RMB 507.8 billion in 2014 from RMB 440.5 billion in 2012, with an annual increase rate of 7.5%. The consulting and management service industry achieved an operating income of RMB 704 billion in 2014 from RMB 617.4 billion in 2012, with an annual increase rate of 6.9%, ranking second among all the subdivided industries for this period. The data content production and processing industry generated an operating income of RMB 424.6 billion in 2014 from RMB 374 billion in 2012, with an annual increase rate of 6.7%, ranking third among all the subdivided industries for this period.

3.4.2 Industrial structure

From 2012 to 2014, subdivided industries of China's information resource industry continued to grow on the back of the rapid development period. As shown in Figure 3.10, the operating incomes of the consulting and management service industry and the agency and brokerage industry were rising quickly, while the developing speed of the publishing and lease industry continued dropping. That further steadied the structure of subdivided industries of the information resource industry for the rapid development period.

Specifically, the proportions of subdivided industries of the information resource industry for this period were shown in Figure 3.11. The proportion of the consulting and management service industry increased to 22.5%, and the total operating income of RMB 2.011 trillion for this period made the consulting and management service industry remain first among all the subdivided industries; from Figure 3.10, the consulting and management service industry kept ahead of the publishing and lease industry in terms of the operating income for the three years, firmly leading the subdivided industries. The proportion of the agency and brokerage industry obviously rose to 16%, and the total operating income of RMB 1.4459 trillion for this period rendered the agency and brokerage industry rank second among all the subdivided industries. The proportion of the publishing and lease industry continued dropping to 14.7%, and the total operating income of RMB 1.3185 trillion for this period made the publishing and lease industry recede to third place. The

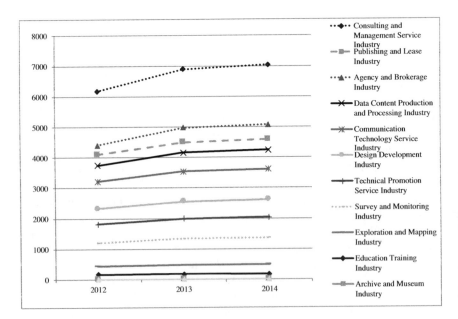

Figure 3.10 Development tendency of subdivided industries of the information resource industry from 2012 to 2014

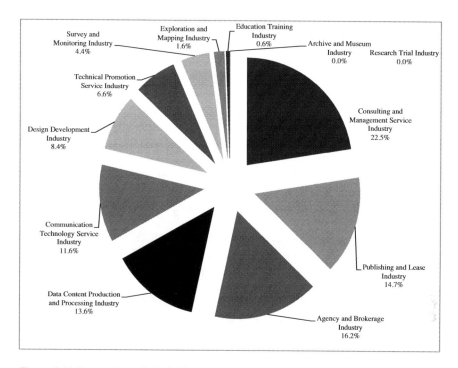

Figure 3.11 Proportions of subdivided industries of the information resource industry from 2012 to 2014

proportion of the communication technology service industry continued decreasing to 11.6%, with the total operating income for this period being RMB 1.0368 trillion. The proportion of the data content production and processing industry increased slightly to 13.6%, with the total operating income for this period being RMB 1.2147 trillion.

Compared with the rapid development period, the total proportions of the design development industry, the technical promotion service industry, the survey and monitoring industry, the exploration and mapping industry, the education training industry, and the archive and museum industry did not change much, and the subdivided industries of the information resource industry were maintained in development in an all-round way; however, obviously, more powerful impetus must be given to developing the subdivided industries.

Additionally, subdivided industries of the information resource industry also demonstrated another characteristic in this period. That is, they were more integrated with other industries, such as the industrial Internet and e-commerce, and they were much more dependent on information resources. They drove rapid development of other types of businesses by exploitation of related data.

3.4.3 Regional disparities

In this period, regional development of the information resource industry was still unbalanced; however, the most prominent characteristic was that East China further gained advantages, South China improved its competitive advantage and North China lost some advantage, thus forming the basic pattern of "East China as the body and North China and South China as the wings." As shown in Figure 3.12, from 2012 to 2014, the provinces in East China again made excellent achievements in the development of the information resource industry with the total operating income up to RMB 3.4635 trillion, continuing to lead the development of China's information resource industry.

The proportion of the information resource industry in South China increased slightly to 16.2% in this period from 15.6% in the rapid development period. Guangdong Province boasted total operating income of RMB 1.1673 trillion, surpassing Beijing and rising to the first place among all provincial-level regions as well as making South China on a par with North China. Meanwhile, in North China, the proportion of the information resource industry dropped only in Beijing, and the operating income of RMB 933 billion from the information resource industry for this period made Beijing recede to second among all provincial-level regions; accordingly, the development level of the industry in North China also declined, with the total operating income for this period being RMB 1.6267 trillion. By contrast, Central China, Southwest, Northeast, and Northwest were still in the low ebb of the development of the information resource industry and had total operating incomes of RMB 800 billion at the most for this period, accounting for no more than 9%, respectively.

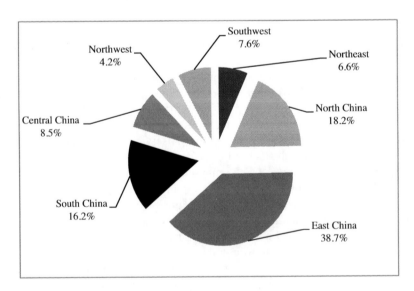

Figure 3.12 Regional distribution of the information resource industry from 2012 to 2014

China's information resource industry underwent the germination period, the initial development period, and the rapid development period, and is now in the steady development period from 1990 until now. Driven by policies, China's information resource industry has grown out of nothing, has grown strong from being weak, and has kept advancing from a lower speed to a higher speed and finally to at a steady speed. The proportions of emerging industries among all subdivided industries of the information resource industry keep increasing while the proportions of traditional industries gradually decrease. The development level of the information resource industry in East China has been on the rise, and currently the regional distribution pattern of the industry of "East China as the body and North China and South China as the wings" has taken shape. Of course, the trajectory also witnessed development deficiencies of China's information resource industry. For example, the overall scale and international competitiveness of the information resource industry remain to be improved, and development levels of the information resource industry differ greatly from region to region and from subdivided industry to subdivided industry, with part of regions and subdivided industries still underdeveloped. Though China's information resource industry has proceeded to the steady development period, it needs more policies for support in the present period given that it is obviously underpowered.

Notes

1 Feng Huiling, "Attaching Importance to Strategic Value of 'Information Resources'," *People's Daily*, October 23, 2014.
2 Youping Zhu, "Ten Issues Concerning Development of China's Information Resource Industry," *China Soft Science*, no. 6 (1996).
3 Jing'an Pang, "Development of China's Information Resource Industry in the Internet Environment," *China Information Review*, no. 3 (1998).
4 Economic Research Department of Development Research Center of the State Council, "Study on Policies for Promoting the Development of Information Resource Industry," December 28, 2005.
5 CCID Consulting, "Annual Research Report of Investment Opportunities for China's Media Industry for 2003," February 2004.
6 CCID Consulting, "Annual Research Report of Investment Opportunities for China's Digital Content Industry from 2004 to 2005," December 2005.
7 Research Group of Information College of Renmin University of China, "Study on Information Market and Policies on Information Resource Industry," April 2005.
8 CCID Consulting, "Information Service Report," February 2002.
9 CCID Consulting, "Annual Research Report of Investment Opportunities for China's Digital Content Industry from 2004 to 2005," December 2005.
10 CCID Consulting, "Annual Report of Development of Digital Television Industry for 2004," February 2005.

4 The supply–demand relation of China's information resource industry

As an industry develops, contradiction is found between in the unity of opposites between supply and demand. Only when the contradiction is properly tackled that demand and supply can reach a balance, an impetus will be given to the industry development. To make possible sound development in our information resource industry, we shall have a good understanding of its supply and demand relationship. Starting with basic analysis of supply and demand factors, this chapter discusses the supply-demand relationship in the information resources industry, and presents conclusions valuable for its industry development and policy setting.

4.1 Analysis of demand factors of information resource industry

Information resource industry grows out of different needs which, in terms of relevance, cover the following four areas: first, transformation and socioeconomic upgrading of information resource industry; second, reforms in politics; third, social undertakings aimed to provide better livelihood; fourth, growing sociocultural needs.

4.1.1 Socioeconomic needs

With the advances in modern information and communication technologies and supporting facilities, information resources are increasingly important in economic development. In addition to the support for other industries, information resource industry is growing into an independent industry that holds a significant position in the national economy. A booming information resource industry is necessary for promoting socioeconomic development and optimizing the socioeconomic structure. It is an important indicator for all countries and regions to measure their economic strength.

It is widely believed in the academic circles at home and abroad that the world is made up of three major elements – materials, energy, and information. Material resources, energy resources, and information resources are the three basic resources for human development. As early as the 1970s, the American sociologist Daniel Bell claimed that: the "transforming resource" of a preindustrial

Supply–demand relation of the industry 97

society is used as natural power, like wind, water, draft animals, and human power. In an industrial society, the transforming resource is created energy, like electricity, oil, gas, coal, and nuclear power. In a postindustrial society or information society, it is information resources represented by computers and data transmission systems. The increase of social wealth is realized through knowledge rather than physical labor.

At present, information is becoming a strategic resource for a country and region to achieve economic growth and raise its regional influence and international status. The scale of information resources is growing by leaps and bounds. Google, for example, processes more than 24 PB (2^{50} bytes) of data a day, and Facebook registers 3 billion hits and uploads daily. These industry leaders at the forefront of innovation regard data as their core assets. With rich information resources, they are pushing forward the industry and dominating the national, regional, or even global economic stage. In China, such trailblazers as Alibaba, Baidu, and Tencent have secured their market share by collecting information resources, tapping their value in an innovative manner, and launching diverse information products and services. As the resource structure shifts its focus toward information resources, we have embraced a more dynamic business environment. It is imperative to optimize the economic structure and develop the information resources industry.

The governments have paid unprecedented attention to information resources. Developing the big data industry; that is, the commercial application of big data, is a key element to promote the development of the information resources industry and the overall economy. For example, the US government announced a $200 million "Big Data Research and Development Initiative" in March 2012. Premier Li Keqiang described in his Government Work Report at the Second Session of the 12th National People's Congress that the country work "to promote information consumption and implement the 'Broadband China' strategy. In August 2015, the Standing Committee of the State Council passed the "Action Outline for Promoting the Development of Big Data," which emphasizes that we need to guide and support the development of the big data industry. We need to develop market-oriented policies to create a fair and flexible environment where enterprises act as the main players. A market-oriented mechanism will be developed to promote innovative application of big data in different industries and create a product system closely aligned with demand.

With the application of new-generation Internet technologies marked by cloud computing, big data, and the Internet of Things, information resource industry has become one of the key factors for economic development for two reasons. Thanks to information and communication technologies, traditional resources are greatly saved and used in a more efficient manner. Unlike the developed countries, China still maintains a higher proportion of primary and secondary industries, consuming a lot of material resources. In 2013, the proportion of service industry in China was lower than 47%, a far cry from the world average of 60%. The industrial structure is attributed to a puny information resource industry that fails to come into play. For a better industrial structure, it is imperative for China to develop its information resources industry. For example, if we can increase the global efficiency of gas-fired

98 Supply–demand relation of the industry

power plants by only 1%, we can save $66 billion of fuel. With reusability and addable value, information resources have become an impressive potential contributor to social and economic development. On the other hand, with better technologies to develop and utilize information resources, information products and services that better meet market needs are offered, creating an optimized product structure. Most information products and services are virtual ones and consume a small amount of energy resources. Many industries, from digital publication to new media, are making products more diversified to meet our needs in work, life, and study. In this way, we will embrace a dynamic, energy-efficient, and high-performing market. It is not necessary to abandon all traditional industries, and an overall upgrade is the right choice. Traditional industries are optimized and upgraded by increasing the content of technology and knowledge which is supplied by information resource industry. Technical patents are critical for the development of manufacturing industries, and even useless patents are used in developed countries for the transformation and upgrade of traditional industries. The practice in Japan shows that, traditional industries can save about two-thirds of the time and 90% of R&D cost by utilizing foreign patents and useless patents for transformation and upgrade. China has promising prospects in this regard. In addition, information resource industry has great potential to stimulate the development of related industries, as its products and services will boost the consumption in the related industries while entering into the final market. As a result, China's economy will embrace inclusive growth. Studies have shown that one yuan increase in the output of online games will yield consumption dividends of 4.16 yuan for the communication industry and 1.77 yuan for information resource industry.

What's more, information products that are original and creative can boost the development of industries like culture, clothing, and toys. The American film *Captain America 2* grossed RMB 709 million during its one-month run in China in 2014. In the same year, *A Bite of China II*, a documentary made by CCTV with an up-front investment of about RMB 30 million, generated hundreds of millions in revenue from sponsorship, copyright sales, and other advertising campaigns. The industrial Internet, relying fully on information resource industry development, has demonstrated its enormous potential in such industries as aviation, railway transportation, power generation, oil and gas development, and health care. Some studies suggest that an increase in efficiency by 1% will make a big difference to the industrial Internet. In commercial aviation, a 1% decrease in fuel consumption means a $30 billion reduction in spending over the next 15 years. If global efficiency of gas-fired power plants increased by 1%, $66 billion will be saved. An additional 1% of efficiency in the health care industry will bring a saving of $63 billion. For the potential of industrial Internet, these are just the tip of the iceberg.

4.1.2 Socio-political needs

Information resource industry development is also subject to demand of political reform. As our economic system develops at a certain stage, we must carry out socialist political restructuring. It is also an inevitable requirement for China to eliminate the drawbacks in the political system and develop socialist democracy. While boosting economic growth, information resource industry has drawn public attention to and promoted political reforms.

As information resource industry and political restructuring share the same goals, we can realize positive efficient reforms in the political system by developing the information resources industry. According to China's *Twelfth Five-Year Plan*, the goal of the political restructuring is to promote what is beneficial and to abolish what is harmful. We need to promote efficient and dynamic socialist democracy that features a high level of democracy and a complete legal system. Our people can better act as the masters of the country, and the productive forces are released and developed. Information resource industry plays its part in two aspects: first, information products and services serve as the tools for political reforms; second, its development can facilitate the disclosure, sharing, and utilization of information.

To be specific, information products and services are essential to socialist democracy realized through political restructuring such as the adjustment of functions and powers. According to *Several Opinions of the General Office of the State Council on Strengthening Services and Supervision over Market Entities by Means of Big Data Analysis* released on July 2015, we need to make full use of advanced concepts, technologies, and resources concerning big data. It is a strategic choice to enhance national competitiveness, and an inevitable requirement to improve government service and supervision. With full access to information, and a more accurate understanding of market demand, the government can deliver effective, targeted services and supervision. By smoothly streamlining administration, delegating power, strengthening regulation, and transforming government functions, government governance will be improved. In the e-government initiative, for example, the information platform, a government affairs microblog network and the national portal for open data are part of the information resources industry. They aim to promote government transformation and political reforms.

It is the purpose and goal of China's political restructuring to promote people's democracy and protect people's rights to act as the masters of the country. To develop information resource industry, we need first to promote the disclosure, integration, and sharing of information resources owned by the government and the entire society. By ensuring public access to information resources, we protect their fair access to and use of information. With these information resources, the public can further participate in or supervise social affairs, making for a service-oriented government. In this light, information resources are indispensable. Therefore, countries like the United States, the United Kingdom, and Canada have realized transformation and upgrade through an open government initiative. Open information and data are fundamental conditions for political restructuring. For most countries, better governance capacity is realized through mature information management plans, such as national initiatives, strategies, and action plans to make public information and data, and international open data association like G8.

100 *Supply–demand relation of the industry*

4.1.3 Needs for better life

The information resource industry also expands rapidly to meet the needs of social undertakings while improving people's livelihoods. Social programs are public services provided by state bodies or other organizations for social welfare purposes. Social programs cover ten aspects: education, health care, labor and employment, social security, science and technology, culture, sports, community construction, tourism, population and family planning. These social programs are all closely related to information resource industry, which provides rich data, technologies, and platforms thus meeting various demands in a more intelligent way. While developing its open data and big data industries, China has emphasized in the *Action Outline for Promoting Big Data Development* that we should first make government data public in such areas concerning people's livelihoods as transportation, health care, employment, and social security, and that we should carry out demonstration projects of big data application in urban construction, social assistance, quality of safety, and community services. In this way, we can improve social governance.

If we want to improve living standards through social programs, we need to establish a system to manage government information resources and optimize public services. In this process, we should promote systematic e-management of government information; build a catalog of government information resources; explore innovative strategic planning, management methods, technical means, and supporting measures; enhance government capacity in information resources management, and tap the potential of government information resources; encourage local governments to incorporate themselves in national management of information resources and to take overall measures in the management, development, and utilization of government information resources. All these are better supported by a strong information resource industry. We should further improve the innovation system and realize innovative integration of information resources. We should build a database of rich information resources; make faster moves in the development and utilization of non-relational databases, data mining, data intelligence analysis, data visualization, and other information resources; support innovation of such information products as high-performance computers, storage equipment, network equipment, intelligent terminals, and large-scale general-purpose database software; build a public platform for information technologies and services; and encourage enterprises with independent intellectual property rights and technological innovation capacity to grow bigger and stronger. In this way, we can lay a solid foundation for social undertakings. Only by growing information resource industry and applying its products innovatively in all social programs can we improve our capacity in social governance, public services, and scientific decision-making. Our people will then live a better life.

Information resource industry development is a key measure for countries seeking to promote social undertakings aimed at people's livelihood. It is clearly defined in the policies of many countries to enhance social governance and make decisions that meet public needs under the support of information resource industry. In

2013, G8 countries, including the United States, the United Kingdom, and Canada, signed the *G8 Open Data Charter*, which stipulated that free access to data in 14 areas like education, transportation, and health care should be provided to social organizations and individuals for commercial application. This will both promote economic innovation and realize in-depth utilization of data value, thus meeting the needs for people's livelihood. These stipulations are later adopted as the basis for G8 countries to develop policies for open data and information resource industry development, and are put into practice in specific action plans.

4.1.4 Sociocultural needs

Information resource industry is also closely related to the ever-growing cultural needs of the people. Information resource industry and the cultural industry are two different sectors that overlap. They affect each other. Cultural needs of the people are satisfied and boosted by information resource industry while information resource industry becomes more mature in the process.

On the one hand, the people have their cultural needs met by consuming information products and services. Amid economic growth, network infrastructures are improved and digital equipment popularized. The public has shifted their focus of cultural needs largely to the digital world. It is a defining trend to promote the integration and sharing of information resources. In the cyber world, in particular, industries like digital publishing, search engine, digital music, online video, online education, and instant information have developed rapidly in recent years. The key driver behind this is that people have gained access to information products when meeting their cultural demands. Under the stimulus, information resource industry has penetrated into the cultural life of the public. Internet companies that aim to meet various cultural needs, for example, Facebook, Wikipedia, Baidu Search, Knowledge Community, Google Scholar, Google Search, and YouTube, have emerged to dominate the global innovation industry and make their contribution to expand information resource industry.

On the other hand, public cultural needs are met in a subtle and real-time manner through information resource industry development. The cultural industry itself keeps generating or acquiring new information resources. For cultural enterprises, their task is how to further understand the needs and preference of subscribers by effectively utilizing massive information resources. In this way, they can produce goods that fit better with target subscribers and increase their corporate value. Intelligent information products such as big data technology have great advantages in analyzing subscriber demand and pushing products and services in time accordingly.

In film and television production, the American drama *House of Cards* is a prime example of big data application. Its producer is neither a TV station nor a traditional movie company. It is a video streaming website. In 2012, Netflix started its trials on drama production. When deciding what and how to shoot, Netflix set aside traditional methods and embraced big data. By accurately analyzing daily clicks of more than 30 million subscribers, for example, save, share, replay, pause,

102 *Supply–demand relation of the industry*

and search, Netflix worked back the production principle. Through the analysis and mining of big data, Netflix found that many of its users subscribed the 1990 BBC drama *House of Cards*, and most audiences favored David Finch and Kevin Spacey. Netflix ventured a prediction that a film combining these elements might be a hit. *House of Cards* was released and became a hit. What's more, Netflix abandoned the traditional pattern of one episode a week and released all episodes in one go at its website. Amid rich and diverse cultural needs, information resource industry will find its opportunities and resources for development.

4.2 Analysis on supply–demand of information resource industry

Information resource industry also develops as driven by various supply factors, and these factors may be different. The main factors include labor input, capital input, urbanization level and population density, changes in supply–demand relationship, innovation and application of science and technology, export and import trade and international competition, cultural and psychological factors, government industrial policies and other industry management factors.

4.2.1 Labor input

Information resource industry is a typical labor-intensive and knowledge-intensive industry. For an industry not mature yet, economic support and talent management policies are important. The former can create a favorable environment where abundant opportunities are available for further industry development; the latter is necessary for the industry to realize rapid growth and establish core competence. At present, positive trends are seen in industry development and its labor input. For example, the Internet industry has been a hot destination for employment groups. The input of labor, especially highly knowledgeable and skilled employees, has been a huge boost for information resource industry.

In Beijing, the number of people working in information resource industry increased from 149,100 in 2009 to 154,600 in 2011, but later declined to 152,100 in 2012, down by 1.6%. In 2013, the figure once again grew, to 159,900, representing a year-on-year increase of 5.15% (see Figure 4.1). In general, a marked increase has been recorded in the number of people working in Beijing's information resource industry. Over the past five years, Beijing's information resource industry has maintained the trend of sustainable growth in operating revenue. It climbed from RMB 283.25 billion in 2009 to RMB 310,908 million in 2013, a year-on-year increase of 2.04%. The figure accounts for 9.75% of the country's total and triples the national average.

4.2.2 Capital input

Information resource industry is distinguished by the following economic features: high investment, high knowledge and labor input, high risk, and high "sunk cost."

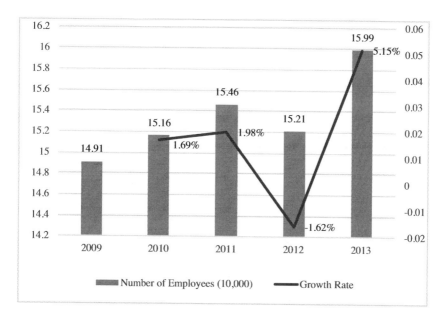

Figure 4.1 2009–2013 demographic change in Beijing Information Resource Industry

Capital input is an important factor for information resource industry development. Generally speaking, capital input is not only an essential condition for industry development in the early stage, but a key element that sustains further expansion. For content-oriented information resource industry, in particular, capital input is all the more important. This is particularly true in the Internet industry.

At websites that provide video, search, and music services, two things are offered by subscriber behaviors: traffic and personal information. First, traffic is the key for online platforms to seize market share, and it is closely related to the advertising revenue of operators. Second, subscribers will provide a collection of personal information which is utilized by operators to optimize their advertising campaigns and subscriber experience. A benign profit model is developed. In other words, subscriber traffic and personal information will become valuable tokens in the process of consumption, and it is reasonable for free plans to prevail. This explains why capital input plays a crucial role in the development of information resources enterprise in the Internet era. From inception to expansion, an enterprise must first provide sufficient information products and services to attract enough subscribers and then achieve profitability through advertising.

In this light, capital input, and more importantly, adequate capital is necessary for information resource industry development. It is a long process to develop technologies, upgrade products or services, or occupy market share. Without continuous capital input, enterprises will struggle to survive. Therefore, many Internet companies tend to make a huge investment in their early operation. However, the

104 Supply–demand relation of the industry

Internet bubble is pushing for more rational capital input to promote information resource industry development.

4.2.3 Urbanization level and population density

Urbanization level and population density, important indicators of economic growth, are also key factors to the development of information resource industry. Generally speaking, the higher a city's urbanization level and population density are, the better its economic development. Such a city has greater demand for economic structure upgrading and information resource consumption, and has a better foundation for information resource industry development: on the one hand, higher demand and a better market environment; on the other hand, better infrastructures, such as network facilities.

According to *2014 Report on China's Information Resource Industry Development*, Beijing sat atop the 2013 information resource industry development index ranking (see Table 4.1). In China, the capital city is the center of politics, culture, science, education, and international exchange, and also the hub for decision-making and management of economic and financial affairs. Beijing takes the lead in both industry value and environment. Its score in the industry value index is 8.42 higher than the North China average and 8.74 higher than the national average. Its score in the industry environment index is 8.11 higher than the North China average and 9.22 higher than the national average. It is one of the domestic cities with the highest level of urbanization and population density.

4.2.4 Changes in supply–demand relationship

The changes in supply–demand relationship is also a factor at play for information resource industry development. When supply is greater than demand, the industry will face the risk of shrinkage; when demand is greater than supply, the industry will embrace opportunities for development and growth. Information resource industry develops a stage when demand is greater than supply. There is great demand for information products and services, involving different contents, aspects, and forms.

According to the *36th Statistical Report on Internet Development in China* released by the China Internet Network Information Center, subscribers of network information resources account for a high proportion of Chinese netizens, and they have huge demand for information search, digital music, video, and books (see Table 4.2). In this context, rich demand for information resources represented by network information resources has created more growth poles, attracting capital, labor, technical, and policy input. That is how information resource industry grows. For example, China's Internet giants like Baidu, Alibaba, and Tencent have risen to fame in China and the world, boosting rapid information resource industry development.

Table 4.1 China's information resource industry development index rankings 2013

Province	Total Points	Ranking	Industry Value	Ranking	Industry Environment	Ranking
Beijing	91.83	1	92.37	2	91.30	1
Zhejiang	90.37	2	90.74	4	89.99	2
Guangdong	90.31	3	92.64	1	87.98	4
Jiangsu	88.62	4	91.86	3	85.37	6
Shanghai	88.41	5	88.30	5	88.53	3
Shandong	87.34	6	86.87	6	87.81	5
Fujian	84.10	7	85.45	9	82.74	8
Chongqing	83.98	8	83.88	12	84.07	7
Tianjin	83.84	9	84.98	11	82.69	9
Hubei	83.72	10	85.71	8	81.73	14
Anhui	83.24	11	85.81	7	80.67	18
Liaoning	82.80	12	83.65	13	81.96	11
Shaanxi	82.72	13	85.37	10	80.07	20
Hunan	81.98	14	82.17	16	81.79	12
Yunnan	81.91	15	83.15	15	80.67	19
Sichuan	81.72	16	80.96	21	82.48	10
Guangxi Zhuang Autonomous Region	81.56	17	83.23	14	79.89	23
Hebei	81.40	18	81.42	19	81.39	15
Heilongjiang	81.30	19	80.84	22	81.77	13
Hainan	80.94	20	81.81	17	80.06	21
Shanxi	80.93	21	81.08	20	80.77	17
Henan	80.87	22	80.66	24	81.07	16
Jiangxi	80.78	23	81.75	18	79.80	24
Jilin	80.30	24	80.60	25	80.00	22
Xinjiang Uygur Autonomous Region	80.08	25	80.79	23	79.37	27
Inner Mongolia Autonomous Region	79.84	26	79.89	28	79.80	25
Guizhou	79.55	27	79.72	29	79.39	26
Ningxia Hui Autonomous Region	79.20	28	79.90	27	78.51	28
Gansu	78.94	29	79.97	26	77.90	29
Qinghai	78.02	30	78.67	30	77.36	31
Tibet Autonomous Region	77.87	31	78.24	31	77.49	30

106 *Supply–demand relation of the industry*

Table 4.2 Subscriber size of the network information resources industry (partial)

Internet Application	Overview	Subscriber Size	Usage Rate
Search Engine	A system that collects Internet information using a specific computer program under a certain strategy, and displays, through information organization and management, all relevant information that a subscriber searches for.	536.15 million	80.3%
Network music	Music works distributed through such wired and wireless methods as the Internet and mobile communication networks. The main feature is a digital model of music production, dissemination, and consumption.	480.46 million	72%
Network video	Audiovisual files provided by network video service providers and broadcast live or on-demand in streaming media.	461.21 million	69.1%
Online game	Multiplayer online games with the Internet as the transmission medium, operator server and subscriber computer as the processing terminal, and game client as the interface for information interaction. They aim to achieve a sustainable experience of entertainment, leisure, communication, and virtual achievement.	380.21 million	56.9%
Digital literature	Literature works, quasi-literary texts, and digital art works containing literary elements. These newly created works are displayed on and transmitted through the Internet and represented by hypertext links and multimedia. Most are original digital works.	28 467	42.6%

4.2.5   *Innovation and application of science and technology*

The innovation and application of science and technology is a direct supply factor for information resource industry development. Technical support involving hardware, software, programs, and many other aspects is mandatory for the development and application of information products and services. Information technology can develop into a separate industry such as the communication technology industry and can become an integral part of information resource industry.

In 2013 (from January through December), the main business income of such key industries as energy conservation and environmental protection, biology, new generation information technology, and new energy reached RMB 16.7 trillion, a year-on-year increase of 15.6%, higher than the overall growth rate of 11.2%. With good economic benefits, key information resource industry industries registered a total profit of RMB 764.32 billion, a year-on-year increase of 20.7%, significantly higher than the overall growth rate of 12.2%. Strategic emerging industries remained a hot destination of social capital. At the end of 2013, the aggregate market value of A-share listed companies in strategic emerging industries accounted for 20.7% of the total market value, an increase of 5.8 percentage points from the end of 2012. In 2013, the new generation of information technology industry maintained steady growth, and the average growth rate of two major industries – software and electronic information manufacturing – stood at 13.5%. Thanks to continuous innovation, an obvious adjustment was realized in the industrial structure. First, with information consumption policies introduced by the State Council, the software service industry maintained rapid innovative growth. Tianhong Zenglibao (Yuebao), China's first Internet fund, has posted RMB 180 billion in scope and 40 million in the number of accounts for half a year after the launch. Rapid growth was also witnessed in big data, cloud computing, mobile Internet, etc. In 2013, the revenue of IT consulting, data processing, and operation increased by more than 30%, respectively, contributing to a annual growth increase of 24.6% in the revenue of software business. Second, amid manufacturing restructuring, some industries were faced with difficulties due to the shortage of innovation. For example, microcomputers and color TV sets registered a negative year-on-year growth in output. The industries that take the lead in technology stood out. The China-led TD-LTE (Enhanced Time Division Synchronous Long Term Evolution) is in commercial use, and the 4G industry developed rapidly. As a result, the main business revenue of the communications equipment manufacturing industry increased by 20.2% year-on-year, 6.1 percentage points higher than that of 2012.

Information technology can promote information resource industry growth by facilitating the development and utilization of information resources that optimized information products and services. For example, the development of the surveying and mapping industry is closely tied to the development and application of 3S technology (GIS, GPS, and RS). China started its development of 3S technology in the 1980s, about 20 years later than its foreign peers. After three stages of start-up, testing, and experiment, China is racing ahead in 3S technology and has developed world-class GIS products. The technology is either directly used in digital navigation products and services or is combined with Internet service, search engines, and other products, boosting industry development. It has been widely used in the navigation products of Baidu, Sogou, Gaode, and Google. China's GIS industry also developed rapidly. It is expected that as the *Twelfth Five-Year Plan* drew to an end, its output value would exceed RMB 200 billion, and by 2020 RMB will reach one trillion. According to the China Mobile Internet Report released by CCNIC in April 2013, navigation apps had reached a certain market size, reaching 35.4% of mobile users.

4.2.6 *Effect of government industrial policies and other industry management factors*

Information resource industry development is also tied to government industrial policies, with such key factors at play as market environment, infrastructures, tax policies, market management, and subsidy support. Generally speaking, the

108 *Supply–demand relation of the industry*

greater support guaranteed by government industrial policies, the better information resource industry develops. However, there is no absolute positive relation due to factors like region, economic development level, and varying degree of positive support from government industrial policies.

By analyzing the frequency of the keywords "surveying and mapping industry" in the policies of various regions across China, we obtain a rough assessment of government attention to the industry. However, the observation and comparison reveal no strict consistency between government attention and industry development. In some regions, government departments pay more attention to the surveying and mapping industry, but the industry is at a low level of development. In other regions, government departments pay less attention to the industry, which develops well. See Table 4.3, Table 4.4, and Figure 4.2 for statistical results and comparison.

The data show that Central China pays a higher level of overall attention to the surveying and mapping industry but ranks sixth in the seven regions in terms of

Table 4.3 Government attention to and development of the surveying and mapping industry in seven regions

Region	Overall Attention	Basic Measures	Result Management	Market Supervision	Operating Revenue (RMB 100 million)
East China	25,964	6,412	3,911	1,284	42.47
South China	8,025	1,747	1,286	290	11.52
Central China	8,879	2,379	1,252	423	9.12
North China	10,379	2,394	1,388	485	21.67
Northwest China	8,442	2,184	1,217	560	6.41
Southwest China	8,053	1,837	1,188	317	15.62
Northeast China	7,946	1,716	905	749	13.63

Table 4.4 Average provincial attention and output of the surveying and mapping industry in seven regions

	South China	East China	Central China	North China	Northeast China	Northwest China	Southwest China
Average Provincial Attention	2,675	3,709	2,960	2,076	2,649	1,688	1,611
Average Provincial Output (RMB 100 million)	3.84	6.07	3.04	4.33	4.54	1.28	3.12

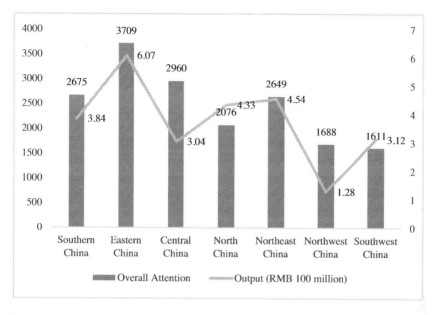

Figure 4.2 Bar chart of average provincial attention and output of the surveying and mapping industry in seven regions

operating income. North China has the same level of attention as Central China, but its business income of the surveying and mapping industry ranks second in the country. There is a striking contrast between Central China and Southwest China, which comes last in the level of attention but exceeds Central China in industry output.

4.3 Analysis of supply–demand relationship of information resource industry

Demand and supply factors are two driving forces that jointly push forward China's information resource industry. In the process, they have different focuses and play different roles. They are not completely independent of one another, but are interrelated. In the initial and developing stages, supply and demand have consistent functions – both are affected by the level of regional economic development. They also have their own features. "Demand" stimulates the participation of information resource industry by adjusting the economic structure, while "supply" gives a direct push to the industry through capital input. Meanwhile, they work on each other. Supply is largely promoted by the increase of demand, and supply input can expand the market by attracting more demand through product increase. A system of mutual promotion is created. As far as China's information resource industry is concerned, supply and demand factors have the commonalities and their respective

110 *Supply–demand relation of the industry*

features. While giving positive impetus, supply and demand factors are also hindering industry growth. Given existing problems and these features of the supply and demand factors, the Chinese government should develop appropriate policies to promote fast, stable, and healthy growth of its information resource industry.

4.3.1 Basic features

1. Indirect effect of the relationship

The indirect role of the supply–demand relationship means that suppliers of industrial resources (supplier) are largely not directly related to the subscribers of information resources (demand). Instead, they trade with each other under a multilateral market system. This is caused in large part by the systems of non-cash payments and third-party payments in domestic consumption of information resources. Subscriber traffic and personal information will become valuable tokens in the process of consumption, and it is reasonable for free plans to prevail. As a result, no cash is used in the consumption behaviors based on personal information and traffic, and the corresponding fee is paid by any third party through advertisement or based on subscriber traffic. This is quite different from such developed regions as the United States and the EU where a large proportion of information consumption is paid by cash.

In this light, the interaction between supply and demand in China's information resource industry is realized to a large extent through other entities or factors. Investors are willing to pitch in funds because they see the value and opportunities revealed by information products and services marketed by advertisers at platforms, and advertisers are willing to launch advertisement because the information products and services can attract sufficient numbers of subscribers to their platforms. Under such circumstance, the relationship between supply and demand grows more complicated, highlighting the indirect effect.

2. Strong supply and demand driven by mass consumption

China is well recognized by its information resource industry achievements. Information resource industry enterprises represented by Alibaba, Tencent, Baidu, and Jingdong are powerful in the global market largely due to substantial supply and demand. China has a surprisingly large subscriber group in terms of information products and services.

On the one hand, China has plenty of subscribers for information resources. There are two implications: first, a broad population is covered by network information resources. In 2015, China had the largest number of netizens in the world, more than 600 million. The subscriber base of major types of network information resources is numbered in the millions, and the usage rate of search engines is up to 80%. Second, network information resources can meet diverse public needs, and the public has strong consumption consciousness of information products and services. Search engines, for example, are the tool for subscribers to obtain information resources and to gain access to various information resources. "Baidu" has become a mantra of Chinese netizens who need information to solve problems in their work and daily life.

On the other hand, mass consumption indicates that the market value of network information resources is demonstrated by strong demand at both the supply and demand side. First, network information products can create profits for their content providers when being launched into the market as direct profitable products. Second, the platform for network information consumption has no limit in space. A massive reach makes it an important priority for marketing, injecting a strong impetus into the development of the industry.

3. Mutual transformation between supply and demand factors

In China's information resource industry, supply factors can be converted into demand factors under certain conditions, and vice versa. For example, the subscribers of network information resources are not only subscribers but also content providers. The traditional model and new sharing model are combined for the consumption of network information resources. On the one hand, with personal information and subscriber traffic, operators are powered to receive advertising revenue or traffic fee from a third party. This is a key point connecting operators and a third party. On the other hand, subscribers contribute and share similar resources on their platforms. At video websites, subscribers will watch videos and upload their own videos. With richer resources, these websites can attract more traffic. At present, video websites with millions of subscribers have a large proportion in user-generated videos. At platforms like "Baidu Knows," one can ask questions or search questions for answers. They are both subscribers and respondents.

4. Subscriber demand represents the unity of content and form

First, content is the foundation of information products to meet subscriber needs. Second, form is a key element for information products to realize competitiveness and generate profits for operators. Based on subscriber demand, we should formally optimize the use of network information products so that we can promote sustainable growth of the network information industry, and in particular, the availability of a user-pay model.

4.3.2 Existing problems

China's information resource industry is troubled by supply–demand imbalance, mainly problems among subscribers, producers, suppliers, and the policy environment.

1. Conflicts between subscribers and content providers

The conflicts between the subscribers of network information resources and their content providers lie in copyright and payment. First, pirated network information

112 *Supply–demand relation of the industry*

resources have won plenty of subscribers. The pirated information resources can meet subscriber demand at a low legal cost, damaging the interests of content providers. Take digital music as an example. In 2010, 71% of music works in China were made in digital form, and the piracy rate hit 99%. Second, subscribers lack the awareness of and even reject pay-for-consumption. This partly explains why our music industry cancels the pay-for-consumption model all this time. In 2012, Xiami, a genuine music website in China, registered tens of millions of subscribers, only 1% of which are paying users. As for e-books, Amazon in 2012 raked in 6.1 billion dollars from online e-book sales, 10% of its total annual revenue. While selling e-books, Amazon has developed a dedicated reader, Kindle, that can be used to purchase, download, and read e-books, newspapers, magazines, blogs, and other electronic media. This is the reason for its success. Kindle not only closely mirrors the print book reading experience (e.g. size, definition), but provides such smart services as playing music and videos. A product that boosts e-book sales with a device marks a prime example of the optimal combination of content and form. Yet Dangdang, China's largest e-commerce platform for books, was met with failure when it started e-book sales in 2012.

2.   Conflicts between subscribers and operators

The imbalance between profitability and subscriber experience results in conflicts between subscribers and operators of network information resources. For the operators driven by a free model, they need to recover their cost with more advertising revenue. Advertisements will disturb the consumption process, causing a poor subscriber experience. Baidu's paid listing mechanism is a typical case. Baidu, which has a huge market share, receives most of its revenue from advertising. Baidu has come in for heavy criticism as advertisements, sometimes mixed with fake information, are displayed prominently on its search engine results page.

3.   Conflicts between subscriber demand and information resource product supply

In the network information resources industry, obvious conflicts exist between subjects and objects of consumption; that is, network information products fail to meet subscriber needs. This is partly demonstrated by the content. Most information resources online are created by the public and are only restricted by laws. Their quality varies greatly due to the lack of strict quality control. This means that subscribers will sometimes get false, low-quality information resources. SNDA Entertainment, for example, introduced a network literature model which allows subscribers to either upload their own works or purchase the available works at the platform. The absence of publisher review, however, results in an inundation of low-quality works. Therefore, the platform experiences the loss of subscribers despite its rich choices. It is also reflected in form. China is still at the early stage of developing network information products, and there is no well-established form.

Supply–demand relation of the industry 113

This is the case with the said e-book failure. Despite its lower price, e-books have not found a market big enough to bring success.

4. A consumption environment without appropriate policies and regulations

The policies and regulations mentioned here target copyright. China has no clear definitions about copyright of all digital resources in its policies and regulations. On April 25, 2013, Yan Xiaohong, Deputy Director of China's National Copyright Administration, introduced at a press conference held by the State Council Information Office the development of China's intellectual property rights in 2012. He emphasized that either charge or free of charge was possible and inevitable for music downloading. It was not until 2015 that copyright of digital music in China was brought under strict control, and the chaos of the digital music industry died away amid the banned dissemination of music products not protected by copyrights. However, copyright disputes still perplex network literature, online video, and online games, and even those in the digital music industry can't all be settled at present immediately.

4.3.3 Policy orientation

China's information resource industry policies strategically deal with the supply–demand imbalance around copyright, content, technologies, and hardware. A highly specific policy orientation should be developed in the following aspects.

1. Copyright

On the one hand, the copyright of network information resources should be defined in a way that will meet the public demand. It means loose copyright policies. First, the people are both content providers and subscribers of network information resources. For some specific network information resources, their owners and subscribers may vary greatly. As far as network information resources are concerned as a whole, there is a big degree of overlap. In this light, we should take a looser approach to defining the copyright of network information resources. Second, network information resources are relatively decentralized, with different dimensions such as industry and stratum. It is imperative to develop a centralized network that properly integrates and allocates network information resources to meet subscriber needs. This also requires a loose approach for copyright definition. Third, network information resources are time-sensitive, and they will lose their value under an excessively strict copyright definition.

On the other hand, copyright definition is necessary. There are two implications. First, we should have a clear copyright definition, either loose or strict. Only a clear definition can provide the consumption of network information resources with legal support and make consumption methods specific. Second, some network information resources require strict copyright definition, which is necessary for

114 *Supply–demand relation of the industry*

creating a standard environment for industries like print books, and video and other industries require strict copyright definition in the network environment to create a standardized development environment.

2. Content

As *Several Opinions of the State Council on Promoting Information Consumption and Boosting Domestic Demand* overlooks or pays little attention to network information resources, we need to intensify efforts in policy formulation. Content is the ultimate impetus to stimulate consumption. Content-free information is just like water without a source. No matter how developed information technologies and hardware are, it is difficult to build a prosperous market for network information resources. Content-oriented policies should focus on the following aspects: first, to coordinate the relationship among copyright, production, and consumption, and to protect legitimate rights of content providers, operators, subscribers, and other stakeholders through policy guidance; second, to encourage the production and operation of network information resources and support the development of relevant platforms with appropriate tax policies and government subsidies; thirdly, to coordinate the competition in the market of network information resources, especially in relevant industries. At present, competition among such leading operators as Baidu, 360, and Tencent has caused many legal disputes, exerting a negative impact on both the market and subscriber behaviors. Therefore, regulated competition should also be a policy focus.

3. Technology and hardware

Information technologies and hardware are key factors to make possible information consumption. In this light, industrial policies should continue to focus on the development of information technology and hardware. This is essential for the enrichment and wide utilization of information resources and is also closely related to the integration, presentation, and consumption of information resources. Only when devices and technologies are available through which subscribers can obtain information and meet diverse needs can we further stimulate and meet market demand. In a word, we need to increase policy support to information resource industry to promote the development of relevant technologies and hardware. In this way, a sound supply chain of information resources will be developed to meet subscriber demand in a timely manner. Meanwhile, better facilities will also stimulate subscriber needs. This is a two-way push for information production and consumption.

5 Structural features of China's information resource industry

According to system theory, the system function is subject to the system structure, which in turn affect the system structure. A thorough understanding of the information resource industry's structure and the relation between industrial functions is critical for developing China's information resource industry and relevant policies. In this chapter, we explore information resource industry's structure and focus on analyzing the features of information resource industry's internal structure and proposing basic methods and a path to optimize information resource industry's structure.

5.1 Composition of China's information resource industry

In March 2015, Premier Li Keqiang stated in his Government report that China should "promote . . . and enhance the quality of the service industry and emerging industries of strategic importance," "drive medium- and high-end transformation of the industrial structure," "grow a number of emerging industries into dominant industries," and "make action plans for the 'Internet +' strategy." Information resource industry is a critical emerging industry of strategic importance. In 2004, the concept of information resource industry and its key position in China's economic and social resource structure were proposed and established in the *Several Opinions on Enhancing the Exploitation and Utilization of Information Resource* issued by the General Office of the Communist Party of China and General Office of the State Council. In the following decades, it has seen various industrial forms. Traditional businesses like literature service, survey and consulting, and book publishing keep growing, while fast, breakthrough development occurs in new areas such as those featuring the widespread application of computer network information technology: digital publishing, Internet content services, and geospatial information development.

5.1.1 Criteria for defining industry attribution

Determining the structure and categorization of information resource industry is a basic task to be completed before studying information resource industry's development. Only when all information resource industry segments are identified can we analyze information resource industry's overall development status based on the data of specific industries and summarize success experiences and shortcomings in

116 *Structural features of the industry*

order to guide the right path for information resource industry's future development. Informetrics methods are adopted, and an information resource industry thesaurus is built after literature analysis. The thesaurus is then used for word frequency analysis of segment names and connotations indicated in the China National Economy Classification Codes (GB/T 4754–2011). After referencing opinions of experts, information resource industry segments are determined. Next, thesaurus analysis and expert evaluation are combined to calculate each segment's dependence on information resources and categorize these segments for further research on the features of information resource industry's structure in China.

Relevant institutions and scholars at home and abroad disagree on the segments of information resource industry. The State Information Center (2006) divides information resource industry into traditional industries, digital industries, and emerging industries. CCID Consulting (2008) proposed the content service industry include core segments and peripheral segments. The 2003 Work Report Shanghai Municipal People's Government indicates that the content industry includes software, information technology, education, animation, media publishing, digital audio and video, digital television programs, video games, etc. In the academic community, He Defang (2005), Lai Maosheng (2008), Yong Gyu Joo from Korea (2008), and other scholars believe that information resource industry or information content industry includes news publishing, radio and television, movies, TV dramas and audiovisual productions, consulting, database, software, social survey, advertising production, Internet information resource services, gaming, animation, mobile content, online learning, and other segments. When analyzing the segments of information resource industry, we believe that the basic connotation of information resource industry should be referenced to define industry attribution. The most important thing is that information resource industry "uses information resources as raw materials" and "creates economic value" in production, processing, disseminating, and providing. It means that the basic definition and connotation of each segment can be utilized to judge whether it is part of information resource industry.

5.1.2 *Analysis of segments of information resource industry*

The thesaurus analysis method (Ma Feicheng, 2011) is used to screen the subject terms of information resource industry. Keywords are collected according to literature-based discovery theory (Liang Zhanping, 2002). First of all, 26 papers related to the "connotation, composition or classification of information resource industry" published between 2003 and 2013 were reviewed, and 97 subject terms describing the features of information resource industry categorization were selected. After removing those repeated ones or those with similar connotation or implications, we calculated the frequency of the remaining 74 subject terms in 12 pieces of highly correlated literature. As there are only a few pieces of literature that are highly related to the composition and categorization of information resource industry, any subject terms seldomly appear. We require that the subject terms should at least be seen in two pieces of literature, or a proportion of at least 15% (Zhang Yunqiu, 2009). Finally, 51 subject terms were selected to judge the segments of information resource industry, as shown in Table 5.1.

Structural features of the industry 117

Table 5.1 Frequency of keywords to identify information resource industry segments (non-exhaustive list)

S/N	Literature No.	01	02	03	04	05	06	07	08	09	10	11	12	Frequency
1	Information evaluation		+	+	+		+	+	+	+		+	+	75.00%
2	Consulting and investigation		+	+	+		+	+		+		+	+	66.67%
3	Information service		+		+		+		+	+	+	+		58.33%
4	Digital content		+				+	+	+	+		+	+	58.33%
5	Data processing		+				+		+	+	+	+	+	58.33%
6	Storage service		+	+			+	+		+	+			50.00%
7	Investigation and monitoring		+	+	+		+			+	+			50.00%
8	Surveying		+	+				+	+			+		41.67%
9	Market survey			+	+	+	+			+				41.67%
10	Quality inspection		+						+	+	+	+		41.67%
···	···	···	···	···	···	···	···	···	···	···	···	···	···	···
43	Planning management	+			+									16.67%
44	Agency						+				+			16.67%
45	Intermediary services						+				+			16.67%
46	Retail and wholesale			+								+		16.67%
47	Call center		+	+										16.67%
48	Publication						+			+				16.67%
49	Convention and exhibition					+				+				16.67%
50	Human resources	+						+						16.67%
51	Labor dispatch			+								+		16.67%

Next, the opinions of 19 experts of economics, management, library and information science, and other fields were solicited through the Delphi method. After referencing the opinions of the expert group and the industrial process as revealed in information resource industry's connotation, the 51 subject terms were categorized into mining, processing, and providing, which are shown in Table 5.2, a list of keywords to identify information resource industry segments.

After information resource industry subject terms were selected, we analyzed 1,095 segments (Class 4 codes) in the China National Economy Classification Codes (GB/T 4754–2011) issued by the National Bureau of Statistics. First, industries such as grain planting, furniture making, and aquaculture that obviously have no connection with information resource industry are excluded according to the segment profile, including name and connotation provided in the code table, as well as with the basic connotation and features of information resource industry. The remaining 207 segments were then subject to frequency analysis. According to the number of information resource industry industry subject terms seen

118　*Structural features of the industry*

Table 5.2 List of keywords to identify information resource industry segments

Category	Keywords
Mining	Investigation and monitoring, surveying and mapping services, market research, quality monitoring, survey and exploration, quality inspection technology, ecological monitoring, meteorology, environmental protection
Processing	Radio and television, film, data processing, storage services, design and development, design services, advertising, news, literary and artistic creation, digital content, recording production, content services, software development, system integration
Providing	Animation, publishing, Internet, information services, agency, consulting and investigation, promotion services, information evaluation, library, museum, archives, professional services, management services, culture and entertainment, education and training, technical services, risk management, legal services, notary services, planning management, agency services, intermediary services, retail and wholesale, call centers, distribution, convention and exhibition, human resources, labor dispatch

Table 5.3 First categorization of the information resource industry

Category	Number of Keywords	Number of Industries
Information resource industry	≥ 5	36
Unidentified	1–4	75
Non-information resource industry	0	96

in the segment profiles (each subject term is counted 1, regardless of repeated occurrence), the segments were categorized for the first time. Segments whose profiles include at least five subject terms were considered part of information resource industry, and those with 1–4 subject terms marked as unidentified, which are subject to the expert group for scoring. The rest without any subject terms were directly excluded. The first round of screening came up with 111 segments (including both identified and unidentified), as shown in Table 5.3.

Next, 75 unidentified segments were scored by the experts independently for second categorization. These segments were analyzed by their connotations, subjects of labor, processing methods, and outcomes, and then rated on a scale of 1–0 (1 indicating high relevance, and 0 no relevance at all), and those segments with an average score above 0.5 are considered part of information resource industry. Second categorization confirms 93 segments of information resource industry. After all segments of information resource industry were identified, they were categorized again by the subject terms seen in the segment profiles. Information resource industry subject terms fall into three categories: mining, processing, and providing. All segments will be marked for each category of subject terms on a scale of 0–6 based on the number of subject terms included in the segment profiles. Last, segment scores for all three categories of subject terms were subject to clustering analysis, and the results, together with opinions of the expert group, contribute to Table 5.4, which shows the segments of information resource industry.

Table 3.4 Second categorization of the information resource industry

Information Resource Category	Number of Segments	Segments
Information Resource Mining	14	Weather services (7410), earthquake services (7420), marine services (7430), hydrological services (7640), ecological monitoring (7462), environmental protection and monitoring (7461), QC technical services (7450), market research (7232), geological survey for energy resources (7471), geological survey for solid mineral resources (7472), geological survey for mineral resources including water and carbon dioxide (7473), basic geological survey (7474), technological service of geological survey (7475), surveying and mapping service (7440)
Information Resource Processing	14	Advertising (7240), journalism (8510), radio (8610), television (8620), TV and video program production (8630), recording (8660), literary and artistic creation and performance (8710), data processing and storing (6540), digital content service (6591), software development (6510), information system integration (6520), integrated circuit design (6550), engineering exploration design (7482), specialized design (7491)
Information Resource Providing	65	Books (8731), archives (8732), museum (8750), information technology consulting (6530), other capital market services (6790), risk and loss evaluation (6891), financial information (6940), lawyer and related legal services (7221), notarization (7222), accounting, audit and taxation services (7231), social and economic consultation (7233), other professional consultation (7239), intellectual property service (7250), credit service (7295), financial trust and management service (6910), engineering management service (7481), planning management (7483), trade agent (5181), other trade agents and brokers (5189), cargo transportation agent (5821), passenger ticket agent (5122), other transportation agency (5829), insurance broker and agent (6850), entertainment agents (8941), sports agents (8942), other cultural and artistic agents and brokers (8949), real estate agency (7030), public employment (7261), talent agent (7262), labor dispatch (7263), other human resources services (7269), convention and exhibition (7292), science and technology agents (7520), book publishing (8521), newspaper publishing (8522), journal publishing (8523), audio-visual product publishing (8524), e-journal publishing (8525), other publications (8529), TV and video program distributing (8640), film screening (8650), wholesale of books (5143), wholesale of newspaper (5144), wholesale of audio-visual products and e-journals (5145), retail of books, newspaper, and periodicals (5243), retail of audio-visual products and e-journals (5244), book renting (7122), audio-visual product renting (7123), promotion of agricultural technologies (7511), promotion of biological technologies (7512), promotion of new material technologies (7513), promotion of energy-saving technologies (7514), promotion of other technologies (7519), other services for promoting and applying technologies (7590), early childhood education (8210), training on vocational skills (8291), sports school and sports training (8292), training on culture and art (8293), auxiliary service for education (8294), other unspecified education services (8299), other telecommunications services (6319), Internet information service (6420), call center (6592), other unspecified information technology services (6599), basic postal service (6010)

Note: The numbers in the parentheses after the name of each segment are industry codes provided in the China National Economy Classification Codes (GB/T 4754–2011).

120 *Structural features of the industry*

5.2 Analysis of the structure of China's information resource industry

We have identified information resource industry's segments according to information resource industry's connotations. Some of these segments use information resources as part of their raw materials for production, and only part of the economic value created in "production, processing, disseminating, and providing" is attributed to the information resource. When analyzing the economic indicators of such segments, if 100% of their data is included for calculating the indicators of information resource industry, it would "amplify" the actual performance of information resource industry and result in inaccurate research conclusions. American economist Marc U. Porat (1977) divided the national information department into primary department and secondary department based on the degree of marketization of information products or services (whether they are available on the market for transaction). Based on Porat's approach for industrial research, we proposed an "information resource dependence" index to solve the problem. Information resource dependence reflects the degree of dependence on "information resource as raw materials" in the process of creating economic value in an industry, and the proportion of value created by information resources in the production process. Here, thesaurus analysis and expert evaluation were combined to calculate the coverage of information resource industry subject terms in information resource segments. Meanwhile, the expert group is required to score on the information resource dependence for each information resource segment. Both results were integrated to produce the information resource dependence of information resource industry segments, which were then categorized accordingly.

5.2.1 *Categories of information resource industry segments in China*

The thesaurus was used to calculate how many information resource segments are covered in information resource industry; that is, coverage was calculated based on information resource industry subject terms determined and the profiles of 93 information resource segments selected. Each segment may be included, to some extent, by all three categories of information resource industry. But to make categorization easier, only those most relevant categories were retained, and other data were deleted. At last, 93 information resource segments were divided into three categories: information resource mining, information resource processing, and information resource providing.

All 93 categorized segments were marked by experts on their information resource dependence. An indicator of "Information Resource Dependence" was proposed, and it ranged from one to three points: one point means that the industrial production involves exploitation and utilization of the information resource, which contributes little to the industry's total output; three points means that almost all economic benefits created by the industry hinges on exploiting and

Structural features of the industry 121

utilizing information resources, and contribution by other types of resources is little. Next, the overall grades provided by the expert group were translated into the industry's coefficient of information resource dependence in value creation. Based on the subject terms coverage marks and expert discussion, 93 segments were categorized into high information resource dependence industry, medium information resource dependence industry, and low information resource dependence industry (see Table 5.5).

Table 5.5 Information resource dependence of the information resource industry

Information Resource Dependence	Information Resource Dependence Coefficient	Category	Segments
High	0.85–1.00	Information Resource Mining	Market research, surveying, and mapping service
		Information Resource Processing	Journalism, TV, and video program production, recording, data processing, and storing, digital content service
		Information Resource Providing	Information technology consulting, financial information, social and economic consultation, other professional consultation, intellectual property service, credit service, book publishing, journal publishing, audiovisual product publishing, e-journal publishing, other publications, TV and video program distributing, retail of books, newspapers, and periodicals, book renting, audiovisual product renting, other telecommunication services, Internet information services, call center, other unspecified information technology services
	0.7–0.85	Information Resource Processing	Radio, TV
		Information Resource Providing	Other capital market service
Medium	0.40–0.70	Information Resource Mining	Weather services, earthquake services, marine services, hydrological services, ecological monitoring, environmental protection and monitoring, QC technical services
		Information Resource Processing	Literary and artistic creation and performance

(*Continued*)

Table 5.5 (Continued)

Information Resource Dependence	Information Resource Dependence Coefficient	Category	Segments
		Information Resource Providing	Museum, risk and loss evaluation, financial information, lawyer and related legal services, notarization, accounting, audit and taxation services, financial trust and management service, science and technology agents, promotion of agricultural technologies, promotion of biological technologies, promotion of new material technologies, promotion of energy-saving technologies, promotion of other technologies, other services for promoting and applying technologies
Low	0.30–0.39	Information Resource Mining	Geological survey for energy resources, geological survey for solid mineral resources, geological survey for mineral resources, including water and carbon dioxide, basic geological survey, technological service of geological survey
		Information Resource Processing	Software development, information system integration, integrated circuit design, engineering exploration design, specialized design
		Information Resource Providing	Library, engineering management service, planning management, insurance broker and agent, real estate agency, public employment, talent agent, labor dispatch, other human resources services, early childhood education, training on vocational skills, sports school and sports training, training on culture and art, auxiliary service for education, other unspecified education services, basic postal service
	0.15–0.29	Information Resource Processing	Advertising
		Information Resource Providing	Archives, trade agent, other trade agents and brokers, cargo transportation agent, passenger ticket agent, other transportation agency, entertainment agents, sports agents, other cultural and artistic agents and brokers, convention and exhibition

5.2.2 Existing structure of China's information resource industry

Analyzing the features of industrial structure, operating revenues, and the number of employees in different regions can reveal the overall industrial landscape (Li Guoping, 2006). Analyzing information resource industry's structure is mainly carried out from approaches from its definition, connotation and existing industry classification (Lai Maosheng, 2008). Based on the composition and categorization of information resource industry, we have analyzed information resource industry's development from the aspects of industry categories, regional features, and dependence on information resources. Basic data needed for evaluating information resource industry development index[1] mainly come from the China Statistical Yearbook, Economic Census Yearbook and Demographic Census Yearbook. Identification of information resource industry segments are guided by the China National Economy Classification Codes (GB/T 4754–2011), which is designed to match with existing statistical calibers and obtain effective statistical data. We have collected 2004–2013 economic data of 31 provinces in mainland China, including operating revenue, number of legal entities, and employed population. Yet this approach is unable to collect all necessary data. The missing data mainly includes indicators of operating income and working population in some regions and some industries. To solve this problem in data collection, we have also designed methods and models for missing data, as shown in Table 5.6.

All data to measure the index have been determined after rounds of estimation and adjustment.

China's information resource industry has witnessed continuous development between 2009 and 2013, with operating revenues reaching new highs, growing from RMB 1801.83 billion in 2009 to RMB 3061.32 billion (5.38% of GDP) in 2013. The same period saw the number of legal entities increasing from more than 600,000 to over one million, and the number of employees increase from 17,127,000 to 28,875,000. The industry has been expanding in scale and influence (see Table 5.7).

1. Information resource industry structure: a perspective from industrial process

All 93 segments of information resource industry are categorized as information resource mining, information resource processing, or information resource providing by the connotation of each segment. The information resource mining industry includes 14 segments, and that of information resource processing and providing industries are 14 and 65, respectively.

Figure 5.1 shows that all three major categories (mining, processing, and providing) experienced growth in both operating revenue and number of employees between 2009 and 2013. As the information resource providing industry has the most segments, it boasts a higher share in information resource industry's total operating revenues, number of legal entities, and number of employees.

Table 5.6 Estimation of missing data for the information resource industry development index

Scenario	Description	Countermeasure	Algorithm
1	Original data lack the operating revenue of a Class 4 industry, and only the number of legal entities of the Class 4 industry is available.	The operating revenue is estimated by referencing and adjusting the operating revenue of the Class 4 industry for last year based on the ratio between the numbers of legal entities in this year and last year.	$A_4^X = \dfrac{C_4^X}{C_4^{X-1}} * A_4^{X-1}$
2	Original data lack all data related to a Class 4 industry, but the number of legal entities of corresponding Class 3 industry is available.	The operating revenue is estimated by referencing and adjusting the operating revenue of the Class 4 industry for last year based on the ratio between the numbers of legal entities of the Class 3 industry in this year and last year.	$A_4^X = \dfrac{C_3^X}{C_3^{X-1}} * A_4^{X-1}$
3	All data of a Class 4 industry and corresponding Class 3 industry are not available.	Data are estimated by referencing the last-year data of the Class 4 industry based on the ratio between the numbers of legal entities of the industry in this year and last year.	$A_4^X = \dfrac{A_3^{X\,whole\,nation}}{A_3^{X-1\,whole\,nation}} * A_4^{X-1}$
4	The numbers of legal entities of the industry in some regions are unavailable.	The numbers are estimated through times-series approach of Exponential smoothing prediction method based on the data of previous years.	$s_t = a \cdot y_t + (1-a)S_{t-1}$

Table 5.7 Operating revenues, legal entity, and employees of the information resource industry (2009–2013)

Year	Operating Revenue (RMB 100 million)	Percentage of GDP	Number of Legal Entities	Number of Employees 10,000	Percentage of The Labor Population
2009	18,018.30	5.29%	616,428	1,712.7	2.26%
2010	21,069.02	5.25%	705,534	2,005.1	2.63%
2011	25 179.50	5.32%	813,032	2,302.9	3.01%
2012	27,608.49	5.32%	911,278	2,615.6	3.41%
2013	30,613.20	5.38%	1,007,119	2,887.5	3.75%

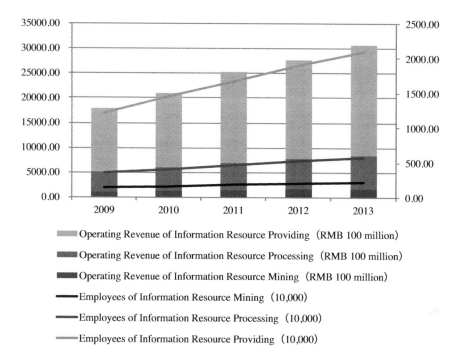

Figure 5.1 Mix of the information resource industry's operating revenue and employees by category (2009–2013)

2. Information resource industry structure: a perspective from dependence

By their dependence on information resources, 93 information resource industry segments can be divided into three categories: high information resource dependence industry (35, scores of 0.7–1.0), medium information resource dependence industry (21, scores of 0.4–0.69), and low information resource dependence industry (37, scores of 0.0–0.39).

Figure 5.2 shows that industries with varying levels of dependence on information resources have seen an increase in both operating revenue and number of employees between 2009 and 2013. The biggest growth was seen in those with low dependence on information resource, followed by high-dependence and medium-dependence ones in sequence. Compared with low-dependence industries, high-dependence industries have fewer employees but higher contribution to the operating revenue. It means that high-dependence industries are knowledge-intensive, and the average value created by the employed population is higher.

126 *Structural features of the industry*

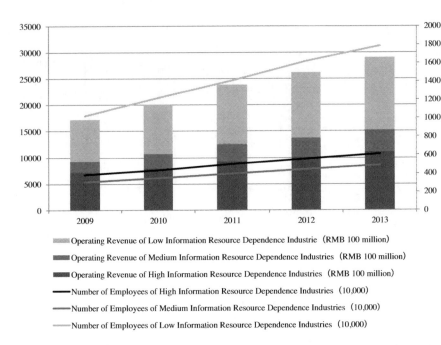

Figure 5.2 The information resource industry's operating revenue and employees by dependence (2009–2013)

3. Information resource industry structure: a perspective from region

China's information resource industry is divided into seven geographical regions: North China, East China, South China, Central China, Southwest China, Northwest China and Northeast China. Figure 5.3 shows the seven regions' proportions in terms of operating revenue, number of legal entities, and employed population in 2013.

Figure 5.3 shows that the employed population and number of legal entities are positively correlated with the operating revenue of information resource industry in each region. Information resource industry in East China is the largest in scale and most advanced in development, while that in Northwest China is underdeveloped.

Analysis of the features of information resource structure reveals that China's information resource industry is doing well, with the following features: (1) Information resource mining, processing, and providing all have steady growth in operating revenue, number of legal entities and employed population, and information resource providing experiences the fastest growth, as it involves most other industries; (2) Being knowledge-intensive, information resource industry can develop faster and create more economic benefits when the level of information resource dependence is higher; (3) There is unbalanced development of

Structural features of the industry 127

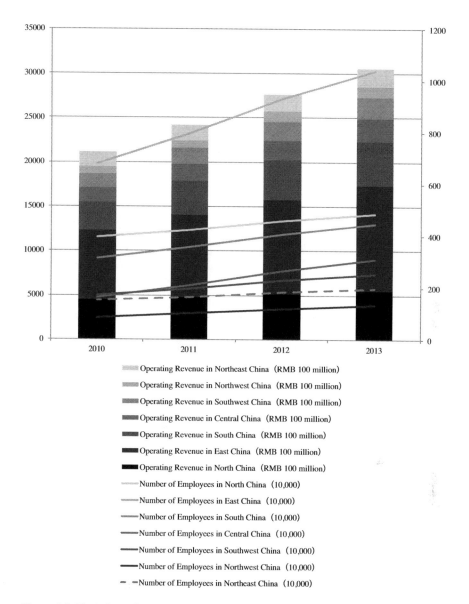

Figure 5.3 The information resource industry's operating revenue and employees by region (2013)

information resource industry across regions, with East China taking the lead with fastest growth, while Northwest China has just started to nurture the industry. It is therefore necessary to intensify support for both information resource mining and providing and to encourage the development of information resource industry. More preferential policies should be implemented to cultivate information

128 *Structural features of the industry*

resource industry in remote regions. In a word, China should secure both rapid and quality development of its information resource industry.

5.3 Optimization of the structure of China's information resource industry

Industrial structure, or sectoral structure of the national economy, refers to the mix of industries and the internal structure of each industry. As China develops its economy, the industrial structure is being adjusted, with the focus shifted from the primary industry to the secondary industry and the tertiary industry. In this process, information resource industry, an important part of the tertiary industry, becomes a major target for the optimization and upgrade of the industrial structure. Optimizing industrial structure is the process in which industries are adjusted for coordinated development, better quality, and higher efficiency. Information resource industry contains an array of segments, and balancing resource distribution among these segments rises to be an urgent problem to be solved. In this section, we briefly introduce the basic principles and concepts of macro-industry structure optimization and provide advice for optimizing information resource industry's structure. Detailed research on information resource industry's structure will be provided afterward.

Many experts and scholars at home and abroad have been studying the issue of structural optimization. Scholars' opinions on the optimization and upgrade of industrial structure evolved as follows: Walt Whitman Rostow in his book *The Stages of Economic Growth* proposed that as economic growth evolves, the dominant groups will be replaced accordingly, which drives the changes in industrial structure. The choice of the right dominant industries can stimulate its faster growth to power economic growth in the region. Building on Rostow's research results, Shinohara Miyohei proposed two benchmarks for optimizing the industrial structure: income-elasticity benchmark (because income-elasticity industries have a larger market demand, it is convenient to take advantage of large-scale economic benefits to improve profits quickly) and productivity-improved benchmark (productivity-increased industries see faster increase in productivity along with faster progress in technology and lower cost of production, which can draw the flow of resources to such industries to boost their development). Albert Otto Hirschman, based on the input–output principle, proposed linkage criteria. He believed that industries with stronger linkage can better drive other industries and facilitate the optimization of the entire economic structure. These industries should be prioritized.

The mechanism of structural optimization is to power sustained and rapid development of the economy through four steps. Step 1: adjusting key factors detrimental to the industrial structure; Step 2: optimizing the industrial structure; Step 3: maximizing the structural effect; Step 4: securing the rapid development of the economy.

The optimization of industrial structure actually emphasizes three things. Firstly, it emphasizes that structural optimization is a dynamic process in which

Structural features of the industry 129

the industrial structure is being improved and upgraded, and there are different measurement standards during different stages of economic development. Secondly, structural optimization prioritizes coordinated development and higher efficiency. Thirdly, structural optimization allocates resources in an optimal manner and maximizes macroeconomic benefits.

Effective strategies should be selected when optimizing the internal structure of information resource industry. A basic method is to select segments with relatively high productivity and large demand in information resource industry to begin with. These segments will receive more support so that they can drive the rapid development of information resource industry. Meanwhile, industries with high linkages will be optimized for better environment to stimulate the prosperity in related industries.

"Information resources are becoming an important production factor and source of social wealth, and how much information a country holds has become an important symbol of its soft power and competitiveness," said President Xi Jinping in a meeting of the Central Leading Group for Cybersecurity and Informatization held in February 2014. Since 2004, China continues expanding its information resource industry, with employed population and number of legal entities on a steady rise. It helps accelerate the pace of China's economic structural transformation and upgrading, and becomes a pillar in the era of the knowledge economy. Meanwhile, exploring the connotation, structure, and development mode of information resource industry has attracted much attention from the academic community in recent years. Beijing, Jiangsu, Zhejiang and other regions have issued local guidance policies for developing information resource industry. These policies lay a solid foundation for furthering information resource industry in China. As more efforts are made in studying information resource industry, the development of information resource industry will be taken to the next level.

Note

1 Information resource industry development index means to reflect the development level of information resources industry in a certain region through quantitative data.

6 Regional features of China's information resource industry

The fast-growing information resource industry has created massive wealth and become a new source of economic growth for China in recent years. Yet seriously unbalanced development of information resource industry across China has not been changed in a fundamental way. Actually, such imbalance is getting worse and worse in a sense. Thanks to superior geographical locations and human resources, East China is way ahead in information resource industry's development, while information resource industry is still in its infancy in Central and West China, despite strong momentum in some provincial-level administrative regions there. In this chapter, we focus on the regional features of information resource industry's development in China. East, Central, and West China are analyzed respectively for its information resource industry development facts and features. We have summarized regional features of information resource industry's development, which can be referenced to when formulating and executing information resource industry policies in China.

6.1 Development by province of China's information resource industry

Balanced development across regions is a key indicator to measure how well the industry's development is optimized. The balanced development of China's information resource industry across regions determines the optimized internal structure of the industry, benefits the healthy development of the industry, and impacts China's economic and social development. This is because whether China's reform and opening-up can equally benefit all people of different ethnic groups from different parts of China is actually crucial to the sustainable and harmonious development of a socialist China. In view of information resource industry's basic features, vigorously developing information resource industry, which requires small investment in existing economy, is an important opportunity for underdeveloped regions in Central and West China to "overtake" other regions, and for China to achieve balanced development of the economy and society. For this reason, both the entire country and all regions, enterprises, and individuals should fully understand and firmly grasp this unprecedented opportunity and play an active role in facilitating the balanced development of information resource industry. To make this happen,

Regional features of the industry   131

we should first have a comprehensive, thorough understanding of information resource industry's development in each region.

To accurately picture information resource industry's development landscape in China, we have, starting from 2014, begun to prepare and publish the *Information Resources Industry Development Report of China* of the previous year. To deliver high-quality reports, we have built an evaluation system for information resource industry's development. The system reveals the development status and features of information resource industry from two dimensions: industrial value and industrial environment.

The system assesses industrial value mainly from four aspects: industrial scale, industrial contribution, industrial development, and industrial structure (four Level 1 indicators); and evaluates the industrial environment from three aspects: infrastructure, policy environment, and decision-making intensity (three Level 1 indicators). Final evaluation results are expressed by the Information Resource Industry Development Index. The latest edition, the *2014 Information Resources Industry Development Report of China* released in 2015, summarizes the development of information resource industry in China's provincial-level administrative regions in 2014 (see Table 6.1).

Table 6.1 China's information resource industry development index rankings 2014 (provincial-level administrative regions)

Provincial-level Administrative Region	Total Points	Ranking	Industry Value	Ranking	Industry Environment	Ranking
Beijing	90.37	2	91.47	2	89.27	3
Zhejiang	89.47	4	89.00	4	89.94	2
Shanghai	87.01	5	86.72	5	87.30	5
Guangdong	89.80	3	91.69	1	87.91	4
Shandong	85.46	6	84.61	6	86.32	6
Jiangsu	91.67	1	91.19	3	92.15	1
Chongqing	81.81	15	82.34	11	81.27	21
Fujian	83.76	7	83.52	9	83.99	9
Tianjin	82.71	10	82.89	10	82.53	15
Sichuan	81.63	16	79.18	22	84.09	8
Liaoning	81.81	14	82.00	13	81.63	18
Hunan	81.12	18	80.69	15	81.54	20
Heilongjiang	80.48	21	79.71	21	81.25	22
Hubei	83.64	8	84.04	8	83.24	11
Hebei	80.61	20	80.10	19	81.11	23
Henan	82.50	11	78.96	23	86.03	7
Shanxi	80.65	19	80.43	18	80.87	24
Anhui	82.99	9	84.27	7	81.72	17

(*Continued*)

132 *Regional features of the industry*

Table 6.1 (Continued)

Provincial-level Administrative Region	Total Points	Ranking	Industry Value	Ranking	Industry Environment	Ranking
Yunnan	80.34	22	80.66	16	80.02	26
Shaanxi	82.44	12	82.15	12	82.73	13
Hainan	79.60	25	80.44	17	78.76	31
Jilin	79.10	26	78.76	25	79.43	27
Guangxi Zhuang Autonomous Region	82.11	13	81.18	14	83.05	12
Jiangxi	80.10	23	79.88	20	80.36	25
Inner Mongolia Autonomous Region	78.70	30	78.07	27	79.34	29
Guizhou	78.92	28	75.20	31	82.67	14
Xinjiang Uygur Autonomous Region	81.37	17	78.84	24	83.90	10
Ningxia Hui Autonomous Region	78.91	29	78.47	26	79.35	28
Gansu	79.81	24	77.88	28	81.74	16
Tibet Autonomous Region	79.02	27	76.45	30	81.59	19
Qinghai	78.05	31	77.06	29	79.05	30

Table 6.1 shows that East China is far ahead of West China in information resource industry development, both in terms of industrial value and industrial environment.

After carefully analyzing the data in Table 6.1, we find that there are three tiers of regional development of information resource industry, in a ladder-like form from the coast to the hinterland. The gaps between regions are huge, and the biggest difference in the development indexes is 13.621 points. In addition to the unbalanced development among regions, information resource industry segments also display obvious differences in terms of development within the same region or between regions. Beijing, for example, boasts relatively balanced development of information resource industry segments, while Guangdong has only a small number of information resource industry segments that are well developed. Such regional differences are also obvious for a number of fundamental information resource industry segments that are immune from geographical differences, such as intellectual property service and quality inspection technology service.

6.2 Features of the information resource industry in East China

East China includes 11 provinces (municipalities directly under the central government): Beijing, Tianjin, Hebei, Liaoning, Shanghai, Jiangsu, Zhejiang, Fujian, Shandong, Guangdong, and Hainan. Most of them are located in the southeast

Regional features of the industry 133

coastal areas that have superior geographical conditions, convenient transportation, and a developed economy. East China is a clear leader in information resource industry's development among all three regions of China considered in this chapter – the East China region, the Central China region, the West China region.

6.2.1 Basic facts about industrial development

Table 6.2 is prepared based on data from the *2014 Information Resources Industry Development Report of China*, and it shows the development of information resource industry in the provincial-level administrative regions of East China in 2014. East China generally has high rankings, with Jiangsu ranked 1st nationwide, seconded by Beijing (2), Guangdong (3), Zhejiang (4), Shanghai (5), Shandong (6), Fujian (7) and Tianjin (10). In other words, eight of the top ten administrative regions are from East China. But Hebei and Hainan lag behind in the ranking, which means there is also a huge gap among provincial-level administrative regions within East China.

As can be seen in Figure 6.1, East China holds a leading position in developing information resource industry nationwide. Guangdong, one of the first places to open to the outside world and one of China's high-tech clusters, scores the highest in terms of industrial value, 91.69, which is 9.7 points higher than the national average. Its industrial environment has high ranking – that is, i.e. 4th, and scores five points higher than the national average. Jiangsu, a developed coastal area, is an early starter in developing information resource industry, and its industrial environment score is 92.15, the highest among all provinces and cities. Beijing is China's center of politics, culture, transportation, scientific research, and education, as well as its hub of economic and financial decision-making and management. Beijing

Table 6.2 Information resource industry development index scores and rankings of provincial-level administrative regions of east China

Provincial-level Administrative Region	Information Resource Industry Development Index Score	National Ranking (excluding Hong Kong, Macau, Taiwan)
Jiangsu	91.67	1
Beijing	90.37	2
Guangdong	89.80	3
Zhejiang	89.47	4
Shanghai	87.01	5
Shandong	85.46	6
Fujian	83.76	7
Tianjin	82.71	10
Liaoning	81.81	14
Hebei	80.61	20
Hainan	79.60	25

134 *Regional features of the industry*

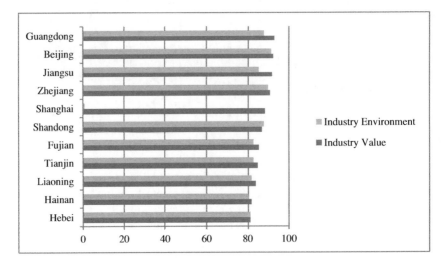

Figure 6.1 Industrial value and industrial environment scores of provincial-level administrative regions of East China

ranks at the top in terms of both industrial value and industrial environmental indicators. Its industrial value and industrial environment scores are 5.77 and 3.8 points higher than the North China average, respectively. The coastal Zhejiang, Shanghai, Guangdong, Shandong, and Fujian see rocketing economic growth, and they are experienced and advanced in exploiting and utilizing information resources. Plus opening wider to the world, they highly depend on information resource industry, and they are all among the top ten by both industrial value and industrial environment. Tianjin and Liaoning rank in the middle thanks to solid economic foundation, unique advantages, and motivation powered by neighboring regions. Hebei and Hainan are late starters, the information industry grows slowly there, and they lag far behind both Beijing and Tianjin.

6.2.2 *Analysis of Level 1 indicators*

Table 6.2 reveals that East China takes the lead in developing information resource industry, but there are still obvious differences within East China. Beijing, Guangdong, Jiangsu, and Zhejiang are information resource industry leaders, while Hebei and Hainan are below the national average.

As shown in the data in the industrial scale indicated in Table 6.3, the average of East China is higher than the national average, but unbalanced development is seen within East China. The average score of East China is 83.67. But the difference of industrial scale ranks is 53, and the average ranking of provincial-level administrative regions is 9th. Beijing, Guangdong, Jiangsu, Zhejiang, Shanghai, and Shandong rank as the Top 6 by industrial scale, and Liaoning, Fujian, and

Table 6.3 Industrial value scores and rankings of provincial-level administrative regions of East China

Provincial-level Administrative Region	Industrial Scale	Ranking	Industrial Contribution	Ranking	Industrial Development	Ranking	Industrial Structure	Ranking
Beijing	94.86	1	90.54	1	85.65	4	83.54	3
Guangdong	94.12	2	82.36	6	96.61	1	82.51	14
Jiangsu	89.60	3	86.57	2	94.70	2	83.08	7
Zhejiang	88.30	4	84.26	4	89.40	3	83.32	4
Shanghai	83.97	5	84.92	3	83.67	7	83.92	2
Shandong	83.17	6	77.62	18	85.41	5	82.62	12
Liaoning	80.48	9	77.80	17	78.50	13	82.37	18
Fujian	78.30	11	80.56	11	82.98	8	83.07	8
Tianjin	77.59	12	83.97	5	80.17	11	81.85	25
Hebei	75.47	20	77.10	19	76.75	17	82.66	11
Hainan	74.50	23	79.61	13	76.23	18	83.00	9
Average	83.67	9	82.30	9	84.55	8	82.90	10
Variance	51.87	53	17.91	46	46.32	35	0.34	47

136   Regional features of the industry

Tianjin rank above average, while Hebei and Hainan lag behind, ranking 20th and 23rd, respectively.

In terms of industrial contribution, East China's average is higher than the national average, indicating that information resource industry contributes to a higher share of the economic development of East China. Beijing ranks first with a score of 90.54, 9.44, and 8.24 points higher than the national average (81.10) and East China average, which means information resource industry is a major contributor to Beijing's economy; Jiangsu, Shanghai, Zhejiang, Tianjin, and Guangdong rank 2nd, 3rd, 4th, 5th, and 6th, with clear clues. Fujian and Hainan also score above average, while Shandong, Liaoning, and Hebei score below both the national average and the East China average (82.30). The data shows that three provinces (autonomous regions) should enhance information resource industry's contribution to the economy. The variance of industrial contribution ranks is 46 for East China. Narrowing internal gaps and maintaining balanced development are top priorities for East China.

Compared with other indicators, East China also excels in terms of industrial development, and that of Central China has relatively high scores. Guangdong, Jiangsu, Zhejiang, Beijing and Shandong rank as the top five, and the other provincial-level administrative regions rank above average. The East China average score of industrial development indicator is 84.55, much higher than the national average (79.26). The average ranking of industrial development is 8th, and the variance of ranks is 35. All these show that it is a fact that the information resource industry of East China is better developed.

In terms of industrial structure, the average ranking of provincial-level administrative regions in East China is 10th, and the variance of ranks is 47, showing a relatively balanced structure of information resource industry, which indicates that structural optimization is relatively balanced in East China. Shanghai, Beijing, and Zhejiang have excellent industrial structure, ranking 2nd, 3rd, and 4th, respectively; Jiangsu, Fujian, Hainan, and Hebei rank 7th, 8th, 9th, and 11th, while Guangdong, Liaoning, and Tianjin rank in the middle. It means that there are regional differences in structural optimization in East China, but it is still well balanced between provinces and cities.

For the policy environment indicator (as shown in Table 6.4), the average ranking of provincial-level administrative regions in East China is 11th, and the average score is 86.37, higher than the national average (82.78). East China generally takes the lead in this aspect, but there is extremely unbalanced development among provincial-level administrative regions, with a variance of ranks as high as 91. Guangdong, Zhejiang, Jiangsu, and Beijing rank 1st, 2nd, 3rd, and 5th, respectively; Shandong, Fujian, Shanghai, and Liaoning rank above average, while Tianjin and Hainan lag behind, ranking 27th and 29th, respectively.

In terms of infrastructure, the average ranking of provincial-level administrative regions in East China is 7th, and the average score is 93.12, higher than the national average (89.94). Beijing, Shanghai, Jiangsu, Shandong, Guangdong, and Zhejiang rank as the Top 6, and Fujian, Tianjin, Liaoning, and Hebei rank above the national average, while Hainan lags behind, ranking 22nd. It means that East

Regional features of the industry   137

Table 6.4 Industrial environment scores and rankings of provincial-level administrative regions of East China

Provincial-level Administrative Region	Policy Environment	Ranking	Infrastructure	Ranking	Decision-making Intensity	Ranking
Beijing	90.65	5	96.17	1	80.40	4
Tianjin	76.21	27	91.52	8	79.00	6
Hebei	81.31	16	89.30	14	72.00	21
Liaoning	82.01	12	90.12	10	72.00	23
Shanghai	85.28	10	96.11	2	79.70	5
Jiangsu	95.44	3	95.76	3	84.95	2
Zhejiang	95.60	2	94.83	6	79.00	6
Fujian	85.29	9	92.20	7	73.75	16
Shandong	86.71	7	95.25	4	76.20	11
Guangdong	96.06	1	95.08	5	72.00	27
Hainan	75.51	29	87.92	22	72.00	28
Average	86.37	11	93.12	7	76.45	14
Variance	54.79	91	9.06	37	19.80	94

China, excluding Hainan, attaches great importance to constructing infrastructure for information resource industry.

In terms of decision-making intensity, the average ranking of provincial-level administrative regions in East China is 14th, a medium ranking. The average score of East China is 76.45, slightly higher than the national average (75.51). Jiangsu, Beijing, Shanghai, and Tianjin ranked 2nd (84.95), 4th (80.40), 5th (79.70), and 6th (79.00), while Hebei, Guangdong, and Hainan have low rankings.

6.2.3   Analysis of development trend

The data in Table 6.5 come from the *2013 Information Resources Industry Development Report of China* and *2014 Information Resources Industry Development Report of China*. As shown in the table, compared with 2013, East China delivered stable performance in industrial contribution and industrial structure in 2014, with little change in average score and variance; there is no obvious change in the average score of industrial scale but an increase in variance from 36.93 to 51.87; for industrial development, the variance almost stays the same, while the sample average decreased from 80.28 to 46.32; as for policy environment, the average score only changes slightly, while the variance increases from 24.23 to 54.79. In terms of infrastructure, the average score grows and the variance decreases; for decision-making intensity, the average drops from 80.44 to 76.45, and the variance rises from 10.57 to 19.80. It shows that information resource industry in East China is steadily going forward, but the regional gap in the policy environment is gradually widening.

138 *Regional features of the industry*

Table 6.5 Information resource industry indicator scores in East China (2013 & 2014)

East China		2013	2014	Growth
Industrial Scale	Average	79.12	83.67	4.55
	Sample Variance	36.93	51.87	14.94
Industrial Contribution	Average	79.26	82.30	3.04
	Sample Variance	15.66	17.91	2.25
Industrial Development	Average	80.28	84.55	4.27
	Sample Variance	32.21	46.32	14.11
Industrial Structure	Average	85.97	82.90	−3.07
	Sample Variance	1.86	0.34	−1.52
Policy Environment	Average	79.99	86.37	6.38
	Sample Variance	24.23	54.79	30.56
Infrastructure	Average	86.39	93.12	6.73
	Sample Variance	19.21	9.06	−10.15
Decision-making Intensity	Average	80.44	76.45	−3.99
	Sample Variance	10.57	19.80	9.23

6.3 Features of the information resource industry in Central China

Central China includes eight provinces: Heilongjiang, Jilin, Shanxi, Anhui, Jiangxi, Henan, Hubei, and Hunan. Central China has moderately developed information resource industry, and regional imbalance is serious. Hubei, Anhui, and Henan rank above average by most indicators, and the majority of remaining provinces are below average; Jilin stays in the bottom by most indicators. Despite strong momentum in Hubei and Anhui, Central China faces serious imbalance in developing information resource industry. That means Central China should maintain some of its existing advantages but also pay attention to solving the imbalance between different provinces.

6.3.1 Basic facts about industrial development

In all three parts of China considered in this chapter – the East China region, the Central China region, the West China region – Central China ranks in the middle. Table 6.6 includes the information resource industry development index scores of various provinces in Central China and their ranks. The average ranking of Information Resource Industry Development Index is 17th for Central China. Hubei and Anhui make it into the top ten, but most of the other provinces rank below average. The variance of ranks for Central China provinces is 46, meaning there is a little difference among these provinces.

According to Figure 6.2, among all Central China provinces, Anhui and Hubei score the highest (84.27, 84.04) for industrial value, above national average, and clue in terms of industrial value when compared with other provinces in Central China.

Table 6.6 Information resource industry development index scores and rankings of Central China provinces

Province	Information Resource Industry Development Index Score	Ranking
Hubei	83.64	8
Anhui	82.99	9
Henan	82.50	11
Hunan	81.12	18
Shanxi	80.65	19
Heilongjiang	80.48	21
Jiangxi	80.10	23
Jilin	79.10	26
Average	81.33	17
Variance	2.45	46

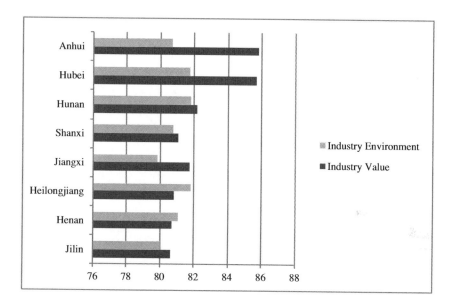

Figure 6.2 Industrial value and industrial environment scores of Central China provinces

As shown in Figure 6.2, Henan scores 86.03 for industrial environment, a good performance. Hubei scores 83.24, around the national average, while other provinces lag far behind.

6.3.2 *Analysis of Level 1 indicators*

Central China ranks in the middle with respect to information resource industry's development, and the industrial value performance of Central China provinces is shown in Table 6.7.

Table 6.7 Industrial value scores and rankings of Central China provinces

Province	Industrial Scale	Ranking	Industrial Contribution	Ranking	Industrial Development	Ranking	Industrial Structure	Ranking
Hubei	81.21	7	81.58	7	84.77	6	80.77	30
Anhui	80.58	8	81.44	9	82.50	9	83.11	6
Hunan	79.46	10	76.42	21	76.15	19	82.19	20
Jiangxi	77.00	15	76.40	22	75.07	22	82.58	13
Henan	75.98	18	74.66	31	74.53	24	82.40	16
Jilin	75.09	21	75.18	26	74.24	25	82.39	17
Heilongjiang	74.94	22	78.30	16	75.78	20	82.02	22
Shanxi	74.15	24	78.90	15	75.47	21	84.03	1
Average	77.30	16	77.86	18	77.31	18	82.44	16
Variance	7.55	44	7.07	67	15.97	49	0.86	83

Regional features of the industry 141

The average score of industrial scale in Central China is 77.30, and the average ranking is 16th, a medium position. Hubei, Anhui, and Hunan rank 7th, 8th, and 10th, while other provinces still see a relatively small-scale information resource industry. The variance of the industrial scale scores in Central China is 7.55, meaning a gap between the provinces in the region.

The average score of industrial contribution in Central China is 77.86, and the average ranking is 18th. Hubei ranks 7th, which means information resource industry makes a huge contribution in Hubei's economic development. In contrast, Jilin and Henan rank 26th and 31st, respectively, below national average. This results in unbalanced performance in terms of industrial contribution and a huge gap between provinces in Central China.

The average score of industrial development in Central China is 77.31, and the average rankings is 18th. Hubei ranks 6th with a well-developed information resource industry, while Henan and Jilin lag behind, ranking 24th and 25th respectively. There is a huge gap between Central China provinces.

The average score of the industrial structure in Central China is 82.44, and the average ranking is 16th. Shanxi holds the first place nationwide with a score of 84.03, and Anhui ranks 6th. Other provinces, however, rank in the bottom sections. It means that structural optimization of information resource industry is still at a low level in Central China provinces.

Table 6.8 shows that Central China provinces generally rank below average overall by all indicators for industrial environment in China. Henan has a high ranking by decision-making intensity, while Hubei leads in all three indicators. There is an obvious gap between these provinces. Hunan and Henan lag behind in terms of building a favorable industrial environment.

The policy environment indicator reflects how well the policy environment is optimized for information resource industry. The average ranking of Central China provinces is 17th, and the average score is 82.16. These provinces mostly rank below average, but there is an obvious imbalance among these provinces. Henan

Table 6.8 Industrial environment scores and rankings of Central China provinces

Province	Policy Environment	Ranking	Infrastructure	Ranking	Decision-making Intensity	Ranking
Shanxi	79.70	22	88.80	17	73.40	19
Jilin	77.41	26	88.10	21	72.00	24
Heilongjiang	80.34	20	87.69	25	75.15	13
Anhui	81.72	13	90.64	9	72.00	25
Jiangxi	79.78	21	88.57	18	72.00	26
Henan	92.63	4	88.41	19	76.90	9
Hubei	84.67	11	89.68	12	74.80	14
Hunan	81.06	18	89.14	16	73.75	17
Average	82.16	17	88.88	17	73.75	18
Variance	22.13	50	0.88	25	3.19	39

142 Regional features of the industry

Table 6.9 Information resource industry indicator scores in Central China (2013 & 2014)

Central China		2013	2014	Growth
Industrial Scale	Average	77.06	77.30	0.24
	Sample Variance	18.40	7.55	−10.85
Industrial Contribution	Average	78.25	77.86	−0.39
	Sample Variance	13.02	7.07	−5.95
Industrial Development	Average	78.72	77.31	−1.41
	Sample Variance	26.39	15.97	−10.42
Industrial Structure	Average	85.63	82.44	−3.19
	Sample Variance	0.92	0.86	−0.06
Policy Environment	Average	78.67	82.16	3.49
	Sample Variance	21.51	22.13	0.62
Infrastructure	Average	84.83	88.88	4.05
	Sample Variance	11.03	0.88	−10.15
Decision-making Intensity	Average	78.98	73.75	−5.23
	Sample Variance	1.34	3.19	1.85

ranks 4th, and Hubei and Anhui take the 11th and 13th places, respectively, above the national average. Other provinces, however, lag far behind. In terms of policy environment, maintaining balanced development is a top priority for Central China provinces.

The average infrastructure ranking of Central China provinces is 17th, and the average score is 88.88, above the national average. Anhui ranks 9th, one of the top ten players, while other provinces are located in the bottom half. It is shown that Anhui invests in more efforts in constructing infrastructure for information resource industry than other Central China provinces do.

The average ranking of decision-making intensity for Central China provinces is 18th, below average, and the average score is 73.75. Compared with other indicators, Central China provinces perform worse in decision-making intensity. Both Anhui and Jiangxi rank below the national average, Henan is among the top 10, and Heilongjiang and Hubei rank in the middle. Decision-making intensity shows how seriously local government departments take information resource industry and how much effort they invest in developing information resource industry. The earlier results show that governments in Central China treat information resource industry like other ordinary industries.

6.3.3 Analysis of development trend

As shown in Table 6.9, compared with 2013, Central China delivered a stable performance in industrial contribution, industrial structure, policy environment, and decision-making intensity in 2014, with little change in average score and variance; there is no obvious change in the average score of industrial scale, but a decrease in variance from 18.40 to 7.55. For industrial development, the average

Regional features of the industry 143

score almost stays the same, while the variance decreases from 26.39 to 15.97; in terms of infrastructure, the average score remains roughly the same, while the variance decreases from 11.03 to 0.88. For decision-making intensity, the average drops from 78.98 to 73.75, and the variance has little change. It shows that information resource industry in Central China is steadily going forward, and there is sufficient space for future growth. Although regional differences in decision-making intensity slightly increase, information resource industry will retain its key role in economic development in Central China.

6.4 Features of the information resource industry in West China

West China includes 12 provincial-level administrative regions: Shaanxi, Gansu, Qinghai, Xinjiang, Ningxia, Yunnan, Sichuan, Guizhou, Tibet, Chongqing, Inner Mongolia, and Guangxi. West China comes last in information resource industry's development, and lags behind in all indicators.

6.4.1 Basic facts about industrial development

Table 6.10 lists the scores of the Information Resource Industry Development Index for West China. The information resource industry development situation for West China is grim. The average score of the Information Resource Industry Development Index is 80.26 for West China, which is lower than the national

Table 6.10 Information resource industry development index scores and rankings of provincial-level administrative regions of West China

Provincial-level Administrative Region	Information Resource Industry Development Index Score	Ranking
Shaanxi	82.44	12
Xinjiang Uygur Autonomous Region	81.37	17
Gansu	79.81	24
Ningxia Hui Autonomous Region	78.91	29
Qinghai	78.05	31
Chongqing	81.81	15
Sichuan	81.63	16
Yunnan	80.34	22
Tibet Autonomous Region	79.02	27
Guizhou	78.92	28
Inner Mongolia Autonomous Region	78.70	30
Guangxi Zhuang Autonomous Region	82.11	13
Average	80.26	22
Variance	1.42	6.50

144 *Regional features of the industry*

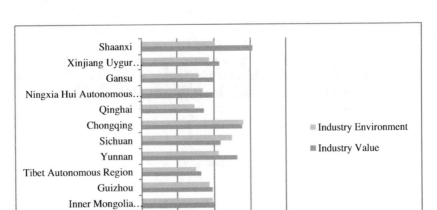

Figure 6.3 Industrial value and industrial environment scores of provincial-level administrative regions of West China

average (82.45). The average ranking of its 12 provincial-level administrative regions is 22nd. Shaanxi and Guangxi boast top positions; Chongqing, Sichuan, and Xinjiang are located in the middle position; Yunnan and Gansu rank below average; and Tibet, Guizhou, Ningxia, Inner Mongolia, and Qinghai are basically at the bottom, ranking 27th, 28th, 29th, 30th, and 31st, respectively. West China must intensify its efforts in developing information resource industry.

Figure 6.3 displays the scores of industrial value. The average score of West China is 78.96, lower than the national average (82.26), and only Chongqing, 82.34, scores higher than the national average. With respect to industrial environment, West China's average score is 81.56, also lower than the national average (82.95), and all nine provincial-level administrative regions except Xinjiang, Sichuan, and Guangxi score below the national average. It shows that West China has a poor environment for developing information resource industry and that more efforts should be invested in optimizing the industrial environment.

6.4.2 *Analysis on Level 1 indicators*

For industry scale performance (Table 6.11), West China has an average score of 74.45, lower than the national average (79.13), and the average ranking of provincial-level administrative regions is 23rd. Shaanxi and Sichuan have high positions in the ranking; Chongqing, Guangxi, and Yunnan rank in the middle; and the other seven regions are below average, in which Xinjiang, Inner Mongolia, and Tibet rank 26th, 25th, and 30th, respectively. West China must continue to intensify its efforts in expanding information resource industry.

Table 6.11 Industrial value scores and rankings of provincial-level administrative regions of West China

Provincial-level Administrative Region	Industrial Scale	Ranking	Industrial Contribution	Ranking	Industrial Development	Ranking	Industrial Structure	Ranking
Sichuan	77.40	13	74.91	30	73.95	27	82.19	19
Shaanxi	77.24	14	80.45	12	79.47	12	82.76	10
Chongqing	76.36	16	80.70	10	80.25	10	83.15	5
Guangxi Zhuang Autonomous Region	76.18	17	81.50	8	77.54	15	81.77	28
Yunnan	75.49	19	79.12	14	77.99	14	82.09	21
Inner Mongolia Autonomous Region	73.94	25	75.01	28	73.95	26	81.82	26
Xinjiang Uygur Autonomous Region	73.38	26	75.12	27	77.40	16	81.82	27
Guizhou	73.21	27	75.55	24	73.33	30	81.97	23
Gansu	72.95	28	75.54	25	73.60	28	81.93	24
Ningxia Hui Autonomous Region	72.46	29	76.48	20	74.56	23	82.51	15
Tibet Autonomous Region	72.44	30	74.93	29	73.59	29	79.33	31
Qinghai	72.30	31	75.64	23	72.89	31	80.85	29
Average	74.45	23	77.08	21	75.71	22	81.85	22
Variance	3.50	40	6.07	57	6.35	55	0.87	58

146 *Regional features of the industry*

For industrial contribution, the average score of West China is 77.08, lower than the national average (81.10). Guangxi ranks 8th, with 81.50, meaning information resource industry makes a great contribution to its economy; Chongqing ranks 10th, with 80.70; Ningxia holds the same position in the middle as last year; Yunnan holds the 14th position, with 79.12; and Xinjiang, Inner Mongolia, Sichuan, and Tibet are in the bottom. Sichuan stands out in West China in terms of industrial scale but only ranks 30th nationwide. It indicates that although Sichuan has a large information resource industry, it has not fully exploited the economic and social benefits brought by information resource industry and has failed to information resource industry's due role in facilitating the regional economy.

In terms of industrial development, the average score of West China is 75.71, lower than the national average (79.26), and the average ranking of provincial-level administrative regions is 22nd. Chongqing and Shaanxi hold high positions; Yunnan ranks above the national average; Gansu, Inner Mongolia, Sichuan, Tibet, and Qinghai are simply in the bottom. Xinjiang saw a significant decrease from its middle position in the last year, evidencing weak momentum in developing information resource industry in Xinjiang. Tibet and Guizhou also experienced a decline in scores, and the development almost became stagnant. The two provinces should intensify their efforts in developing information resource industry.

For industrial structure, the average score of West China is 81.85, lower than the national average (82.38), and the average ranking of provincial-level administrative regions is 22nd. Chongqing and Shaanxi rank 5th and 10th, showing strong momentum. Ningxia ranks 15th, better than last year; Yunnan, which ranked 10th last year, fell to the 21st place, showing worse performance of information resource industry than that of last year; Xinjiang, Inner Mongolia, Qinghai, and Tibet lag far behind, and structural adjustment is a must for information resource industry in West China.

For policy environment performance (Table 6.12), the average score of West China is 79.89, lower than the national average (82.78), and the average ranking of provincial-level administrative regions is 20th. Sichuan ranks 6th with 88.23, and Shaanxi 8th with 86.40, indicating that both provinces have created a favorable policy environment for developing information resource industry; Guangxi, Chongqing, Gansu, and Xinjiang rank below average, while Inner Mongolia, Ningxia, Qinghai, and Tibet are in the bottom, and it is necessary to issue more preferential industrial policies. The average infrastructure score of West China is 87.73, which is lower than the national average (89.94), and the average ranking of provincial-level administrative regions is 23rd. Sichuan has the highest ranking, 11th, showing sufficient infrastructure has been built in Sichuan. Chongqing, and Shaanxi rank in the middle positions, while other provincial-level administrative regions lag behind. In a word, the construction of information resource industry infrastructure in West China falls behind, and more effort should be invested in infrastructure construction so as to lay a solid foundation to power information resource industry's development.

For decision-making intensity, the average score of West China is 75.82, slightly higher than the national average (75.51), and the variance of scores is 20.39. The

Regional features of the industry 147

Table 6.12 Industrial environment scores and rankings of provincial-level administrative regions of West China

Provincial-level Administrative Region	Policy Environment	Ranking	Infrastructure	Ranking	Decision-making Intensity	Ranking
Inner Mongolia Autonomous Region	77.53	25	87.72	24	72.00	22
Guangxi Zhuang Autonomous Region	81.42	15	88.25	20	79.00	8
Chongqing	81.44	14	89.63	13	72.00	29
Sichuan	88.23	6	89.80	11	73.75	18
Guizhou	79.52	23	87.63	26	72.00	30
Yunnan	78.93	24	87.09	28	73.40	20
Tibet Autonomous Region	72.65	31	85.04	31	86.70	1
Shaanxi	86.40	8	89.23	15	72.00	31
Gansu	81.30	17	86.79	29	76.67	10
Qinghai	74.56	30	86.39	30	75.50	12
Ningxia Hui Autonomous Region	75.77	28	87.22	27	74.33	15
Xinjiang Uygur Autonomous Region	80.92	19	87.91	23	82.50	3
Average	79.89	20	87.73	23	75.82	17
Variance	18.68	62	1.75	43	20.39	96

average ranking of provincial-level administrative regions is 17th. Tibet and Xinjiang rank 1st and 3rd, respectively, meaning that the intensity of decision-making will become a major factor in changing the development of information resource industry in both regions. Sichuan, Yunnan, and Inner Mongolia are at a medium level, while Chongqing, Guizhou, and Shaanxi lag behind, ranking 29th, 30th, and 31st. These provincial-level administrative regions still need to intensify their decision-making efforts.

6.4.3 Analysis of development trend

Table 6.13 lists and compares the scores of various indicators for information resource industry development in West China in 2013 and 2014.

Information resource industry in West China is still underdeveloped when compared to other parts of China. Shaanxi presents stable performance, with high scores and little fluctuation. Xinjiang's rankings have risen significantly to the middle place, up eight places from last year. Good momentum is also seen in

148   *Regional features of the industry*

Table 6.13 Information resource industry indicator scores in West China (2013 & 2014)

West China		2013	2014	Growth
Industrial Scale	Average	74.60	74.45	−0.15
	Sample Variance	3.80	3.50	−0.30
Industrial Contribution	Average	77.90	77.08	−0.82
	Sample Variance	15.16	6.07	−9.09
Industrial Development	Average	76.60	75.71	−0.89
	Sample Variance	6.60	6.35	−0.25
Industrial Structure	Average	85.20	81.85	−3.35
	Sample Variance	0.68	0.87	0.19
Policy Environment	Average	77.50	79.89	2.39
	Sample Variance	10.72	18.68	7.96
Infrastructure	Average	82.50	87.73	5.23
	Sample Variance	6.45	1.75	−4.70
Decision-making Intensity	Average	79.10	75.82	−3.28
	Sample Variance	1.90	20.39	18.49

Gansu, and its scores and rankings slightly increased compared to last year. Qinghai and Ningxia are in the bottom for all aspects. They show no indication of improvement in any indicator, and the development has become stagnant. These two regions must improve everything to create a favorable environment for developing information resource industry.

7 Evaluation of the development of China's information resource industry

Evaluating industrial development is a process or behavior of making judgments on the state of industrial development based on certain evaluation criteria and methods. In a certain sense, industrial development evaluation is a key policy instrument. Scientific evaluation has an indispensable role in guiding and motivating information resource industry's development by resource allocation and diagnosis when information resource industry experiences a special period of development opportunities. This chapter introduces the basic principles and methods of the system developed by the team to evaluate information resource industry development. This system is also utilized to evaluate and analyze information resource industry's development in 2013 and 2014.

7.1 Proposal of the system for evaluating the development of China's information resource industry

Information resource industry, an emerging industry of strategic importance, has a fundamental impact on the overall economic and social development of the country. Ensuring its healthy and orderly development requires positive actions from all communities. Industrial development is powered by attention and efforts of all kinds from all members of the society, including enterprises of the industry, capitalists who intend to enter the industry, government agencies intending to promote and protect the industrial development through industrial policies, as well as the public, who are subscribers of information products and information service. The basic premise of such attention and efforts is to ensure that these members can correctly understand and evaluate the actual development of information resource industry. Without such recognition and evaluation, all efforts are useless and unable to obtain effective returns. To meet such needs, the research team has developed an information resource industry development evaluation system which is used as a tool and means for all members of society to correctly understand China's information resource industry development situation. This evaluation system can help all members to accurately understand the development situation, regional differences, industry composition, difficult obstacles, policy effects, lessons learned, and direction of efforts, in order to better guide resource investment,

150   *Evaluation of the industry's development*

product development, management, consumption decisions, and policy formulation for China's information resource industry.

7.1.1   *Relevant research*

The definition of information resource industry determines what would be evaluated for industrial development. Therefore, a basic task before exploring the evaluation of information resource industry development is required. Many scholars have looked into this issue. Dong Baoqing (2005) believes that information resource industry is a sector of the national economy that specializes in producing and processing information resources, as well as providing products and services with information resources as basic content to the public.[1] After summarizing existing research at home and abroad, Lai Maosheng et al. (2008) conclude that information resource industry takes information resources and information content as its source, and has a mature business model that makes profits by information products and services.[2] Zhao Jing and Niu Xiaohong (2012) state that information resource industry is a high-tech, high-intelligence, high-growth, high-value-added industry with various segments, wide application, large scale, and a long value chain.[3] Feng Huiling et al. (2011) point out the differences between information resource industry and the information industry, the content industry, the information service industry, the cultural and creative industry, and other relevant industries, and define information resource industry as "an economic department that uses information resources as materials to produce, process, spread, and provide products or services in the form of information, and creates economic value via such activities."[4] We believe that Professor Feng Huiling and other scholars' explanation and definitions of the connotation of information resource industry reflect the essential features of the industry. The analysis assists a deeper exploration of the basic composition, basic functions, and development laws of information resource industry in relevant theoretical research, helps identify the industrial boundaries when developing the industry, and matches with the basic laws and basic requirements of industrial development. The research team therefore adopts this definition.

As for evaluation of industrial development, most research efforts focus on industrial competitiveness, especially the competitive advantage theory put forward by Porter. Deng Fei and other scholars (2013) proposed a model to evaluate the competitiveness of China's construction industry, and it adopted the diamond model proposed by Porter as a conceptual framework to develop a competitiveness index system with 34 potential influencing factors.[5] Trisha Lin (2012) combined Porter's Five Force model with other analytical frameworks to design evaluation indicators for the factors affecting the competitiveness of China's mobile TV market.[6] Liang Shanshan et al. (2007) studied the method to evaluate the competitiveness of China's coal industry based on Porter's diamond model.[7] According to the theory of competitive advantage, whether a country's specific industry is competitive depends on four key factors: production factors, demand conditions, the performance of related industries and supporting industries, and the company's

Evaluation of the industry's development 151

own strategic structure and competitors. Other influential factors include the role of the government and the opportunities provided by the government for the development of information resources industry.[8] A large number of domestic and foreign scholars borrowed Porter's theory of competitive advantage to varying extents when studying the evaluation of industrial competitiveness. Although Porter proposed the theory of competitive advantage initially for studying national competitiveness, the competitive model can also be used to describe the competitiveness of industries within the region.

In addition, research on the design of the index system for development evaluation and competitiveness has inspired the design of the information resource industry development index system. The evaluation system of China's urban cultural industry development issued by Renmin University of China, for example, analyzes the development of urban cultural industry from the three dimensions: industrial productivity, industrial influence, and industrial driving force. Level 2 indicators mainly involve industrial scale, social influence, resource richness, human resource environment, market environment, public environment, and innovation environment.[9] The China Cultural Industry Development Index System published by Shanghai Jiaotong University is composed of connotation index and representation index, and it covers factors including the development stage of the cultural industry, its economic impact, and how its development impacts the society and culture.[10] The Global Competitiveness Index (GCI) published by the World Economic Forum includes Level 1 indicators such as basic requirements, performance improvement, and innovation and social factors.[11] Existing research on the evaluation of industrial competitiveness mostly approaches from the internal and external. But existing industry evaluation index system pay insufficient attention to government policies and government decision-making. In China, government guidance and support plays a decisive role, to a certain extent, in developing most emerging industries. When building the indicator system, we should focus on how to better reflect the impact of government factors in industrial development.

7.1.2 Constructing the framework of the indicator system

The information resource industry development evaluation system is a collection of evaluation factors (evaluator, evaluation object, evaluation standard, evaluation indicator, evaluation method, etc.) required to ensure the scientific and effective evaluation of industrial development and the corresponding organizational structure, systems, procedures, and resource conditions. We believe that among all factors of the evaluation system, the construction of the evaluation index system plays a key part. It is the value scale on which the evaluation of the industry is based; in other words, it helps propose specific and systematic evaluation criteria and prescribes the selection of basic conditions or direction method for other factors to play their due roles. To this end, we concentrated our efforts on building the framework for the industrial development evaluation index system and the proposed Information Resource Industry Development Index (IRIDI), which can

152 *Evaluation of the industry's development*

reflect both information resource industry's industrial value and external environment of industrial development as well as ensure that the basic data required for index calculation is collectable.

The evaluation index system proposed needs quantitative data to show the development of information resource industry at a specific time and in a specific region. But as China is experiencing industrial restructuring and economic restructuring, industrial development cannot be measured by economic indicators alone. Such indicators to reflect industrial development also include social contribution, industrial structure, infrastructure, and policy environment. To this end, this study reveals the development status and features of information resource industry from two dimensions: industrial value and industrial environment.

Industrial value and industrial environment are complementary. Higher industrial value helps optimize the industrial environment, and a better industrial environment can boost the increase in industrial value. Both are positive indicators for evaluating the development of information resource industry. Industrial value is subject to four factors: industrial scale, industrial contribution, industrial development, and industrial structure, and these four indicators are adopted to calculate industrial value. Industrial environment is evaluated by three indicators: infrastructure, policy environment, and decision-making intensity. An index system to evaluate information resource industry's development is therefore built, including 70 indicators of four levels. There are 2 indicators at Level 1, 7 at Level 2, 17 at Level 3, and 44 at Level 4. Level 1, 2, and 3 indicators and their calculation methods are shown in Table 7.1.

Table 7.1 Level 1, 2, and 3 indicators to evaluate information resource industry's development and their estimation

Level 1 Indicators	Level 2 Indicators	Level 3 Indicators	Estimation Method
Industrial Value	Industrial Scale	Industrial Value	Fitted by the economic scale of industries that are highly, moderately, and lowly dependent on information resources
		Number of Employees	Fitted by the employed population of industries that are highly, moderately, and lowly dependent on information resource
		Number of Legal Entities	Fitted by the number of legal entities of industries that are highly, moderately, and lowly dependent on information resource
		Scale of Public Companies	Fitted by the number of public information resource industry companies and their return on net worth and gross revenue

Level 1 Indicators	Level 2 Indicators	Level 3 Indicators	Estimation Method
	Industrial Contribution	Contribution to Employment	Fitted by the employed population of information resource industry and employed population of the region
		Contribution to GDP	Fitted by the operating revenues of information resource industry and regional GDP
	Industrial Development	Development of Scale	Fitted by information resource industry's scale data in the past 10 years
		Development of Legal Entities	Fitted by information resource industry's numbers of legal entities in the past 10 years
		Development of Employed Population	Fitted by information resource industry's employed population in the past 10 years
	Industrial Structure	Industrial Resource Structure	Fitted by the share of completely dependent information resource industry segments
		Industrial Factor Intensity	Fitted by industrial value density and population breadth
Industrial Environment	Public Policy	Fitted by the number of policies to measure the supply of industrial policies	Fitted by the data on government open interaction: data fitting between government website and weibo
	Infrastructure	Development of Industrial Parks	Fitted by the number of industrial parks and prices
		Utilization of Information Technologies	Fitted by the utilization factors of the Internet, phone, radio, and TV
	Decision-making Intensity	Attention from Decision Makers	Fitted by the attention intensity of leaders and governments
		Government Work Intensity	Fitted by the data included in the government work report

7.2 Construction of the system for evaluating the development of China's information resource industry

With a conceptual framework for evaluating information resource industry's development, how to determine the specific weight of indicators at all levels and how to ensure the evaluation system is stable become important issues in constructing

154 *Evaluation of the industry's development*

the system. The research team used the factor analysis method to determine the weights of indicators at all levels.

7.2.1 *Determining the weight of indicators*

Factor analysis is a statistical method of extracting common factors from multiple variables, in order to reduce the number of variables and dimensionality. For the variable group, the variable weight is determined by the factor analysis result, and for the indicator group, equal-weight method is adopted. The weights of indicators are shown in Table 7.2.

Both sensitivity analysis and robustness analysis are needed to make sure that the information resource industry development index is designed in a reasonable way. Sensitivity analysis targets single or multiple indicators and aims to avoid the excessive dependence of the calculation results on individual indicators and the failure of other indicators. A sensitivity coefficient was used to analyze how much each indicator affects the final result (sensitivity coefficient = percentage change of target value/percentage change of parameter value), and multifactor

Table 7.2 The weights of level 1, 2, and 3 indicators to evaluate information resource industry's development

Level 1 Indicators	Weight	Level 2 Indicators	Weight	Level 3 Indicators	Weight
Industrial Value	0.500	Industrial Scale	0.280	Industrial Value	0.272
				Number of Employees	0.272
				Number of Legal Entities	0.271
				Scale of Public Companies	0.185
		Industrial Contribution	0.242	Contribution to Employment	0.500
				Contribution to GDP	0.500
		Industrial Development	0.260	Development of Scale	0.336
				Development of Legal Entities	0.332
				Development of Employed Population	0.332
		Industrial Structure	0.218	Industrial Resource Structure	0.500
				Industrial Factor Intensity	0.500
Industrial Environment	0.500	Policy Environment	0.322	Supply of Industrial Policies	0.500
				Opening and Interaction of Government Affairs	0.500
		Infrastructure	0.354	Development of Industrial Parks	0.500
				Utilization of Information Technologies	0.500
		Decision-making Intensity	0.324	Attention from Decision Makers	0.500
				Government Work Intensity	0.500

Evaluation of the industry's development 155

sensitivity analysis was also carried out. Robustness analysis shows how much the evaluation results are affected by the model parameters and environmental parameters, and it means that the indicator system should be able to handle abnormalities and adapt to dynamic changes. We checked the influence of environmental parameters on the index results by detecting changes in the non-dimensionalization method, sample capacity, and data vibration so as to examine the robustness of the index system.

In the case of changes in the non-dimensionalization method, the research team has adopted four methods of range standardization, maximization, minimization, mean value, and Z-score to process the variables, and used the Kendall coefficient of concordance to measure how the changes in method affect the outcome. The Kendall coefficient of concordance has a value range of [0,1], and the larger the coefficient, the smaller the influence of the non-dimensionalization methods on the model.

It was found that the Kendall coefficient of concordance ranges between [0.9, 1.0] for provincial-level administrative regions in China. The test results were subject to a significance test with $\alpha = 0.01$ and $\alpha = 0.05$, respectively, and the critical significant values of the Kendall coefficient of concordance were examined. We found that all Kendall coefficients of concordance were significant, and the evaluation results of 31 provincial-level administrative regions were consistent when using different non-dimensionalization methods. In addition to the non-dimensionalization method test, the results of both sample capacity change and data vibration test show that the Information Resource Industry Development Index we developed delivers excellent performance in terms of robustness.

7.2.2 Processing of evaluation indicators

Data processing is a key step in the empirical analysis of IRIDI. In addition to weight design, linear weighting method in the comprehensive scoring method was used to calculate IRIDI:

$$F = \sum p_i \cdot w_i$$

where F refers to IRIDI, p the result of Indicator i after the non-dimensionalization method, and w is the weight of Indicator i.

Basic data needed for IRIDI mainly come from the "China Basic Statistical Units Yearbook," "China Economic Census Yearbook," "China Economic and Social Development Statistical Database," "Evaluation Report on China Government Affairs Microblogs," "Report on the Sixth Census," "China Electronic Information Industry Statistical Yearbook," provincial- and municipal-level economic census yearbooks, information resource exploitation and utilization reports, and the public financial reports of listed information resource industry companies. Identification of information resource industry segments is guided by the China National Economy Classification Codes (GB/T 4754–2011), which is designed to

156 *Evaluation of the industry's development*

Table 7.3 Estimation of missing data for the information resource industry development index

Scenario	Description	Countermeasure	Algorithm
1	Original data lack the operating revenue of a Class 4 industry, and only the number of legal entities (employed population) of the Class 4 industry is available	The operating revenue is estimated by referencing and adjusting the operating revenue of the Class 4 industry in last year based on the ratio between the numbers of legal entities in this year and last year	$A_4^X = \dfrac{C_4^X}{C_4^{X-1}} * A_4^{X-1}$
2	Original data lack all data related to a Class 4 industry, but the number of legal entities of corresponding Class 3 industry is available	The operating revenue is estimated by referencing and adjusting the operating revenue of the Class 4 industry in last year based on the ratio between the numbers of legal entities of the Class 3 industry in this year and last year	$A_4^X = \dfrac{C_3^X}{C_3^{X-1}} * A_4^{X-1}$
3	All original data of a Class 4 industry and corresponding Class 3 industry are not available	Data are estimated by referencing the last-year data of the Class 4 industry based on the ratio between the numbers of legal entities of the industry in this year and last year	$A_4^X = \dfrac{A_3^{X\,whole\,nation}}{A_3^{X-1\,whole\,nation}} * A_4^{X-1}$
4	The original numbers of legal entities of the industry in some regions are unavailable	The numbers are estimated through times-series approach of Exponential smoothing prediction method based on the data of previous years	$s_t = a \cdot y_t + (1-a) S_{t-1}$

match with existing statistical calibers. We have collected 2004–2013 economic data of 31 provinces on the mainland, including operating revenue, number of legal entities, and employed population.

Standardized processing is to eliminate dimensional differences between IRIDI indicators. These standardized processing methods include range standardization, maximization, minimization, mean value method, and Z-score. Range standardization was adopted for data dimensioning. The formula of the range standardization method is as follows:

$$X' = \frac{X - X_{min}}{X_{max} - X_{min}}$$

where X' marks the target value, X the original value, X_{min} the minimum value in the indicator data set, and X_{max} the maximum value in the indicator data set.

Evaluation of the industry's development 157

When processing data related to information resource industry's development, we found that indicator data for a small number of segments or a region may be missing or distorted. This requires data estimation and correction, in order to reduce the impact of missing or distorted data on IRIDI. The missing data mainly include indicators of operating income and working population in some regions and some industries. To solve this problem in data collection, we have also designed methods and models for different missing data, as shown in Table 7.3. All data to measure the index have been determined after rounds of estimation and adjustment.

7.3 Empirical analysis of evaluation of the development of China's information resource industry

To verify the effectiveness of IRIDI system, the research team has used China's information resource industry data in 2013 for an empirical analysis and compared it with that.

7.3.1 Ranking by indicators

By measuring information resource industry data of 31 provinces, municipalities and autonomous regions in China in 2013 and 2014, we obtained the IRIDI ranks in 2014 and the changes from the 2013 ranking, as shown in Table 7.4.

Table 7.5 shows the industrial value ranking for IRIDI in 2014, and the changes compared with 2013.

Table 7.6 shows the industrial environment ranking for IRIDI in 2014 and the changes compared with 2013.

7.3.2 Explanation of ranking by indicators

Industrial value and industrial environment, two Level 1 indicators of IRIDI, respectively reflect the economic value created by information resource industry and the environmental factors that affect information resource industry in each region. The evaluation and analysis of IRIDI reveal the following.

In 2014, China's information resource industry maintained good momentum, and there is little change in the rankings by each region when compared with 2013. The overall scale was on a steady increase, and there are high scores for infrastructure, industrial structure, and public policy. Comparison between IRIDI and the economic development index between regions shows a clear correlation between the two: the better the economy in a region, the better the information resource industry development in that region. However, there are still certain problems concerning information resource industry's development. Unbalanced development across China is a major problem, with "East China Outperforming West China."

1. Information resource industry infrastructure is being improved, and the utilization level of information resources needs to be improved

Level 2 indicators include industrial scale, industrial contribution, industrial development, industrial structure, public policy, infrastructure, and decision-making intensity.

Table 7.4 China's information resource industry development index rankings 2014 (provincial-level administrative regions)

Provincial-level Administrative Region	Total Points	Ranking	Ranking of Last Year	Industry Value	Ranking	Industry Environment	Ranking
Jiangsu	91.67	1	4	91.19	3	92.15	1
Beijing	90.37	2	1	91.47	2	89.27	3
Guangdong	89.80	3	3	91.69	1	87.91	4
Zhejiang	89.47	4	2	89.00	4	89.94	2
Shanghai	87.01	5	5	86.72	5	87.30	5
Shandong	85.46	6	6	84.61	6	86.32	6
Fujian	83.76	7	7	83.52	9	83.99	9
Hubei	83.64	8	10	84.04	8	83.24	11
Anhui	82.99	9	11	84.27	7	81.72	17
Tianjin	82.71	10	9	82.89	10	82.53	15
Henan	82.50	11	22	78.96	23	86.03	7
Shaanxi	82.44	12	13	82.15	12	82.73	13
Guangxi Zhuang Autonomous Region	82.11	13	17	81.18	14	83.05	12
Liaoning	81.81	14	12	82.00	13	81.63	18
Chongqing	81.81	15	8	82.34	11	81.27	21
Sichuan	81.63	16	16	79.18	22	84.09	8
Xinjiang Uygur Autonomous Region	81.37	17	25	78.84	24	83.90	10
Hunan	81.12	18	14	80.69	15	81.54	20
Shanxi	80.65	19	21	80.43	18	80.87	24
Hebei	80.61	20	18	80.10	19	81.11	23
Heilongjiang	80.48	21	19	79.71	21	81.25	22
Yunnan	80.34	22	15	80.66	16	80.02	26
Jiangxi	80.12	23	23	79.88	20	80.36	25
Gansu	79.81	24	29	77.88	28	81.74	16
Hainan	79.60	25	20	80.44	17	78.76	31
Jilin	79.10	26	24	78.76	25	79.43	27
Tibet Autonomous Region	79.02	27	30	76.45	30	81.59	19
Guizhou	78.92	28	27	75.20	31	82.67	14
Ningxia Hui Autonomous Region	78.91	29	28	78.47	26	79.35	28
Inner Mongolia Autonomous Region	78.70	30	26	78.07	27	79.34	29
Qinghai	78.05	31	30	77.06	29	79.05	30

Table 7.5 Industrial value ranking for China's information resource industry

Province	Industrial Value	Ranking	Last Year Ranking	Industrial Scale	Industrial Contribution	Industrial Development	Industrial Structure
Guangdong	91.69	1	1	94.12	82.36	96.61	82.51
Beijing	91.47	2	2	94.86	90.54	85.65	83.54
Jiangsu	91.19	3	3	89.60	86.57	94.70	83.08
Zhejiang	89.00	4	4	88.30	84.26	89.40	83.32
Shanghai	86.72	5	5	83.97	84.92	83.67	83.92
Shandong	84.61	6	6	83.17	77.62	85.41	82.62
Anhui	84.27	7	7	80.58	81.44	82.50	83.11
Hubei	84.04	8	8	81.21	81.58	84.77	80.77
Fujian	83.52	9	9	78.30	80.56	82.98	83.07
Tianjin	82.89	10	11	77.59	83.97	80.17	81.85
Chongqing	82.34	11	12	76.36	80.70	80.25	83.15
Shaanxi	82.15	12	10	77.24	80.45	79.47	82.76
Liaoning	82.00	13	13	80.48	77.80	78.50	82.37
Guangxi Zhuang Autonomous Region	81.18	14	14	76.18	81.50	77.54	81.77
Hunan	80.69	15	16	79.46	76.42	76.15	82.19
Yunnan	80.66	16	15	75.49	79.12	77.99	82.09
Hainan	80.44	17	17	74.50	79.61	76.23	83.00
Shanxi	80.43	18	20	74.15	78.90	75.47	84.03
Hebei	80.10	19	19	75.47	77.10	76.75	82.66
Jiangxi	79.88	20	18	77.00	76.40	75.07	82.58

(*Continued*)

Table 7.5 (Continued)

Province	Industrial Value	Ranking	Last Year Ranking	Industrial Scale	Industrial Contribution	Industrial Development	Industrial Structure
Heilongjiang	79.71	21	22	74.94	78.30	75.78	82.02
Sichuan	79.18	22	21	77.40	74.91	73.95	82.19
Henan	78.96	23	24	75.98	74.66	74.53	82.40
Xinjiang Uygur Autonomous Region	78.84	24	23	73.38	75.12	77.40	81.82
Jilin	78.76	25	25	75.09	75.18	74.24	82.39
Ningxia Hui Autonomous Region	78.47	26	27	72.46	76.48	74.56	82.51
Inner Mongolia Autonomous Region	78.07	27	28	73.94	75.01	73.95	81.82
Gansu	77.88	28	26	72.95	75.54	73.60	81.93
Qinghai	77.06	29	30	72.30	75.64	72.89	80.85
Tibet Autonomous Region	76.45	30	31	72.44	74.93	73.59	79.33
Guizhou	75.20	31	29	73.21	75.55	73.33	75.78

Table 7.6 Industrial environment ranking for China's information resource industry

Province	Industry Environment	Ranking	Ranking of Last Year	Policy Environment	Infrastructure	Decision-making Intensity
Jiangsu	92.15	1	6	95.44	95.76	84.95
Zhejiang	89.94	2	2	95.60	94.83	79.00
Beijing	89.27	3	1	90.65	96.17	80.40
Guangdong	87.91	4	4	96.06	95.08	72.00
Shanghai	87.30	5	3	85.28	96.11	79.70
Shandong	86.32	6	5	86.71	95.25	76.20
Henan	86.03	7	16	92.63	88.41	76.90
Sichuan	84.09	8	10	88.23	89.80	73.75
Fujian	83.99	9	8	85.29	92.20	73.75
Xinjiang Uygur Autonomous Region	83.90	10	27	80.92	87.91	82.50
Hubei	83.24	11	14	84.67	89.68	74.80
Guangxi Zhuang Autonomous Region	83.05	12	23	81.42	88.25	79.00
Shaanxi	82.73	13	20	86.40	89.23	72.00
Guizhou	82.67	14	26	79.52	87.63	80.40
Tianjin	82.53	15	9	76.21	91.52	79.00
Gansu	81.74	16	29	81.30	86.79	76.67
Anhui	81.72	17	18	81.72	90.64	72.00
Liaoning	81.63	18	11	82.01	90.12	72.00
Tibet Autonomous Region	81.59	19	30	72.65	85.04	86.70
Hunan	81.54	20	12	81.06	89.14	73.75
Chongqing	81.27	21	7	81.44	89.63	72.00
Heilongjiang	81.25	22	13	80.34	87.69	75.15
Hebei	81.11	23	15	81.31	89.30	72.00
Shanxi	80.87	24	17	79.70	88.80	73.40
Jiangxi	80.36	25	24	79.78	88.57	72.00
Yunnan	80.02	26	19	78.93	87.09	73.40
Jilin	79.43	27	22	77.41	88.10	72.00
Ningxia Hui Autonomous Region	79.35	28	28	75.77	87.22	74.33
Inner Mongolia Autonomous Region	79.34	29	25	77.53	87.72	72.00
Qinghai	79.05	30	31	74.56	86.39	75.50
Hainan	78.76	31	21	75.51	87.92	72.00

162 *Evaluation of the industry's development*

The industrial scale indicator reflects the relative scale of information resource industry in a region, which is measured by four indicators: operating revenue, employed population, number of legal entities, and the size of public companies. Beijing (94.9), Guangdong (94.1), and Jiangsu (89.6) ranked in the top three, while the national average score was only 78.5, and the standard deviation was 6.1. There were 21 provincial-level administrative regions scoring lower than the national average. All top six places were held by East China, and all bottom seven places by West China. In terms of industrial scale indicators, information resource industry is still quite small in China, and there are significant differences between regions, with most provincial administrative regions lagging behind in information resource industry's development.

The industrial contribution indicator reflects how much information resource industry contributes to a region's economy, which is measured by two indicators: contribution to employment and contribution to economy. The highest score belongs to Beijing (90.5), the lowest Henan (74.7). The national average score is 79.1, and the standard deviation is 4.0. To sum up, information resource industry has not contributed significantly to China's economy. Compared with other industries, information resource industry still plays a secondary role in the different province in China economy and is still weak.

The industrial development indicator shows the dynamic development of information resource industry in a region since 2004. It is measured by the development of industrial scale, the development of the number of legal entities, and the development of employed population. The highest score goes to Guangdong (96.6), the lowest score is Qinghai (72.9). The national average score is 79.3, and the standard deviation is 6.2. A total of 19 provincial-level administrative regions score lower than the national average. In conclusion, China's information resource industry development is growing at varying paces between regions.

The industrial structure indicator depicts the optimization of information resource industry structure in a region, and it is measured by two indicators: industrial resource structure and industrial factor intensity. The highest score belongs to Shanxi (84.0), the lowest Guizhou (75.8). The national average score is 82.2, and the standard deviation is 1.5. Information resource industry structure is relatively reasonable across China, with little difference between regions, which means that all regions share similar paths to develop information resource industry.

The policy environment indicator represents the optimization of information resource industry policy environment in a region, and it is measured by two indicators: supply of industrial policies and opening and interaction of government affairs. Guangdong has the highest score (96.1) and Tibet the lowest score (72.7). The national average score is 82.8, and the standard deviation is 6.3. There is a huge gap between the supply of information resource industry policies and the opening of government affairs in various regions of China. Many regions fail to pay enough attention to developing information resource industry. The government needs to step up efforts in constructing information resource industry, make reasonable planning, establish uniform standards, and strengthen the construction of the legal system and security system.

Evaluation of the industry's development 163

The infrastructure indicator shows how well supporting infrastructure is provided for information resource industry, and it is measured by two indicators: development of industrial parks development and utilization of information technologies. The highest score belongs to Beijing (96.2), the lowest one is Tibet (85.0). The national average score is 89.9, and the standard deviation is 3.1. It is worth noting that the lowest score in 2013 was with Gansu (79.2), with an average score of 86.1 and a standard deviation of 4.4. This indicates that in 2014, all provincial-level administrative regions have made great progress in constructing information resource industry infrastructure, and the infrastructure gap between these regions is being closed.

The decision-making strength indicator represents the amount of attention paid by the government to develop information resource industry and the intensity of relevant government work. It is measured by two indicators: attention from decision makers and government work intensity. The highest score goes to Tibet (86.7), and the bottom scores are seen in ten provinces and cities (72.0), including Inner Mongolia. The national average score is 75.8 and the standard deviation is 4.1. It should be noted that the lowest score for 2013 belongs to Jilin (77.5), with an average score of 80.2 and a standard deviation of 3.3. In other words, all regions across China still have not paid enough attention to and worked hard enough in developing information resource industry in 2014, and the performance in 2013 is even worse.

In all indicators listed in Figure 7.1, the lowest score (75.8) of 2014 is with decision-making intensity, the highest (89.9) with infrastructure. Correspondingly, Level 3 indicators – attention from decision makers and government work intensity score low points, while the development of industrial parks and

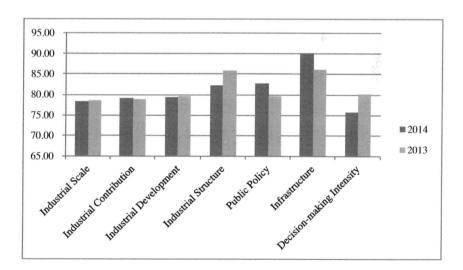

Figure 7.1 Level 2 indicators for the information resource industry's development in China (2013–2014)

164   *Evaluation of the industry's development*

utilization of information technologies score high points. The evaluation of the development index of information resources industry means China has come a long way in constructing industrial parks and advancing informatization, along with smooth progress in economic restructuring. However, information resource industry's development has not drawn enough attention, and the decision-makers have not guided it in the right way, which becomes a top constraint on information resource industry's development. The scores of industrial structure and public policy indicators are 82.2 and 82.8, relatively high. The scores of industrial scale, industrial contribution, and industrial development are 78.5, 79.1, and 79.3, respectively, still large gaps from the three indicators mentioned earlier. It is evidenced that the construction of information resource industry is far from being perfect, and the exploitation and utilization of information resources are still at a primitive stage, and the industrial scale is small, so there is much room for future growth.

2. Stable information resource industry rankings by regions, with some provincial-level administrative regions catching up

As shown in Table 7.4, the comprehensive IRIDI rankings of all regions have changed, but only to a slight extent, except for a small number of provincial-level administrative regions. The rankings of Henan, Xinjiang Uygur Autonomous Region, and Gansu saw the biggest increase of 11, 8, and 5 places, respectively, while Chongqing, Yunnan, and Hainan were down 7, 7, and 5 places, respectively. As shown in Table 7.6, Henan, Xinjiang Uygur Autonomous Region, and Gansu experienced a substantial increase in industrial environment from last year, while Chongqing, Yunnan, and Hainan deteriorated in this indicator, a major reason for obvious changes in the comprehensive rankings of these provincial-level administrative regions.

3. Development is unbalanced across China, with "East China Outperforming West China"

The information resource industry gap between different parts of China is still very large in 2014 (see Figure 7.2). All six provincial-level administrative regions with the highest scores of development index come from East China: Jiangsu, Zhejiang, Beijing, Guangdong, Shanghai, and Shandong, and their scores are obviously higher than the national average and also higher than the averages of Central China, Northeast China, and West China. West China lags behind in terms of information resource industry's development. Shaanxi and Guangxi stand out in developing information resource industry, but Tibet, Guizhou, Ningxia, Inner Mongolia, and Qinghai rank in the bottom. In terms of growth rate, the average IRIDI score of East China increased by 1.64% year on year in 2014, while Central, Northeast, and West China saw a year-on-year growth of 0.32%, 1.12%, and 0.63%, respectively, still slower than that of East China. East China boasts a clear edge in developing information resource industry, yet there are still obvious gaps

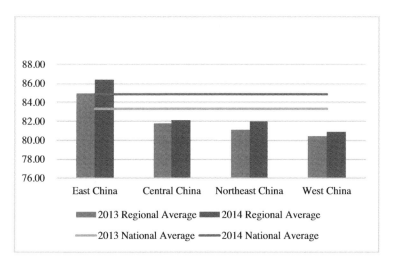

Figure 7.2 Average information resource industry development index of provincial-level administrative regions (2013–2014)

Table 7.7 Pearson correlation coefficient for per capita GDP and IRIDI

		Development Index	*Per Capita GDP*
Development Index	Pearson Correlation	1	0.670**
	Sig.(2-tailed)		0.000
	N	31	31
Per Capita GDP	Pearson Correlation	0.670**	1
	Sig.(2-tailed)	0.000	
	N	31	31

Note: ** significance level is only 0.01 (double-sided).

between the regions. The development of information resource industry still needs to be furthered.

4. IRIDI and economic index complement each other

Analysis of IRIDI and per capita GDP reveals that they have a correlation coefficient as high as 0.67 (see Table 7.7). The two-variable scatter plot is shown in Figure 7.3.

Generally speaking, information resource industry is better developed in regions that lead in the economy, and it lags behinds in regions where the economy lags behind. There are, however, some issues to be addressed. As seen in the per capita GDP rankings in Table 7.8, eight of the top ten provincial-level administrative provinces by per capita GDP come from East China; evidence shows that these

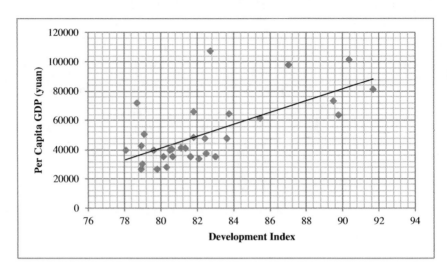

Figure 7.3 Information resource industry development index scores and rankings of provincial-level administrative regions in 2014

Table 7.8 Information resource industry development index scores and rankings of provincial-level administrative regions in 2014

Provincial-level Administrative Region	Per Capita GDP (yuan)	Per Capita GDP Ranking	Development Index	Development Index Ranking
Tianjin	106,796.02	1	82.71	10
Beijing	100,864.38	2	90.37	2
Shanghai	97,554.77	3	87.01	5
Jiangsu	81,080.48	4	91.67	1
Zhejiang	73,032.02	5	89.47	4
Inner Mongolia Autonomous Region	71,146.06	6	78.70	30
Liaoning	65,208.61	7	81.81	14
Fujian	63,740.75	8	83.76	7
Guangdong	63,600.57	9	89.80	3
Shandong	61,054.37	10	85.46	6
Jilin	50,172.32	11	79.10	26
Chongqing	48,031.65	12	81.81	15
Hubei	47,192.69	13	83.64	8
Shaanxi	46,997.72	14	82.44	12
Ningxia Hui Autonomous Region	42,068.82	15	78.91	29
Xinjiang Uygur Autonomous Region	40,913.75	16	81.37	17
Hunan	40,427.56	17	81.12	18

Provincial-level Administrative Region	Per Capita GDP (yuan)	Per Capita GDP Ranking	Development Index	Development Index Ranking
Hebei	40,123.71	18	80.61	20
Qinghai	39,626.23	19	78.05	31
Heilongjiang	39,215.96	20	80.48	21
Hainan	39,101.96	21	79.60	25
Henan	37,116.84	22	82.50	11
Sichuan	35,200.02	23	81.63	16
Shanxi	35,151.91	24	80.65	19
Jiangxi	34,737.02	25	80.12	23
Anhui	34,576.27	26	82.99	9
Guangxi Zhuang Autonomous Region	33,212.48	27	82.11	13
Tibet Autonomous Region	29,510.0	28	79.02	27
Yunnan	27,343.04	29	80.34	22
Gansu	26,470.93	30	79.81	24
Guizhou	26,414.7	31	78.92	28

regions are prosperous. Among these eight regions, only Beijing, Shanghai, Zhejiang, Fujian, and Jiangsu score high in IRIDI, and Tianjin's IRIDI ranking is nine places below than its GDP ranking. Information resource industry is developing at a pace slower than economic growth, and it is not yet a new engine to power the economic growth in the region. The Inner Mongolia Autonomous Region, Jilin, Ningxia Hui Autonomous Region, Qinghai, and other regions in West China have sparse population and inconvenient transportation; its IRIDI is low, and the ranking lag compared to economic ranking is 24, 15, 14, and 12 places, respectively, the Top 4 provincial-level administrative regions see the largest gap between information resource industry's development and economic growth. Natural resources such as water, minerals, natural gas, and tourism are abundant in West China, but they have not been fully utilized due to information block and insufficient utilization of information resources. Attention should be paid to improving the ability of exploiting and utilizing information resources in West China, and potential advantages of all kinds should be transformed into real productivity, thus driving economic development. Information resource industry in parts of Central China such as Anhui and Henan is growing at a pace faster than their economies, and their IRIDI rankings are 17 and 11 places higher than their economic ranking. Information resource industry will undoubtedly become a new driver for their economic development.

7.3.3 Research on development strategies

Given China's information resource industry development, government authorities should focus on the following three aspects while formulating industrial policies.

168   *Evaluation of the industry's development*

1. To encourage regional coordinated development for win–win results

There are many reasons behind regional disparities, such as regional economic foundation, the policy environment, and infrastructures. The central government should optimize policies concerning regional coordinated development to pool strengths in different regions. First, the government should increase policy support for backward regions. For areas with poor information resource industry development, policy support should be increased to strengthen infrastructure construction, introduce professionals, and input support funds. Second, backward areas should learn from developed regions, which in turn give more assistance. The central government should build a positive policy environment for regional cooperation. In its *12th Five-year Plan of Industrial Development*, Shanghai Municipal People's Government has outlined a strategic plan to build an information-based city, fully reflecting the city's attention to information resource industry development. For this purpose, Shanghai introduced policies like developing smart information industries, promoting industry innovation, and enhancing the construction of an e-city. These policies and practices have provided a model for other regions in China to develop local information resources industry.[12] Finally, government departments may consider launching pilot projects in backward regions. For example, some capital cities in the western region can serve as pilot areas to promote the development of their surrounding areas. As a result, regional disparities will be narrowed.

2. To promote information resources consumption with greater policy support

Information consumption is the direct force that drives the growth of industry. A poor level of consumption is the core reason for the weak industry development and a low contribution rate to employment. To promote information consumption, we should enhance the supply of information products and boost subscriber demand. At the supply side, the government should break down barriers to introduce market mechanisms to the monopolistic areas so that traditional industries are transformed and optimized by information resources; increase the number of information resource industry enterprises; and formulate financing and tax policies conducive to the development of these enterprises. At the demand side, information resource industry enterprises should be guided to develop emerging markets based on internal demand, focus on overseas markets, and enhance the quality of information products and services. Policy support should be increased for information resource industry to adjust the supply–demand relation through market leverage. In this way, we can increase the industry scale and promote information consumption. In addition to policy guidance at the supply and demand side, we can also learn from developed countries in this respect. In the United States, information resource industry is largely dependent on market mechanisms. The administration can concentrate more on developing policies targeting infrastructure construction and talent development, along with some financial policies. To guide and promote information resource industry development, a country should put more effort on policies concerning talents, funding, and regulation. As a result, more vitality will be injected into the industry through market competition.

3. To accelerate management system reform and optimize industrial policy environment

China should advance the construction of relevant information resource industry departments, deepen the reform of the management system, and improve the management functions of government departments. Feasible laws, regulations, and policies should be formulated in a tailored manner to suit information resource industry's actual situation, so as to help create a better policy environment for information resource industry. Firstly, local governments can make targeted regulatory measures and assign specific departments and personnel to supervise the execution of relevant policies. That means putting written proposals into practice and maximizing the use of every penny of the fund. Secondly, detailed talent assessment, management systems, and talent reward and punishment systems should be established. This will ensure that relevant technical personnel engaged in the industry reach certain qualifications in business handling and management, and should attract more high-tech talent into information resource industry. Thirdly, strict market access system should be established and executed to ensure a stable information resource industry market in good order. Fourthly, more effort should be made in protecting intellectual property rights. Innovation is a core driver of information resource industry, and better protecting intellectual property rights can encourage innovation and facilitate the healthy development of information resource industry. In addition, relevant government departments across China should learn the success of foreign countries in developing information resource industry and adjust relevant policies based on China's facts to stimulate the rapid development of information resource industry.

Notes

1 Baoqing Dong, "Facilitating the Exploitation and Utilization of National Information Resource and Archival Information Resource," *China Archives*, no. 6 (2005): 15–17.
2 Maosheng Lai, Hui Yan and Jian Long, "Information Resource Industry and Its Scope," *Information Science*, no. 4 (2008): 481–490.
3 Jing Zhao and Xiaohong Niu, "Thoughts on the Strategies for Developing Information Resource Industry in China," *Research on Library Science*, no. 15 (2012): 44–50.
4 Feng Huiling and Hongyan Yang, "Connotation of Information Resource Industry and Its Relations with Relevant Industries," *Information and Documentation Services*, no. 2 (2011): 10–14.
5 F. Deng, G.W. Liu and Z.G. Jin, "Factors Formulating the Competitiveness of the Chinese Construction Industry: Empirical Investigation," *Journal of Management in Engineering* 29, no. 4 (October 1, 2013): 435445,11.
6 T.T.C. Lin, "Market Competitiveness of Mobile TV Industry in China," *Telecommunications Policy*, 36 (November–December, 2012): 10–11, 943–954, 12. Special Issue: SI.

170 *Evaluation of the industry's development*

7 Shanshan Liang and Min Zhou, "Research on the Competitiveness of China's Coal Industry with Porter's 'Diamond Model'," *Resources & Industries*, no. 2 (2007): 37–42.
8 M.E. Porter, *Competitive Advantage: Creating and Sustaining Superior Performance* (New York: Free Press, 1998).
9 Yi Peng, *Research on the Evaluation System of Urban Cultural Industry Development in China* (Beijing: China Renmin University Press, 2011).
10 Key Philosophy and Social Science Research Project of the Ministry of Education. Chinese Strategies for Developing the Culture Industry (08JZD0034) Research Team, "Report on the Research of Chinese Cultural Industry Development Index (CCIDI)," [EB/OL], (7/19/2014) [2014-7-19 17:18], http://cciidi.sjtu.edu.cn/news_view.asp?newsid=365.
11 World Economic Forum, "The Global Competitiveness Report 2008–2009," [2014-12-29], www.weforum.org/reports/global-competitiveness-report-2008-2009.
12 Shanghai Municipal People's Government, "Notice of Shanghai Municipal People's Government on Issuing Shanghai's 12th Five-Year Plan of Industrial Development," [2014-8-13], www.shanghai.gov.cn/shanghai/node2314/node2319/node12344/u26ai30908.html.

Afterword

Feng Huiling, Zhao Guojun, Qian Minghui

This book in its Chinese version is attributed to the "Research on the Development Policies and Management of Information Resource Industry in China" Project (No. 将":"删去 71133006), a key project supported by the National Natural Science Foundation.

For all members of the project, it has been a happy academic journey accompanied by difficulties. We are happy that the project has attracted wide attention from its declaration to approval and to actual research lasting for five years. As information resource industry gains popularity, it is gaining importance in the economy and social development. More and more people start to get involved in and accept the topic. The difficulties come from the countless unknown and uncertain things, ranging from concepts and principles to basic judgments. We had to do many things from scratch, and we were being watched by many stakeholders from varying communities. Fortunately, the project started at the perfect time, and we were lucky to move forward with it. We have visited more than 100 domestic and overseas organizations for literature research. Proposing an idea, overthrowing the idea (or partly), and proposing another idea – the process has been repeated for thousands of times to write this book on issues including field definition and basic theories, core features, and development evaluation. We hope that our exploratory moves can also support those marching on the same path.

Authors of the book include Feng Huiling, Yang Hongyan, Yang Jianliang, Zhang, Zhao Guojun, Hou Weizhen, Qian Minghui, Chao Yuemen, Hui Xinyu (in the order of the number of strokes of the first name), and editors include Feng Huiling, Zhao Guojun, and Qian Minghui. We would like to extend heartfelt gratitude to all the people who have helped us in the research, to all experts and enterprises receiving the survey and offering data, and to Editor Song Yiping with China Renmin University Press for his excellent work! Any advice on supplementing and modifying any part of the book would be appreciated!

References

"According to the World Bank Data." Accessed December 2012. www.worldbank.org.

A. D. Team. "Webviewclient Hooks List." http://developer.android.com/reference/android/webkit/WebViewClient.html.

Armstrong, M. "Competition in Two-Sided Markets." *RAND Journal of Economics* 37, no. 3 (2006): 668691.

BCC Research. "Remote Sensing Technologies and Global Markets." [2013–09–19]. Accessed August 8, 2020. www.giichinese.com.cn/report/bc223038-remote-sensing-technologies-global-markets.html.

Beijing Informatization Office. *Development Report for Beijing's Information Service Industry in 2004*. Beijing: China Development Press, 2005.

Bell, D. *The Coming of Post-Industrial Society: A Venture in Social Forecasting*. New York: Basic Books, 1973.

Bell, D. "Welcome to the Post-Industrial Society." *Physics Today*, no. 2 (1976): 535563.

Cai, Huaishun. "Research on the Information Consumption of College Students." *Journal of Jiangsu Institute of Education (Social Science Edition)*, no. 7 (2004).

Cai, Xiaojun, Li, Shuangjie and Liu, Qihao. "Research on the Formation Mechanism and Stability of the Production Chain in Eco-Industry Parks." *Soft Science*, no. 3 (2006).

CCID Consulting. *Report on the Development of Digital TV Industry (2004)*.

CCID Consulting. *Report on Investment Opportunities in China's Media Industry (2003)*.

CCID Consulting. *Report on Investment Opportunities in China's Digital Content Industry (2004–2005)*. http://www.ccidreport.com/pub/html/market/report/report2006/index.html.

Chen, Xile. "Comparison of the Development and Management of Scientific and Technological Information Resources between the Chinese Mainland and Taiwan." *Studies in Science of Science*, no. 4 (2000): 18.

Cheng, Jinhua, Chen, Jun and Duan, Pingzhong. "Evaluation of the Effective Supply of Non-Renewable Energy in China in the Past 15 Years." *China Soft Science*, no. 11 (2006).

CPC. *Communique of the Fourth Plenum of Central Committee of the CPC (Separate Edition)*. Beijing: People's Publishing House, 2014.

Cui, Hongming. "Analysis of the Structure of Information Resource Industry Chain: The Digital Publishing Industry as an Example." *Information and Documentation Services*, no. 1 (2014).

Cui, Hongming and Guojun, Zhao. "Research on Value Flow of Information Resources Industry Chain: On the Value Beam of Information Resources Products." *Journal of Intelligence*, no. 8 (2013).

References 173

Deng, F., Liu, G.W. and Jin, Z.G. "Factors Formulating the Competitiveness of the Chinese Construction Industry: Empirical Investigation." *Journal of Management in Engineering* 29, no. 4, October 1 (2013): 435445, 11.

Dutton, William H. "Putting Things to Work: Social and Policy Challenges for the Internet of Things." *Source: Info* 16, no. 3 (2014): 121.

Dyson, Esther. *Release 2.0: A Design for Living in the Digital Age.* Translated by Yong Hu and Haiyan Fan. Haikou: Hainan Publishing House, 1998.

The Editorial Team. *Compilation of Documents for the 17th CPC National Congress.* Beijing: People's Publishing House, 2012.

Einstein, A. "Does the Inertia of a Body Depend Upon Its Energy Content?" *Annalen der Physik* 18, no. 13 (1905): 639641.

Einstein, A. "Über einen die erzeugung und verwandlung des lichtes betreffenden heuristischen gesichtspunkt (on a Heuristic Viewpoint Concerning the Production and Transformation of Light)." *Annalen der Physik* 17, no. 6 (1905): 132148.

Ernst, M.L. "At the Heart of Evolving Literacy: A Framework for Action." www.pirp.harvard.edu/pubs_pdf/ernst/ernst-p973.pdf, 1997.

European Commission. "I2000. [20101231]." http://ec.europa.eu/information-society/eeurope/i2010/index-en.htm.

European Commission. "Info 2000 (4-Year Work Program 1996–1999)." *European Commission*, 1996.

Forfás. "A Strategy for the Digital Content Industry in Ireland." Translated by Jinjing Zhang. *Informatization Reference*, no. 5 (2004).

Galvin, T.J. *Rights in Conflict: Public Policy in an Information Age, New Worlds in Information and Documentation: Proceedings of the 46th FID Conference and Congress.* The Hague, the Netherlands: FID, 1994: 5966.

Gong, Qinlin. "On the Construction of Industrial Chain and Urban-Rural Coordinated Development." *Economist*, no. 3 (2004).

Hadida, A.L. and Paris, T. "Managerial Cognition and the Value Chain in the Digital Music Industry." *Technological Forecasting and Social Change* 83 (2014): 8497.

Han, Yun. "Information Resource Industry and Its Development Strategy in China." *Journal of Library Science in China*, no. 6 (2006).

Hartley, R.V. "Transmission of Information." *Bell System Technical Journal* 7, no. 3 (1928): 535563.

He, Shaohua and Sun, Gaojian. "Research on the Integrated Management of Government Information Resources." *Library and Information Service*, no. S2 (2010).

Hou, Jinchuan. "Research on the Physical Features of Information: The Unity of Matter, Energy and Information." *Journal of Xiangtan University (Philosophy and Social Sciences)*, no. 5 (1997).

Hou, Jinchuan. "Research on the Physical Features of Information: The Unity of Matter, Energy and Information (II)." *Library*, no. 2 (1995).

Hou, Jinchuan. "Research on the Physical Features of Information: The Unity of Matter, Energy and Information (III)." *Library*, no. 3 (1995).

Hou, Jinchuan. "Research on the Physical Features of Information: The Unity of Matter, Energy and Information (IV)." *Library*, no. 4 (1995).

Hou, Jinchuan and Yang, Liangquan. "Research on the Physical Features of Information: The Unity of Matter, Energy and Information (I)." *Library*, no. 1 (1995).

Hu, Xiaopeng. "Industrial Symbiosis: Theoretical Definition and Internal Mechanism." *China Industrial Economics*, no. 9 (2008).

Huang, Yunwu. *Dictionary of Market Economy.* Wuhan: Wuhan University Press, 1993.

174   References

Huiling, Feng. "No Time Left to Exploit and Utilize Information Resources." *Guangming Daily*, May 17 (2014).

Huiling, Feng. "Paying Sufficient Attention to the Strategic Value of 'Information Resources'." *People's Daily*, October 23 (2014).

Huiling, Feng and Chao, Lemen. "Research on the Evolution Law and Optimization Strategy of Consumption Structure of the Information Resource Industry." *Information Studies: Theory & Application*, no. 5 (2014).

Huiling, Feng and Yang, Hongyan. "Connotation of Information Resource Industry and Its Relations with Relevant Industries." *Information and Documentation Services*, no. (2011).

Ji, Baocheng. "On the Essence and Function of Market Order." *Journal of Renmin University of China*, no. 1 (2004).

Ji, Hanlin. "Model Research on Pricing Methods in Bilateral Markets." *Industrial Economics Research*, no. 4 (2006).

Jiang, Guojun and Jiang, Mingxin. "Research on Industrial Chain Theory and Its Stability Mechanism." *Journal of Chongqing University (Social Science Edition)*, no. 1 (2004).

Jiang, Yanbo. *Research on Antitrust in the Network Industry*. Beijing: China Social Sciences Press, 2008.

Jiang, Zemin. "Development of China's Information Technology Industry in the New Age." *Journal of Shanghai Jiaotong University*, no. 10 (2008).

Jing, Haiying and Yang, Zhaoyu. "Analysis of the Complexity in Renewable Resources Development Activities." *Complex Systems and Complexity Science*, no. 4 (2004): 1.

Jintao, Hu. *Hold High the Great Banner of Socialism with Chinese Feature and Strive for New Victories in Building a Moderate Prosperous Society in All Respects: Report on the 17th CPC National Congress*. Beijing: People's Publishing House, 2007.

Jöckel, S., Will, A. and Schwarzer, F. "Participatory Media Culture and Digital Online Distribution: Reconfiguring the Value Chain in the Computer Game Industry." *The International Journal on Media Management* 10, no. 3 (2008): 102111.

Lai, Maosheng, Yan, Hui and Long, Jian. "Information Resource Industry and Its Scope." *Information Science*, no. 4 (2008).

Lai, Maosheng, Yang, Xiudan, Hu, Xiaofeng and Xu, Bo. "Research on the Basic Theories for Exploiting and Utilizing Information Resources." *Information Studies: Theory & Application*, no. 3 (2004).

Lancaster, F.W. and Burger, R.H. "Macroinformatics, Microinformatics and Information Policy." In *The Information Environment: A World View Studies in Honor of Professional A.I. Mikhailov*. North-Holland: Elsevier, 1990.

Li, Guifu. "Research on China's Industrial Chain for Cable TV." *Industrial Technology & Economy*, no. 3 (2007).

Li, X. and Cheng, G. "Research on Measurement Index System of Information Consumption Level in Rural Areas." *Journal of Luoyang Institute of Science and Technology (Social Science Edition)* 2 (2012): 14.

Li, Zhengfen. "Powered by Independent Innovation, GIS Platform Software Embraced the Cloud Era." *China High-Tech Industry Herald*, October 13 (2014).

Liang, Shanshan and Zhou, Min. "Research on the Competitiveness of China's Coal Industry with Porter's Diamond Model." *Resources & Industries*, no. 2 (2007).

Lin, T.T.C. "Market Competitiveness of Mobile TV Industry in China." *Telecommunications Policy* 36, no. 10–11, November–December (2012): 943954, 12, Special Issue:SI.

Liu, Dongqing. "The Policy System of China's Information Network Environment." *Journal of Library Science in China (Bimonthly)*, no. 4 (2002).

References 175

Liu, Guifu. "Research on the Basic Connotation of Industrial Chain." *Industrial Technology & Economy*, no. 8 (2007).

Liu, Guifu. "Research on the Structural Model of the 'Inside Chain' of the Industry Chain." *Taxation and Economy*, no. 2 (2008).

Liu, Runda, Zhu, Wenbo and Zhu, Yunqiang. "Analysis of Key Issues in the Operational Service Stage of National Science and Technology Basic Condition Platform." *Journal of Modern Intelligence*, no. 11 (2012): 32.

Liu, Shulin and Niu, Haitao. *Industrial Economics*. Beijing: Tsinghua University Press, 2012.

Liu, Ying, Li, Qi and Wang, Xiaofan. "Analysis of the Complexity of Chinese Traditional Medicine Industry Chain Structure." *Journal of Chinese Materia Medica*, no. 16 (2014).

Liu, Ying, Zhang, Tieying, Jin, Xiaolong and Cheng, Xueqi. "Personal Privacy Protection in the Era of Big Data." *Journal of Computer Research and Development*, no. 1 (2015).

Logan, R.K. "What Is Information?: Why Is It Relativistic and What Is Its Relationship to Materiality, Meaning and Organization." *Information* 3, no. 1 (2012): 6891.

Lu, Chao and Liu, Qing. "Analysis of China's Open Access Policies." *Journal of Intelligence*, no. 1 (2011): 30.

Lu, Peng, Miao, Liangtian, Mo, Jinian, Li, Zhixiong, Li, Xueliang, Sun, Shihong, and Wang, Song. "Explanation on Drafting the Regulations of the People's Republic of China on Scientific Data Sharing (Proposal)." *Recent Development in World Seismology*, no. 8 (2008).

Lu, Xueyi and Lu, Liusheng. *Social Modernization: Taicang Practice* (Vol. 1 & 2). Beijing: Social Sciences Academic Press, 2012.

Ma, Feicheng and Lai, Maosheng. *Information Resource Management*. Beijing: Higher Education Press, 2006.

Ma, Feicheng, Gang, Li, Xianjin, Cha. *Information Resource Management*. Wuhan: Wuhan University Press, 2001: 206.

Manuel, C. and Aoyama, Y. "Paths Towards the Information Society: Employment Structure in G7 Countries 1920–1990." *International Labor Review* 133, no. 1 (1994): 533.

Naisbitt, J. *Megatrends: Ten New Directions Transforming Our Live*. New York: Warner Books, 1982.

OECD. "Content as a New Growth Industry." DSTI/ICCP/IE(96)6/FINAL.OECD, 1998.

Oettinger, A.G. "Knowledge Innovations: The Endless Adventure." *Bulletin of the American Society for Information Science and Technology* 27, no. 2 (2001): 1015.

Oettinger, A.G. "National Politics and the Telecommunications World." www.pirp.harvard.edu/pubs_pdf/oetting/oetting-other-90.pdf, January, 1990.

Pang, Jing'an. "Development of China's Information Resource Industry in the Age of Internet." *China Information Review*, no. 3 (1998).

Peng, Yi. *Research on the Evaluation System of Urban Cultural Industry Development in China*. Beijing: China Renmin University Press, 2011.

Porat, Marc U. *The Information Economy*. Changsha: Hunan People's Publishing House, 1987.

Porter, M.E. *Competitive Advantage: Creating and Sustaining Superior Performance*. New York: Free Press, 1998.

Porter, M.E. "Location, Competition, and Economic Development: Local Clusters in a Global Economy." *Economic Development Quarterly* 14, no. 1 (2000): 1534.

Qiao, Chaofei. "The Connotation and Classification of Geographic Information Industry." *Journal of Geomatics*, no. 47 (2012).

Qiao, Chaofei and Sun, Wei. "Analysis of the Facts and Trends of International Geographic Information Industry Development." In *China Geographic Information Industry Development Report 2011*. Beijing: Social Sciences Academic Press, 2011.

176 References

Ren, Juan. "Research on Information Resource Management of Private Technology Enterprises." *Management World*, no. 3 (2006).

Renner, G.T. "Geography of Industrial Localization." *Economic Geography* 23, no. 3 (1947): 167189.

Rourke, J.O. "Information Resources in Canada." *Special Libraries* 61, no. 2 (1970): 5965.

Rui. Mingjie, Liu, Mingyu and Ren, Jiangbo. *On the Integration of Industrial Chain*. Shanghai: Fudan University Press, 2006.

Sakaiya, Taichi. *Knowledge-Value Revolution: Huang, Xiaoyong*. Beijing: Shanghai Joint Publishing House, 1987.

Salamon, L. and Lund, M.S. *Beyond Privatization*. Washington, DC: Urban Institute Press, 1989: 3439.

Salehi-Sangari, E, Nath, A.K. and Saha, P. "Transforming Supply Chains in Digital Content Delivery: A Case Study in Apple." *IFIP International Federation for Information Processing* 255, no. 1 (2010).

School of Economics at Osaka City University. *Dictionary of Economics*. Tokyo: Iwanami Shoten, 1999.

Sepstrup, P. *Consumption of Mass Communication: Construction of a Model on Information Consumption Behaviour*. ERIC 1977.

Servan-Schreiber, J.J. *Le Défi mondial*. Paris: LGF, 1981.

Shao, Chang and Li, Jian. "Research on the 'Wave-Particle Duality' of the Industrial Chain: The Features, Structure and Integration of the Industrial Chain." *China Industrial Economics*, no. 9 (2009).

Shen, Manhong and He, Lingqiao. "Classification of Externalities and Evolution of the Externality Theory." *Journal of Zhejiang University (Humanities and Social Sciences)*, no. 1 (2002).

The State Council. *Several Opinions of the State Council on Promoting Information Consumption and Boosting Domestic Demand*. Beijing: People's Publishing House, 2013.

Sun, Dongchuan. *Introduction to Systems Engineering*. Beijing: Tsinghua University Press, 2004.

Sun, Gennian. "The Transformation of Matter-Energy-Information (MEI) and Sustainable Development of Human Beings." *Studies in Dialectics of Nature*, no. 8 (1999): 15.

Sun, Jingshui. "Research on Measurement Methods of Market Structure and Market Performance." *Statistical Research*, no. 5 (2002).

Susskind, L. *The Cosmic Landscape: String Theory and the Illusion of Intelligent Design*. New York: Little Brown, 2005.

Tan, Xueyu. "American Digital Publishing News." *Modern Publishing*, no. 3 (2011).

Toffler, A. *Power Shift: Knowledge, Wealth and Violence at the Edge of the 21st Century*. New York: Bantam Books, 1990.

Toffler, A. [The United States]. *The Third Wave*. Translated by Mingjian Huang. Beijing: CITIC Press, 2006.

Tong, Shuquan. "China's Satellite Navigation Industry Will Value RMB 400 Billion in 2020." *Beijing Daily*, December 11 (2014).

Umpleby, S.A. "Physical Relationships among Matter, Energy and Information." *Systems Research and Behavioral Science* 24, no. 3 (2007): 369372.

Wang, Qiuju. "Analysis of the Connotation and Structure of the Industry Chain." *Logistics Sci-Tech*, no. 5 (2012).

Wang, Yang, Xiao, Xu and Yu, Shuyan. *Research on the Development Model of the Software Industry*. Beijing: Science Press, 2009.

Wang, Zhenzhen and Bao, Xinghua. "Research on the Development and Application of Industrial Symbiosis Theory." *East China Economic Management*, no. 10 (2012).

References   177

Weiner, N. *Cybernetics: Or Control and Communication in the Animal and the Machine.* Paris: Hermann & Cie & Cambridge, MA: MIT Press, 1948.

Wen, Jiabao. "Several Questions on the Development of Social Undertakings and Improvement of People's Livelihood." *Qiushi*, no. 7 (2010).

Whittaker, S. "Personal Information Management: From Information Consumption to Curation." *Annual Review of Information Science and Technology* 45, no. 1 (2011): 162.

World Economic Forum. "The Global Competitiveness Report 2008–2009 [20141229]." www.weforum.org/reports/global-competitiveness-report-2008-2009.

Wu, Kun. "Material Thinking·Energy Thinking·Information Thinking: The Three Leaps of Human Scientific Thinking Mode." *Academics*, no. 2 (2002).

Xi, Youmin, Ge, Jing, Han, Wei and Chen, Jian. "The Significance and Value of Harmonious Management Theory." *Chinese Journal of Management*, no. 4 (2005): 2.

Xiao, Zhongdong, Liu, Yongqing and Sun, Linyan. "Food Chain Research on the Industrial Symbiosis System." *Science & Technology Progress and Policy*, no. 3 (2008).

Xie, Kefan. *Research on the Allocation and Use of Regional Science and Technology Resources.* Wuhan: Wuhan University of Technology, 2005.

Xu, Cai and Guo, Fenghai. "The Origin and Essence of Matter, Energy, Information and Human Intelligence." *Studies in Dialectics of Nature* (1992): 22–26.

Xu, Deming. *Report on China's Geographic Information Resources Industry 2011.* Beijing: Social Sciences Academic Press, 2011.

Xuan, Xiaohong. *Preliminary Study on the Development of Information Resources Market.* Beijing: China Federation of Literary and Art Circles Publishing House, 2008.

Yacci, M. and Rozanski, E.P. "Student Information Consumption Strategies: Implications of the Google Effect." *Proceedings of the 2012 iConference*. ACM, 2012: 248253.

Yang, Chuanming. "Research on the Modularization of Online Game Industry." *Journal of Intelligence*, no. 7 (2008).

Yang, Gongpu and Xia, Dawei. *Modern Industrial Economics.* Shanghai: Shanghai University of Finance and Economics Press, 1999.

Ye, Yi. "Boom of the Geological Information Industry." *Think Tank*, no. 10 (2014).

Yu, Xiangping. "The Structure and Effect of Exhibition Industry Chain." *Economic Forum*, no. 1 (2008).

Yu, Yihong and Guan, Xizhan. *Vertical Control of Industrial Chain and Economic Regulation.* Shanghai: Fudan University Press, 2006.

Zemin, Jiang. *Compilation of Documents for the 16th CPC National Congress.* Beijing: People's Publishing House, 2002.

Zhang, Aixia and Shen, Yulan. "Analysis of the Construction of the American Government's Science and Technology Reporting System." *Information Science*, no. 4 (2007): 26.

Zhang, Yuxiang. "Incomplete Information and Solutions in Library Information Services." *Sci-Tech Information Development & Economy*, no. 12 (2011): 21.

Zhang, Zhang and Guojun, Zhao. "Research on China's State Control of Information Resources." *Chinese Public Administration*, no. 6 (2012).

Zhao, Yulin and Zhang, Zhongfang. "Empirical Analysis of the Impact of Hi-Tech Industry Development on the Optimization and Upgrade of Industrial Structure." *Science Research Management*, no. 3 (2008): 29.

Zhe-Ming, M.A. "Research on Mechanism of Information Consumption." *Information Science* 12 (2012): 8.

Zheng, Xinli. "Accelerating the Transformation of Economic Development Mode." *Economic Daily*, June 28 (2010).

178 References

Zhong. Yixin. *Science in Information*. Beijing: Guangming Daily Press, 1988.

Zhou, Jizhong. *Science and Technology Resources*. Xi'an: Shaanxi People's Education Press, 1999.

Zhu, Jiajun, Tang, Hongzhen and Liu, Jin. "Comparative Research on the Whole-Chain Development Modes of the Animation Industry." *Science and Technology Management Research*, no. 11 (2014).

Zhu, Yongbin, Liu, Changxin, Wang, Zhen and Shi, Yajuan. "Analysis on the Evolution Trend of China's Industrial Structure and Its Emission Reduction Potential." *China Soft Science*, no. 2 (2013).

Zhu, Youping. "Ten Problems in the Development of Information Resource Industry in China." *China Soft Science*, no. 6 (1996).

Index

Note: Page numbers in *italics* indicate figures and those in **bold** indicate tables.

American Association of Software and Information Industries 3
Annual Research Report for Investment Opportunities of Chinese Digital Content Industry from 2004 to 2005 (CCID Consulting Co., Ltd.) 5

Basic Research Report for Creative Industry in Hong Kong 3
Bell, Daniel 29, 96–97
"Bohr atom" model, industrial chain 57–58
British Special Working Team for Creative Industry 3
'Broadband China' strategy 97

Cai, Xiaojun 52
capital input, supply-demand of information resource industry and 102, 103–104
CCID Consulting Co., Ltd. 5, 116
Central China information resource industry 138–143; development trend analysis 142–143; indicator scores in 142; industrial development 138–139, 139, *139*; industrial environment scores/rankings of 141; industrial value scores/rankings of 140; Level 1 indicators, analysis of 139–142; overview of 138
Chen, Yu 2
China Cultural Industry Development Index System 151
China Internet Network Information Center 104
China's IT Industry Development in the New Era (Jiang Zemin) 19–20
connotation of information resource industry 1–4

consumer participation 66
Content As a New Growth Industry (OECD) 3, 4
content-oriented policies 114
copyright definition 113–114
creative industry, defined 3
Cui, Hongming 58
cultural creative-related industry 3–4, 6

demand, features of 109
Deng, Fei 150
Deng, Xiaoping 75
denotation of information resource industry 4–5
development evaluation, China's information resource industry 149–169; construction of system for 153–157; empirical analysis of 157–167; evaluation indicators, processing of 155–157; indicator rankings 157, 158–161, 162–167, *163*, 165, *165*, *166*, 166–167; indicator system, framework of 151–152, 152–153; overview of 149; relevant research 150–151; strategies, research on 167–169; system proposed for 149–152, 152–153; weight of indicators 154, 154–155
development theories, China's information resource industry 26–72; *see also individual theories*; dynamic resource triangle theory 26–37; industrial chain theory 55–66; industrial symbiosis theory 47–55; information consumption theory 37–47; limited government intervention theory 66–72; overview of 26
development trajectory, China's information resource industry 75–95;

180 *Index*

germination period 75, 76, 77–78; industrial distribution, concentration of 78; industrial structure 80–82, *81*, 87, *88*, 92–93, *92–93*; initial development period 76, 78–84; overview of 75, 76, 79–80, *80*, 84–85, *85*, *86*, 90–91, *91*; rapid development period 76, 84–89; regional disparities *82*, 82–84, *83*, 88–89, *89*, *94*, 94–95; related industries, scale/competitiveness of 77–78; steady development period 76, 89–95
digital content industry concept 3
direct consumption mode of information consumption *42*
direct network effect 62
Dong, Baoqing 150
dynamic resource triangle barycenter curve (DB curve) 27–37; displacement path of 32, *33–35*, 36–37; features of 31; function expression 36; mathematical features of 32
dynamic resource triangle (DRT) model 29–30
dynamic resource triangle theory 26–37; barycenter curve analysis 30, 31, 32, *33–35*, 36–37; construction/ characteristic analysis of 29–30; overview of 26–27; retrospective analysis of 27, *28–29*, 29

East China information resource industry 132–137; development index scores/rankings 133; development trend analysis 137, 138; industrial development 133–134, *134*; industrial environment scores/rankings of 137; industrial value scores/rankings of 135; Level 1 indicators, analysis of 134–137; overview of 132–133
economic development, information resource industry and 11
economic features, information resource industry and 12–13
economic function of information resource industry 14–15
economies of scale theory 68
effect failure, market 67
evolution, information consumption and 43–45, 44
explanation model 38–39, *39*
externality, defined 41

Feng, Huiling 150
function failure, market 67

Global Competitiveness Index (GCI) 151
Gong, Qinlin 56
Guan, Xizhan 56

Hadida, A. L. 58
Han, Yun 2
He, Defang 116
Hirschman, Albert Otto 128
"Hoffmann Theorem" 69
Hu, Xiaopeng 52

incomplete consumability of information products 61
indirect consumption mode of information consumption *42*
indirect network effect 62
industrial chain theory 55–66; *see also* information products; "Bohr atom" model of 57–58; connotation of 56–57; definitions of 56–57; evolution of 55–56; information products, effects of features of 60–66, *64–65*; information resource 58–60; information resource industry and 13–14; structure of 57–58
Industrial Symbiosis (Danish Kahlenburg Company) 47
industrial symbiosis theory 47–55; composition/features of 47–48, *49*; equation 53; formations and types of 48, 50, 50–51; influencing factors/ measurement of 51–53; new formation of, for policies and management 53–55, *54*; overview of 47
industry attribution, defining 115–116
Info 2000 (4-Year Work Program 1996–1999) 3
"Information Conference for Seven Western Countries" 3
information consumption markets 41
information consumption theory 37–47; evolution features of 43–45, 44; explanation model for 38–39, *39*; externality and 41; foreign literature regarding 38; information resource exploitation and 37–38; information technologies/hardware and 114; market features of 40–41, 41; material/energy consumption and 43; motive/behavior separation in 43; overview of 37–38; policy demand features of 45–47; structural features of *42*, 42–43; two-sided/multi-sided markets and 40–41
information products: consumer participation and 66; effects of features

of 60–66, *64–65*; enterprise replacement and 64, *64–65*, 65; incomplete consumability of 61; network effect of 62; network operators and 63–64; non-substantiality of 60–61; physical exchange and 62–63; production efficiency and 65–66; timeliness of 61–62

information resource exploitation: Chinese Government documents concerning 38; described 37–38; industrial symbiosis theory and 47–48, *49*; information consumption theory and 37–38

information resource industrial chain 58–60; definition of 59–60; schematic diagram of *59*; studies on 58–59

information resource industry: copyright of 113–114; development by province of China's 130–131, 131–132, 132; development index rankings, 2013 105; development tendency of, 2012–2014 *91*; development tendency of operating incomes, 2008–2011 *86*; development tendency of subdivided industries, 2012–2014 *92*; limited government intervention and development of 70–72, 71; market failure in 67–68; network, subscriber size of 106; regional distribution of, 2004–2007 *82*, *83*; regional distribution of, 2012–2014 *94*; regional operating incomes, 2008–2011 *85*, *89*; subdivided industries, 2004–2007 changes of *80*; subdivided industries, 2004–2007 proportions of *81*; subdivided industries, 2008–2011 proportions of *88*; subdivided industries, 2012–2014 proportions of *93*

information resource industry, China's; *see also individual headings*: concept of 1–24; development evaluation of 149–169; development theories on 26–72; development trajectory of 75–95; regional features of 130–148; strategic value of 17–24; structural features of 115–129; supply-demand relation of 96–114

information resource industry concept 1–24; characteristics of 2; classifications of 6–10, 7, 8–10; connotation of 1–4; definition of 5–10; denotation of 4–5; economic development and 11; economic features and 12–13; economic function of 14–15; features of 10–14; functions of 14–17; industrial chain and

13–14; as object of labor 10; overlap with other related industries 2–4, 6–7, *7*; political function of 15–16; profit output and 10–11; social function of 16–17; strategic value of 17–24; as value source 11

Information Resource Industry Development Index (IRIDI) 151–152, 155; *see also* development evaluation, China's information resource industry; data processing step 155, 156, 156–157; effectiveness of 157, 158–161, 162–167, *163*, *166*, 166–167

Information Resource Policy Research Center 27

International Intellectual Property Alliance 3

IRIDI *see* Information Resource Industry Development Index (IRIDI)

Irish Development Strategies for Digital Content Industry 3

Japanese Association of Science, Technology and Economics 3

Japanese Content Promotion Law 3

Jiang, Guojun 56

Jiang, Mingxin 56

Jiang, Zemin 19–20, 77

Jöckel, S. 58

KOCCA (The Korea Creative Content Agency) 3

"Kuznets Growth Theory" 69

labor input, supply-demand of information resource industry and 102, *103*

Lai, Maosheng 116, 150

late-developing superiority theory 68–69

Li, Guifu 58

Li, Jian 57

Li, Jiatu 68–69

Li, Keqiang 97, 115

Li, Shuangjie 52

Liang, Shanshan 150

limited government intervention theory 66–72; economies of scale theory and 68; information resource industry development and 70–72, 71; late-developing superiority theory and 68–69; market failure theory and 67–68; national interest theory and 70; overview of 66–67; structural transformation theory and 69; technological development theory and 70

182   *Index*

Lin, Trisha 150
Liu, Guifu 57
Liu, Qihao 52
Liu, Ying 58
Liu, Yongqing 51

marginal cost: defined 40; marginal benefit and 40
market failure theory 67–68
material/energy consumption, information consumption and 43
mechanism failure, market 67
multi-sided markets 40–41

Nai, Maosheng 2
national interest theory 70
network effect of information products 62
network operators, information products and 63–64
Niu, Xiaohong 150
non-substantiality of information products 60–61

Oettinger, Anthony G. 26, 27
Organization for Economic Cooperation and Development (OECD) 3, 4

Pang, Jing'an 1, 77
"Petty-Clark Theorem" 69
policy demand, information consumption and 45–47; information consumers, personal privacy protection 46; information content provider, rights/ interests protection 45–46; market order standards 46–47
political function of information resource industry 15–16
population density, supply-demand of information resource industry and 104, 105
Porat, Marc U. 120
Porter, Michael 56, 150–151
profit output, information resource industry and 10–11

regional features, China's information resource industry 130–148; *see also individual regions*; in Central China 138–143; development by province 130–132; development index rankings, 2014 131–132; in East China 132–137, 138; overview of 130; in West China 143–148

resource triangle *see* dynamic resource triangle theory
Rostow, Walt Whitman 128

Salehi-Sangari, E. 58
Several Opinions of the General Office of the CPC Central Committee and the General Office of the State Council on Strengthening Information Resource Exploitation (State Council) 66–67, 78–79
Several Opinions of the General Office of the State Council on Strengthening Services and Supervision over Market Entities by Means of Big Data Analysis (State Council) 99
Several Opinions on Enhancing the Exploitation and Utilization of Information Resource (State Council) 115
Several Opinions on Promoting Information Consumption and Expanding Domestic Demand (State Council) 37, 89, 114
Shao, Chang 57
Shinohara, Miyohei 128
Smith, Adam 56; *see also* industrial chain theory
social development, China's 20–24; development resource structure and 22–23; information resources and 23–24; strategic problems in 20–21
social function of information resource industry 16–17
Stages of Economic Growth, The (Rostow) 128
State Information Center 116
strategic value of China's information resource industry 17–24; China's social development and 20–24; overview of 17; structure vital to 17–20
structural features, China's information resource industry 115–129; analysis of 120–128; categories of 120–121, 121–122; composition of 115–118, 119; dependence perspective of 125, 126; industrial perspective of 123, 124, *125*; industry attribution, defining 115–116; information resource dependence of 121–122; optimization of 128–129; overview of 115; region perspective of 126–128, *127*; segment analysis of 116–118, 117, 118, 119

Index 183

structural transformation theory 69
Sun, Linyan 51
supply, features of 109
supply-demand relation, China's
information resource industry 96–114;
analysis of 109–114; better life needs
and 100–101; capital input 102,
103–104; changes in 104, 106;
demand factors 96–102; existing
problems of 111–113; features of
110–111; government industrial
policies, effect of 107–109, 108;
industry management factors of
107–109, 108, *109*; labor input
102, *103*; overview of 96; policy
orientation 113–114; population
density and 104, 105; science/
technology innovation and application
106–107; sociocultural needs and
101–102; socioeconomic needs and
96–98; socio-political needs and
98–99; urbanization level and 104, 105
symbiosis 47–48, *49*; *see also* industrial
symbiosis theory

technological development theory 70
timeliness of information products 61–62
two-sided markets 40–41

urbanization level, supply-demand of
information resource industry and
104, 105

value, information resource industry
and 11

Wang, Qiuju 57
Wen, Jiabao 20
West China information resource industry
143–148; development index scores/
rankings 143; development trend
analysis 147–148, 148; industrial
development 143–144, *144*; industrial
environment scores/rankings of 147;
industrial value scores/rankings of 145;
level 1 indicators, analysis of 144–147;
overview of 143
White Paper of Digital Content 3

Xi, Jinping 129
Xia, Dawei 56
Xiao, Zhongdong 51
Xuan, Xiaohong 2

Yan, Xiaohong 113
Yang, Chuanming 58–59
Yang, Gongpu 56
Yong Gyu, Joo 116
Yu, Xiangping 58
Yu, Yihong 56

Zhao, Guojun 58
Zhao, Jing 150
Zhu, Jiajun 59
Zhu, Youping 1, 77